As I Was Saying

A CHESTERTON READER

Edited By
ROBERT KNILLE

REGENT COLLEGE PUBLISHING
· VANCOUVER, BRITISH COLUMBIA ·

First published 1985 by William B. Eerdmans Publishing Co.
255 Jefferson Ave., SE, Grand Rapids, Mich. 49503 U.S.A.

This edition published 2006 by
Regent College Publishing
5800 University Boulevard, Vancouver, B.C. V6T 2E4 Canada

Grateful acknowledgment is given to the following for permission to reprint excerpts from the works of G. K. Chesterton.

A. P. WATT LTD. for permission granted by Miss Dorothy E. Collins to reprint excerpts from all the works of G. K. Chesterton for which she holds the copyright. These include the following volumes, originally copyright © by G. K. Chesterton or his estate in the years indicated: *All I Survey* (1933); *All Is Grist* (1931); *As I Was Saying* (1936); *Autobiography* (1936); *Avowals and Denials* (1934); *Come to Think of It* (1930); *The Common Man* (1950); *A Miscellany of Men* (1912); *St. Thomas Aquinas* (1933); *Sidelights on New London and Newer York* (1932); *The Thing: Why I Am a Catholic* (1929); *Tremendous Trifles* (1909); *The Well and the Shallows* (1935); *What I Saw in America* (1922).

DODD, MEAD & COMPANY, INC., for permission (U.S.) to quote material from the following works of G. K. Chesterton: *The Collected Poems of G. K. Chesterton*, copyright © 1932 by Dodd, Mead & Company, copyright renewed in 1959 by Oliver Chesterton; *The Everlasting Man*, copyright © 1925 by Dodd, Mead & Company, copyright renewed in 1953 by Oliver Chesterton; *The Innocence of Father Brown*, copyright © 1911 by Dodd, Mead & Company, copyright renewed in 1938 by Frances B. Chesterton; *The Scandal of Father Brown*, copyright by G. K. Chesterton, copyright renewed in 1963 by Oliver Chesterton; *The Secret of Father Brown*, copyright © 1927 by G. K. Chesterton, copyright renewed in 1954 by Oliver Chesterton.

OXFORD UNIVERSITY PRESS for permission to quote "A Hymn" by G. K. Chesterton.

A cataloguing record for this publication is available from
Library and Archives Canada

ISBN 1-57383-381-9

CONTENTS

CONTENTS

CONTENTS

As I Was Saying

INTRODUCTION

CHESTERTON FOR ALL

George Bernard Shaw called him a "colossal genius." When being awarded an honorary doctoral degree by the University of Notre Dame, he was referred to as a "defender of the Christian tradition, whose keen mind, right heart, and versatile literary genius have been valiantly devoted to eternal truth, goodness and beauty, in literature and in life." And Pope Pius XI called him a devoted son of the Holy Church and a gifted defender of the Faith. The wisdom of Gilbert Keith Chesterton (1874–1936) remains an inspiration for us today.

Chesterton was a dominant figure in English letters during the first third of this century, as well as the ablest and most exuberant proponent of orthodox Christianity of his time—a time characterized by spiritual doubt, pessimism, and skepticism. The recent reawakening of interest in his writings and the recognition of the present importance of his social and moral ideas began in the 1970's. The Chesterton Society was founded in 1974, the centenary of GKC's birth, and *The Chesterton Review* began publication the same year. In the past decade over a dozen books about GKC have been published, as well as several anthologies of his writings and reprints of his works. Notable among these is the edition of GKC's complete works, being published by Ignatius Press.

Chesterton was a prolific writer, having produced nearly a hundred books. Nevertheless, he considered himself primarily a journalist, writing articles for 75 different British periodicals (over 1500 essays for *The Illustrated London News* alone) and for about 50 different American magazines. His bibliographer, Mr. John Sullivan, speaks of his "apparently inexhaustible nature. There seems no end of him." Included in his huge output are literary criticism, religious and philosophical argumentation, biographies, detective stories, novels and short stories, economic and political writings, social commentary, humorous writing and nonsense verse, plays, and poetry.

Chesterton's great range of personal interests and intellectual involvements makes his writings of almost universal appeal. The noted American journalist Joe Breig summarizes his broad appeal as follows:

Chesterton is recognized by essayists as one of the greatest of essayists; by poets as a magnificent poet; by humorists as a humorist of tremendous versatility; by philosophers as a profound philosopher; by controversialists as a deadly but lovable master of controversy; by political economists as a man of deep political insights; by novelists as a most able novelist; and by theologians as one who saw, sometimes, far deeper than they are able to see into theological truth.

[From *Ave Maria*, 9 May 1959]

And, as Karl G. Schmude points out in *The Man Who Was Chesterton*,

No one understood the common man better than Chesterton; no one had a deeper appreciation of his loves and hungers. All his life he fought, through his writings, for the freedom and dignity, the normal loyalties and elementary rights of the ordinary person. Unlike many revolutionaries and reformers, Chesterton understood the people about whom he talked and for whom he professed to speak; his popular sympathies . . . could really survive any intimacy with the populace.

But the remarkable variety and universality of Chesterton's expressiveness is of less importance than the grounding of his life and thought in a clearly unified context of wonder, praise, and faith. He related everything to ultimate beliefs in man, his reason, his religious faith, and his supernatural destiny. He was deeply aware that each of us has been just saved, gratuitously, from non-existence, and he had a constant sense of being within the palpable presence of divine governance and truth, under the cope of eternity.

Paul Claudel, the eminent Catholic novelist and playwright, was the French ambassador to the United States during Chesterton's 1930–1931 trip to America. At this time Claudel remarked:

Chesterton thoroughly understands that in our religion Mystery is wed with Evidence, and our eternal responses with the most pressing and present exigencies. He is the man that threw the doors wide open: and upon a world pallid and sick he sent floods of poetry, of joyousness, of noble sympathies, of radiant and thundering humor—all drawn from unfailing sources of orthodoxy. His onward march is the verification of that divine saying: "The truth will make you free."

If I were to state his essential quality, I would say that it is a sort of triumphant common sense—that *gaudiam de veritate*, of which philosophers discourse; a joyous acclaim towards the splendor and the powers of the soul, those faculties that were overburdened and numbed by a century of false science [and] of pedantic pessimism. . . . In the sparkling and irresistible dialectics of a great poet, he keeps always bringing us back to that infallible promise of Christ: And I will refresh you: *Et Ego reficiam vos.*

4

INTRODUCTION

[From Paul Claudel, *Chestertoniana*, published by Holy Cross College, 1930]

Chesterton's longtime friend and journalistic collaborator, W. R. Titterton, had this to say of GKC in 1936, shortly after Chesterton's death:

> Let me rather hint at the effect that G. K. C. had upon me. . . . He taught me the value of common things and ordinary people; he taught me to understand for the first time the meaning of democracy. For G. K. C. was not a democrat, he was democracy. He was really at home with all sorts and ranks of people, with kings and cobblers, with learned men and ignorant men, with wise men and fools, so long as they were not cocky, intrusive fools. He taught me to fight without rancour, and to love the enemy while I hated his creed. And, from first to last, he amazed me, overpowered me, with his innocence and humility. Extensively he has influenced the world most by his great powers as a controversialist. But intensively the influence of his personality, his example, his way of life, was far greater. "To know him was a benediction."

[From W. R. Titterton, *G. K. Chesterton: A Portrait*]

✤ 1 ✤

EXCERPTS FROM *AUTOBIOGRAPHY*

B OWING down in blind credulity, as is my custom, before mere
authority and the tradition of the elders, superstitiously swallow-
ing a story I could not test at the time by experiment or private judgment, I am firmly of the opinion that I was born on the 29th of May, 1874,
on Campden Hill, Kensington; and baptised according to the formu-
laries of the Church of England in the little church of St. George opposite the large Waterworks Tower that dominated that ridge. I do not
allege any significance in the relation of the two buildings; and I indignantly deny that the church was chosen because it needed the whole
water-power of West London to turn me into a Christian.

Nevertheless, the great Waterworks Tower was destined to play its
part in my life, as I shall narrate on a subsequent page; but that story is
connected with my own experiences, whereas my birth (as I have said) is
an incident which I accept, like some poor ignorant peasant, only because it has been handed down to me by oral tradition. And before we
come to any of my own experiences, it will be well to devote this brief
chapter to a few of the other facts of my family and environment which I
hold equally precariously on mere hearsay evidence. Of course what
many call hearsay evidence, or what I call human evidence, might be
questioned in theory, as in the Baconian controversy or a good deal of
the Higher Criticism. The story of my birth might be untrue. I might be
the long-lost heir of The Holy Roman Empire, or an infant left by
ruffians from Limehouse on a door-step in Kensington, to develop in
later life a hideous criminal heredity. Some of the sceptical methods
applied to the world's origin might be applied to my origin, and a grave
and earnest inquirer come to the conclusion that I was never born at all.
But I prefer to believe that common sense is something that my readers
and I have in common; and that they will have patience with a dull
summary of the facts.   [Beginning of Chapter 1]

THE very first thing I can ever remember seeing with my own eyes was a young man walking across a bridge. He had a curly moustache and an attitude of confidence verging on swagger. He carried in his hand a disproportionately large key of a shining yellow metal and wore a large golden or gilded crown. The bridge he was crossing sprang on the one side from the edge of a highly perilous mountain chasm, the peaks of the range rising fantastically in the distance; and at the other end it joined the upper part of the tower of an almost excessively castellated castle. In the castle tower there was one window, out of which a young lady was looking. I cannot remember in the least what she looked like; but I will do battle with anyone who denies her superlative good looks.

To those who may object that such a scene is rare in the home life of house-agents living immediately to the north of Kensington High Street, in the later seventies of the last century, I shall be compelled to admit, not that the scene was unreal, but that I saw it through a window more wonderful than the window in the tower; through the proscenium of a toy theatre constructed by my father; and that (if I am really to be pestered about such irrelevant details) the young man in the crown was about six inches high and proved on investigation to be made of cardboard. But it is strictly true to say that I saw him before I can remember seeing anybody else; and that, so far as my memory is concerned, this was the sight on which my eyes first opened in this world. And the scene has to me a sort of aboriginal authenticity impossible to describe; something at the back of all my thoughts; like the very back-scene of the theatre of things. I have no shadow of recollection of what the young man was doing on the bridge, or of what he proposed to do with the key; though a later and wearier knowledge of literature and legend hints to me that he was not improbably going to release the lady from captivity. It is a not unamusing detail of psychology that, though I can remember no other characters in the story, I do remember noting that the crowned gentleman had a moustache and no beard, with a vague inference that there was another crowned gentleman who had a beard as well. We may safely guess, I imagine, that the bearded one was by way of being a wicked king; and we should not need much more converging evidence to convict him of having locked up the lady in the tower. All the rest is gone; scenes, subject, story, characters; but that one scene glows in my memory like a glimpse of some incredible paradise; and, for all I know, I shall still remember it when all other memory is gone out of my mind.

Apart from the fact of it being my first memory, I have several reasons for putting it first. I am no psychologist, thank God; but if psychologists are still saying what ordinary sane people have always said: that early impressions count considerably in life, I recognise a sort of symbol of all that I happen to like in imagery and ideas. All my life I have loved edges; and the boundary-line that brings one thing sharply against another. All my life I have loved frames and limits; and I will maintain that the largest wilderness looks larger seen through a window. To the grief of all grave dramatic critics, I will still assert that the perfect drama must strive to rise to the higher ecstasy of the peep-show. I have also a pretty taste in abysses and bottomless chasms and everything else that emphasises a fine shade of distinction between one thing and another; and the warm affection I have always felt for bridges is connected with the fact that the dark and dizzy arch accentuates the chasm even more than the chasm itself. I can no longer behold the beauty of the princess; but I can see it in the bridge that the prince crossed to reach her. And I believe that in feeling these things from the first, I was feeling the fragmentary suggestions of a philosophy I have since found to be the truth. For it is upon that point of truth that there might perhaps be a quarrel between the more material psychologists and myself. If any man tells me that I only take pleasure in the mysteries of the window and the bridge because I saw these models of them when I was a baby, I shall take the liberty of telling him that he has not thought the thing out. To begin with, I must have seen thousands of other things before as well as after; and there must have been an element of selection and some reason for selection. And, what is still more obvious, to date the occasion does not even begin to deal with the fact. If some laborious reader of little books on child-psychology cries out to me in glee and cunning: "You only like romantic things like toy theatres because your father showed you a toy theatre in your childhood," I shall reply with gentle and Christian patience: "Yes, fool, yes. Undoubtedly your explanation is, in that sense, the true one. But what you are saying, in your witty way, is simply that I associate these things with happiness because I was so happy. It does not even begin to consider the question of why I was so happy. Why should looking through a square hole, at yellow pasteboard, lift anybody into the seventh heaven of happiness at any time of life? Why should it specially do so at that time of life? That is the psychological fact that you have to explain; and I have never seen any sort of rational explanation."

I apologise for this parenthesis; and for mentioning child psychology or anything else that can bring a blush to the cheek. But it happens to be a point on which I think some of our psycho-analysts display rather unblushing cheek. I do not wish my remarks confused with the horrible and degrading heresy that our minds are merely manufactured by accidental conditions, and therefore have no ultimate relation to truth at all. With all possible apologies to the freethinkers, I still propose to hold myself free to think. And anybody who will think for two minutes will see that this thought is the end of all thinking. It is useless to argue at all, if all our conclusions are warped by our conditions. Nobody can correct anybody's bias, if all mind is all bias.

The interlude is now over, thank you; and I will proceed to the more practical relations between my memory and my story. . . .

[From Chapter 2]

IN truth, the story of what was called my Optimism was rather odd. When I had been for some time in these, the darkest depths of contemporary pessimism, I had a strong inward impulse to revolt; to dislodge this incubus or throw off this nightmare. But as I was still thinking the thing out by myself, with little help from philosophy and no real help from religion, I invented a rudimentary and makeshift mystical theory of my own. It was substantially this; that even mere existence, reduced to its most primary limits, was extraordinary enough to be exciting. Anything was magnificent compared with nothing. Even if the very daylight were a dream, it was a day-dream; it was not a nightmare. The mere fact that one could wave one's arms and legs about (or those dubious external objects in the landscape which were called one's arms and legs) showed that it had not the mere paralysis of a nightmare. Or if it was a nightmare, it was an enjoyable nightmare. In fact, I had wandered to a position not very far from the phrase of my Puritan grandfather, when he said that he would thank God for his creation if he were a lost soul. I hung on to the remains of religion by one thin thread of thanks. I thanked whatever gods might be, not like Swinburne, because no life lived forever, but because any life lived at all; not, like Henley for my unconquerable soul (for I have never been so optimistic about my own soul as all that) but for my own soul and my own body, even if they could be conquered. This way of looking at things, with a sort of mystical minimum of gratitude, was of course, to some extent assisted by those few of the fashionable writers who were not pessimists; especially by Walt Whitman, by Browning and by Stevenson; Browning's "God must be glad one loves his world so much," or Stevenson's "belief in the ultimate decency of things." But I do not think it is too much to say that I took it in a way of my own; even if it was a way I could not see clearly or make very clear. What I meant,

9

whether or no I managed to say it, was this; that no man knows how much he is an optimist, even when he calls himself a pessimist, because he has not really measured the depths of his debt to whatever created him and enabled him to call himself anything. At the back of our brains, so to speak, there was a forgotten blaze or burst of astonishment at our own existence. The object of the artistic and spiritual life was to dig for this submerged sunrise of wonder; so that a man sitting in a chair might suddenly understand that he was actually alive, and be happy. There were other aspects of this feeling, and other arguments about it, to which I shall have to return. Here it is only a necessary part of the narrative; as it involves the fact that, when I did begin to write, I was full of a new and fiery resolution to write against the Decadents and the Pessimists who ruled the culture of the age.

[From Chapter 4]

THE profound problem of how I ever managed to fall on my feet in Fleet Street is a mystery; at least it is still a mystery to me. It used to be said by critics that falling on my feet was only a preliminary to standing on my head. But in fact Fleet Street, not to mention my head, was a rather seasick and earthquaky sort of thing to stand on. On the whole, I think I owe my success (as the millionaires say) to having listened respectfully and rather bashfully to the very best advice, given by all the best journalists who had achieved the best sort of success in journalism; and then going away and doing the exact opposite. For what they all told me was that the secret of success in journalism was to study the particular journal and write what was suitable to it. And, partly by accident and ignorance and partly through the real rabid certainties of youth, I cannot remember that I ever wrote any article that was at all suitable to any paper.

On the contrary, I think I became a sort of comic success by contrast. I have a notion that the real advice I could give to a young journalist, now that I am myself an old journalist, is simply this: to write an article for the *Sporting Times* and another for the *Church Times*, and put them in the wrong envelopes. Then, if the articles were accepted and were reasonably intelligent, all the sporting men would go about saying to each other, "Great mistake to suppose there isn't a good case for us; really brainy fellows say so"; and all the clergymen would go about saying to each other, "Rattling good writing on some of our religious papers; very witty fellow." This is perhaps a little faint and fantastic as a theory, but it is the only theory upon which I can explain my own undeserved survival in the journalistic squabble of the old Fleet Street. I wrote on a Nonconformist organ like the old *Daily News* and told them all about French cafés and Catholic cathedrals; and they loved it, because they had never heard of them before. I wrote on a robust Labour organ like the old *Clarion* and defended medieval theology and all the things their readers had never heard of; and their readers did not mind me a bit. What is really the matter, with almost every paper, is that it is much too full of things suitable to the paper. But in these later days of the solidification of journalism, like everything else, into trusts and monopolies, there seems to be even less likelihood of anyone repeating my rare and reckless and unscrupulous manoeuvre; of anyone waking up to find himself famous as the only funny man on the *Methodist Monthly;* or the only serious man on *Cocktail Comics.*

[From Chapter 8]

. . . one of the most admirably absurd correspondences I have ever seen in the columns of journalism. It all began, if I remember right, with my brother writing something about the meeting between H. G. Wells and Booker Washington, the famous Negro publicist in America, in which some doubt was thrown on how far Mr. Wells understood the difficulties of Mr. Washington, and by inference those of the White South in which he worked. This view was enforced and exaggerated in a letter dated from Bexley, which warned everybody of the real dangers of racial admixture and intermarriage; it was signed "White Man." This produced a fiery letter from Mr. Wells, humorously headed, "The White Man of Bexley," as if the man were a sort of monster. Mr. Wells said he did not know what life was like "among the pure whites of Bexley," but that elsewhere meeting people did not always mean marrying them; "The etiquette is calmer." Then I think, a real Negro intervened in the debate about his nature and destiny; and signed his letter, "Black Man." Then came a more detached query, I should guess from some Brahmin or Parsee student at some college, pointing out that the racial problem was not confined to the races of Africa; and asking what view was taken of intermarriage with the races of Asia. He signed his letter "Brown Man." Finally, there appeared a letter, of which I remember almost every word; for it was short and simple and touching in its appeal to larger and more tolerant ideals. It ran, I think, as follows:

"Sir,

May I express my regret that you should continue a correspondence which causes considerable pain to many innocent persons who, by no fault of their own, but by the iron laws of nature, inherit a complexion uncommon among their fellow-creatures and attractive only to the élite. Surely we can forget all these differences; and, whatever our race or colour, work hand in hand for the broadening of the brotherhood of humanity.

Yours faithfully,
Mauve Man with Green Spots."

This correspondence then ceased.

[From Chapter 8]

I remember another rather ridiculous private incident which had more of what is called public interest. For it involved the meeting of Belloc and a very famous and distinguished author; and I think the meeting was the most comic comedy of cross-purposes that ever happened in the world. One could write books about its significance, social, national, international and historic. It had in it all sorts of things; including the outside and the inside of England. And yet as an anecdote it would probably seem pointless, so subtle and penetrating is the point.

One summer we took a house at Rye, that wonderful inland island, crowned with a town as with a citadel, like a hill in a medieval picture. It happened that the house next to us was the old oak-panelled mansion which had attracted, one might almost say across the Atlantic, the fine aquiline eye of Henry James. For Henry James, of course, was an American who had reacted against America; and steeped his sensitive psychology in everything that seemed most antiquatedly and aristocratically English. In his search for the finest shades among the shadows of the past, one might have guessed that he would pick out that town from all towns and that house from all houses. It had been the seat of a considerable patrician family of the neighbourhood, which had long ago decayed and disappeared. It had, I believe, rows of family portraits, which Henry James treated as reverently as family ghosts. I think in a way he really regarded himself as a sort of steward or custodian of the mysteries and secrets of a great house, where ghosts might have walked with all possible propriety. The legend says (I never learned for certain if it was true) that he had actually traced that dead family-tree until he found that there was far away in some manufacturing town, one unconscious descendant of the family, who was a cheerful and commonplace commercial clerk. And it is said that Henry James would ask this youth down to his dark ancestral house, and receive him with funereal hospitality, and I am sure with comments of a quite excruciating tact and delicacy. Henry James always spoke with an air which I can only call gracefully groping; that is not so much groping in the dark in blindness as groping in the light in bewilderment, through seeing too many avenues and obstacles. I would not compare it, in the unkind phrase of Mr. H. G. Wells, to an elephant trying to pick up a pea. But I agree that it was like something with a very sensitive and flexible proboscis, feeling its way through a forest of facts; to us often invisible facts. It is said, I say, that these thin straws of sympathy and subtlety were duly split for the benefit of the astonished commercial gentleman, while Henry James, with his bowed dome-like head, drooped with unfathomable apologies and rendered a sort of silent account of his stewardship. It is also said that the commercial gentleman thought the visit a great bore and the ancestral home a hell of a place; and probably fidgeted about with a longing to go out for a B and S and the *Pink 'Un*.

Whether this tale be true or not, it is certain that Henry James inhabited the house with all the gravity and loyalty of the family ghost; not without something of the oppressive delicacy of a highly cultured family butler. He was in point of fact a very stately and courteous old gentleman; and, in some social aspects especially, rather uniquely gracious. He proved in one point that there was a truth in his cult of tact. He was serious with children. I saw a little boy gravely present him with a crushed and dirty dandelion. He bowed; but he did not smile. That restraint was a better proof of the understanding of children than the writing of *What Maisie Knew*. But in all relations of life he erred, if he erred, on the side of solemnity and slowness; and it was this, I suppose, that got at last upon the too lively nerves of Mr. Wells; who used, even in those days, to make irreverent darts and dashes through the sombre house and the sacred garden and drop notes to me over the garden wall. I shall have more to say of Mr. H. G. Wells and his notes later; here we are halted at the moment when Mr. Henry James heard of our arrival in Rye and proceeded (after exactly the correct interval) to pay his call in state.

Needless to say, it was a very stately call of state; and James seemed to fill worthily the formal frock-coat of those far-off days. As no man is so dreadfully well-dressed as a well-dressed American, so no man is so terribly well-mannered as a well-mannered American. He brought his brother William with him, the famous American philosopher; and though William James was breezier than his brother when you knew him, there was something finally ceremonial about this idea of the whole family on the march. We talked about the best literature of the day; James a little tactfully, myself a little nervously. I found he was more strict than I had imagined about the rules of artistic arrangement; he deplored rather than depreciated Bernard Shaw, because plays like *Getting Married* were practically formless. He said something complimentary about something of mine; but represented himself as respectfully wondering how I wrote all I did. I suspected him of meaning why rather than how. We then proceeded to consider gravely the work of Hugh Walpole, with many delicate degrees of appreciation and doubt; when I heard from the front-garden a loud bellowing noise resembling that of an impatient fog-horn. I knew, however, that it was not a fog-horn; because it was roaring out, "Gilbert! Gilbert!" and was like only one voice in the world; as rousing as that recalled in one of its former phrases, of those who

> Heard Ney shouting to the guns to unlimber
> And hold the Beresina Bridge at night.

I knew it was Belloc, probably shouting for bacon and beer; but even I had no notion of the form or guise under which he would present himself.

I had every reason to believe that he was a hundred miles away in France. And so, apparently, he had been; walking with a friend of his in the Foreign Office, a co-religionist of one of the old Catholic families; and by some miscalculation they had found themselves in the middle of their travels entirely without money. Belloc is legitimately proud of having on occasion lived, and being able to live, the life of the poor. One of the Ballades of the *Eye-Witness*, which was never published, described tramping abroad in this fashion:

> To sleep and smell the incense of the tar,
> To wake and watch Italian dawns aglow
> And underneath the branch a single star,
> Good Lord, how little wealthy people know.

In this spirit they started to get home practically without money. Their clothes collapsed and they managed to get into some workmen's slops. They had no razors and could not afford a shave. They must have saved their last penny to recross the sea; and then they started walking from Dover to Rye; where they knew their nearest friend for the moment resided. They arrived, roaring for food and drink and derisively accusing each other of having secretly washed, in violation of an implied contract between tramps. In this fashion they burst in upon the balanced tea-cup and tentative sentence of Mr. Henry James.

Henry James had a name for being subtle; but I think that situation was too subtle for him. I doubt to this day whether he, of all men, did not miss the irony of the best comedy in which he ever played a part. He had left America because he loved Europe, and all that was meant by England or France; the gentry, the gallantry, the traditions of lineage and locality, the life that had been lived beneath old portraits in oak-panelled rooms. And there, on the other side of the tea-table, was Europe, was the old thing that made France and England, the posterity of the English squires and the French soldiers; ragged, unshaven, shouting for beer, shameless above all shades of poverty and wealth; sprawling, indifferent, secure. And what looked across at it was still the Puritan refinement of Boston; and the space it looked across was wider than the Atlantic.

It is only fair to say that my two friends were at the moment so disreputable that even an English inn-keeper was faintly at fault in his unfailing nose for gentlemen. He knew they were not tramps; but he had to rally his powers of belief to become completely convinced that they were a Member of Parliament and an official at the Foreign Office. But, though he was a simple and even stupid man, I am not sure that he did not know more about it than Henry James. The fact that one of my friends insisted on having a bottle of port decanted and carrying it through the streets of Rye, like a part of a religious procession, completely restored his confidence in the class to which such lunatics belonged. I have always been haunted by the contradictions of that comedy; and if I could ever express all that was involved in it, I should write a great book on international affairs. I do not say I should become the champion of an Anglo-American Alliance; for any fool can do that, and indeed generally does. But I should begin to suggest something which is often named and has never been even remotely approached: an Anglo-American Understanding.

[From Chapter 10]

WHEN people ask me, or indeed anybody else, "Why did you join the Church of Rome?" the first essential answer, if it is partly an elliptical answer, is, "To get rid of my sins." For there is no other religious system that does *really* profess to get rid of people's sins.

It is confirmed by the logic, which to many seems startling, by which the Church deduces that sin confessed and adequately repented is actually abolished; and that the sinner does really begin again as if he had never sinned. And this brought me sharply back to those visions or fancies with which I have dealt in the chapter about childhood. I spoke there of the indescribable and indestructible certitude in the soul, that those first years of innocence were the beginning of something worthy, perhaps more worthy than any of the things that actually followed them. I spoke of the strange daylight, which was something more than the light of common day, that still seems in my memory to shine on those steep roads down from Campden Hill, from which one could see the Crystal Palace from afar. Well, when a Catholic comes from Confession, he does truly, by definition, step out again into that dawn of his own beginning and look with new eyes across the world to a Crystal Palace that is really of crystal. He believes that in that dim corner, and in that brief ritual, God has really remade him in His own image. He is now a new experiment of the Creator. He is as much a new experiment as he was when he was really only five years old. He stands, as I said, in the white light at the worthy beginning of the life of a man. The accumulations of time can no longer terrify. He may be grey and gouty; but he is only five minutes old.

I am not here defending such doctrines as that of the Sacrament of Penance; any more than the equally staggering doctrine of the Divine love for man. I am not writing a book of religious controversy; of which I have written several and shall probably, unless violently restrained by my friends and relatives, write several more. I am here engaged in the morbid and degrading task of telling the story of my life; and have only to state what actually were the effects of such doctrines on my own feelings and actions. And I am, by the nature of the task, especially concerned with the fact that these doctrines seem to me to link up my whole life from the beginning, as no other doctrines could do; and especially to settle simultaneously the two problems of my childish happiness and my boyish brooding. And they specially affected one idea; which I hope it is not pompous to call the chief idea of my life; I will not say the doctrine I have always taught, but the doctrine I should always have liked to teach. That is the idea of taking things with gratitude, and not taking things for granted. Thus the Sacrament of Penance gives a new life, and reconciles a man to all living, but it does not do it as the optimists and the hedonists and the heathen preachers of happiness do it. The gift is given at a price, and is conditioned by a confession. In other words, the name of the price is Truth, which may also be called

Reality; but it is facing the reality about oneself. When the process is only applied to other people, it is called Realism.

I began by being what the pessimists call an optimist; I have ended by being what the optimists would very probably call a pessimist. And I have never in fact been either, and I have never really changed at all. I began by defending vermillion pillar-boxes and Victorian omnibuses although they were ugly. I have ended by denouncing modern advertisements or American films even when they are beautiful. The thing that I was trying to say then is the same thing that I am trying to say now; and even the deepest revolution of religion has only confirmed me in the desire to say it. For indeed, I never saw the two sides of this single truth stated together anywhere, until I happened to open the Penny Catechism and read the words, "The two sins against Hope are presumption and despair."

I began in my boyhood to grope for it from quite the other end; the end of the earth most remote from purely supernatural hopes. But even about the dimmest earthly hope, or the smallest earthly happiness, I had from the first an almost violently vivid sense of those two dangers; the sense that the experience must not be spoilt by presumption or despair. To take a convenient tag out of my first juvenile book of rhymes, I asked through what incarnations or prenatal purgatories I must have passed, to earn the reward of looking at a dandelion. Now it would be easy enough, if the thing were worth while even for a commentator, to date that phrase by certain details, or guess that it might have been worded otherwise at a later time. I do not believe in Reincarnation, if indeed I ever did; and since I have owned a garden (for I cannot say since I have been a gardener) I have realised better than I did that there really is a case against weeds. But in substance what I said about the dandelion is exactly what I should say about the sunflower or the sun, or the glory which (as the poet said) is brighter than the sun. The only way to enjoy even a weed is to feel unworthy even of a weed. Now there are two ways of complaining of the weed or the flower; and one was the fashion in my youth and another is the fashion in my later days; but they are not only both wrong, but both wrong because the same thing is right. The pessimists of my boyhood, when confronted with the dandelion, said with Swinburne:

> I am weary of days and hours,
> Blown buds of barren flowers,
> Desires and dreams and powers
> And everything but sleep.

And at this I cursed them and kicked at them and made an exhibition of myself; having made myself the champion of the Lion's Tooth, with a dandelion rampant on my crest. But there is a way of despising the dandelion which is not that of the dreary pessimist, but of the more offensive optimist. It can be done in various ways; one of which is saying, "You can get much better dandelions at Selfridge's," or "You can get much cheaper dandelions at Woolworth's." Another way is to observe with a casual drawl, "Of course nobody but Gamboli in Vienna really understands dandelions," or saying that nobody would put up with the old-fashioned dandelion since the super-dandelion has been grown in the Frankfurt Palm Garden; or merely sneering at the stinginess of providing dandelions, when all the best hostesses give you an orchid for your buttonhole and a bouquet of rare exotics to take away with you. These are all methods of undervaluing the thing by comparison; for it is not familiarity but comparison that breeds contempt. And all such captious comparisons are ultimately based on the strange and staggering heresy that a human being has a *right* to dandelions; that in some extraordinary fashion we can demand the very pick of all the dandelions in the garden of Paradise; that we owe no thanks for them at all and need feel no wonder at them at all; and above all no wonder at being thought worthy to receive them. Instead of saying, like the old religious poet, "What is man that Thou carest for him, or the son of man that Thou regardest him?" we are to say like the discontented cabman, "What's this?" or like the bad-tempered Major in the club, "Is this a chop fit for a gentleman?" Now I not only dislike this attitude quite as much as the Swinburnian pessimistic attitude, but I think it comes to very much the same thing; to the actual loss of appetite for the chop or the dish of dandelion-tea. And the name of it is Presumption and the name of its twin brother is Despair.

This is the principle I was maintaining when I seemed an optimist to Mr. Max Beerbohm; and this is the principle I am still maintaining when I should undoubtedly seem a pessimist to Mr. Gordon Selfridge. The aim of life is appreciation; there is no sense in not appreciating things; and there is no sense in having more of them if you have less appreciation of them. I originally said that a cockney lamp-post painted pea-green was better than no light or no life; and that if it was a lonely lamp-post, we might really see its light better against the background of the dark. The Decadent of my early days, however, was so distressed by it that he wanted to hang himself on the lamp-post, to extinguish the lamp, and to let everything relapse into aboriginal darkness. The modern millionaire comes bustling along the street to tell me he is an Optimist and has two million five thousand new lamp-posts, all ready painted not a Victorian pea-green but a Futuristic crome yellow and electric blue, and that he will plant them over the whole world in such numbers that nobody will notice them, especially as they will all look exactly the same. And I cannot quite see what the Optimist has got to be Optimistic about. A lamp-post can be significant although it is ugly. But he is not making lamp-posts significant; he is making them insignificant.

In short, as it seems to me, it matters very little whether a man is discontented in the name of pessimism or progress, if his discontent does in fact paralyse his power of appreciating what he has got. The real difficulty of man is not to enjoy lamp-posts or landscapes, not to enjoy dandelions or chops; but to enjoy enjoyment. To keep the capacity of really liking what he likes; that is the practical problem which the philosopher has to solve. And it seemed to me at the beginning, as it seems to me now in the end, that the pessimists and optimists of the modern world have alike missed and muddled in this matter; through leaving out the ancient conception of humility and the thanks of the unworthy. This is a matter much more important and interesting than my opinions; but, in point of fact, it was by following this thin thread of a fancy about thankfulness, as slight as any of those dandelion clocks that are blown upon the breeze like thistledown, that I did arrive eventually at an opinion which is more than an opinion. Perhaps the one and only opinion that is really more than an opinion.

For this secret of antiseptic simplicity was really a secret; it was not obvious, and certainly not obvious at that time. It was a secret that had already been almost entirely left to, and locked up with, certain neglected and unpopular things. It was almost as if the dandelion-tea really were a medicine, and the only recipe or prescription belonged to one old woman, a ragged and nondescript old woman, rather reputed in our village to be a witch. Anyhow, it is true that both the happy hedonists and the unhappy pessimists were stiffened by the opposite principle of pride. The pessimist was proud of pessimism, because he thought nothing good enough for him; the optimist was proud of optimism, because he thought nothing was bad enough to prevent him from getting good out of it. There were valuable men of both these types; there were men with many virtues; but they not only did not possess the virtue I was thinking of, but they never thought of it. They would decide that life was no good, or that it had a great deal of good; but they were not in touch with this particular notion, of having a great deal of gratitude even for a very little good. And as I began to believe more and more that the clue was to be found in such a principle, even if it was a paradox, I was more and more disposed to seek out those who specialised in humility, though for them it was the door of heaven and for me the door of earth.

For nobody else *specialises* in that mystical mood in which the yellow star of the dandelion is startling, being something unexpected and undeserved. There are philosophies as varied as the flowers of the field, and some of them weeds and a few of them poisonous weeds. But they none of them create the psychological conditions in which I first saw, or desired to see, the flower. Men will crown themselves with flowers and brag of them, or sleep on flowers and forget them, or number and name all the flowers for a parade of learning and pedantry, or cultivate the flowers only in order to grow a super-flower for the Imperial International Flower Show; or, on the other hand, trample the flowers like a stampede of buffaloes, or root up the flowers as a childish camouflage of the cruelty of nature, or tear the flowers with their teeth to show that they are enlightened philosophical pessimists. But this original problem with which I myself started, the utmost possible imaginative appreciation of the flower—about that they can make nothing but blunders, in that they are ignorant of the elementary facts of human nature; in that, working wildly in all directions, they are all without exception going the wrong way to work. Since the time of which I speak, the world has in this respect grown even worse. A whole generation has been taught to talk nonsense at the top of its voice about having "a right to life" and "a right to experience" and "a right to happiness." The lucid thinkers who talk like this generally wind up their assertion of all these extraordinary rights, by saying that there is no such thing as right and wrong. It is a little difficult, in that case, to speculate on where their rights came from; but I, at least, leaned more and more to the old philosophy which said that their real rights came from where the dandelion came from; and that they will never value either without recognising its source. And in that ultimate sense uncreated man, man merely in the position of the babe unborn, has no right even to see a dandelion; for he could not himself have invented either the dandelion or the eyesight.

I have here fallen back on one idle figure of speech from a fortunately forgotten book of verses; merely because such a thing is light and trivial, and the children puff it away like thistledown; and this will be most fitting to a place in which formal argument would be quite a misfit. But lest anyone should suppose that the notion has no relation to the argument, but is only a sentimental fancy about weeds or wild flowers, I will lightly and briefly suggest how even the figure fits in with all the aspects of the argument. For the first thing the casual critic will say is "What nonsense all this is; do you mean that a poet cannot be thankful for grass and wild flowers without connecting it with theology; let alone your theology?" To which I answer, "Yes, I mean he cannot do it without connecting it with theology, unless he can do it without connecting it with thought. If he can manage to be thankful when there is nobody to be thankful to, and no good intentions to be thankful for, then he is simply taking refuge in being thoughtless in order to avoid being thankless."

[From Chapter 16]

THIS story, therefore, can only end as any detective story should end, with its own particular questions answered and its own primary problem solved. Thousands of totally different stories, with totally different problems, have ended in the same place with their problems solved. But for me my end is my beginning, as Maurice Baring quoted of Mary Stuart, and this overwhelming conviction that there is one key which can unlock all doors brings back to me my first glimpse of the glorious gift of the senses; and the sensational experience of sensation. And there starts up again before me, standing sharp and clear in shape as of old, the figure of a man who crosses a bridge and who carries a key; as I saw him when I first looked into fairyland through the window of my father's peepshow. But I know that he who is called Pontifex, the Builder of the Bridge, is also called Claviger, the Bearer of the Key; and that such keys were given him to bind and loose when he was a poor fisher in a far province, beside a small and almost secret sea.

[From Chapter 16]

❧ 2 ☙

RELIGIOUS POEMS

The Donkey

When fishes flew and forests walked
    And figs grew upon thorn,
Some moment when the moon was blood
    Then surely I was born.

With monstrous head and sickening cry
    And ears like errant wings,
The devil's walking parody
    On all four-footed things.

The tattered outlaw of the earth,
    Of ancient crooked will;
Starve, scourge, deride me: I am dumb,
    I keep my secret still.

Fools! For I also had my hour;
    One far fierce hour and sweet:
There was a shout about my ears,
    And palms before my feet.

[From *The Wild Knight*]

The Ballad of God-Makers

A bird flew out at the break of day
    From the nest where it had curled,
And ere the eve the bird had set
    Fear on the kings of the world.

22

The first tree it lit upon
    Was green with leaves unshed;
The second tree it lit upon
    Was red with apples red;

The third tree it lit upon
    Was barren and was brown,
Save for a dead man nailed thereon
    On a hill above a town.

That night the kings of the earth were gay
    And filled the cup and can;
Last night the kings of the earth were chill
    For dread of a naked man.

"If he speak two more words," they said,
    "The slave is more than the free;
If he speak three more words," they said,
    "The stars are under the sea."

Said the King of the East to the King of the West,
    I wot his frown was set,
"Lo, let us slay him and make him as dung,
    It is well that the world forget."

Said the King of the West to the King of the East,
    I wot his smile was dread,
"Nay, let us slay him and make him a god,
    It is well that our god be dead."

They set the young man on a hill,
    They nailed him to a rod;
And there in darkness and in blood
    They made themselves a god.

And the mightiest word was left unsaid,
    And the world had never a mark,
And the strongest man of the sons of men
    Went dumb into the dark.

Then hymns and harps of praise they brought,
    Incense and gold and myrrh,
And they throned above the seraphim,
    The poor dead carpenter.

"Thou art the prince of all," they sang,
  "Ocean and earth and air,"
Then the bird flew on to the cruel cross,
  And hid in the dead man's hair.

"Thou art the sun of the world," they cried,
  "Speak if our prayers be heard."
And the brown bird stirred in the dead man's hair,
  And it seemed that the dead man stirred.

Then a shriek went up like the world's last cry
  From all nations under heaven,
And a master fell before a slave
  And begged to be forgiven.

They cowered, for dread in his wakened eyes
  The ancient wrath to see;
And the bird flew out of the dead Christ's hair,
  And lit on a lemon-tree.

[From *The Wild Knight*]

Ultimate

The vision of a haloed host
  That weep around an empty throne;
And, aureoles dark and angels dead,
  Man with his own life stands alone.

"I am," he says his bankrupt creed;
  "I am," and is again a clod:
The sparrow starts, the grasses stir,
  For he has said the name of God.

[From *The Wild Knight*]

The Wood-Cutter

We came behind him by the wall,
  My brethren drew their brands,
And they had strength to strike him down—
  And I to bind his hands.

Only once, to a lantern gleam,
 He turned his face from the wall,
And it was as the accusing angel's face
 On the day when the stars shall fall.

I grasped the axe with shaking hands,
 I stared at the grass I trod;
For I feared to see the whole bare heavens
 Filled with the face of God.

I struck: the serpentine slow blood
 In four arms soaked the moss—
Before me, by the living Christ,
 The blood ran in a cross.

Therefore I toil in the forests here
 And pile the wood in stacks,
And take no fee from the shivering folk
 Till I have cleansed the axe.

But for a curse God cleared my sight,
 And where each tree doth grow
I see a life with awful eyes,
 And I must lay it low.

        [From *The Wild Knight*]

The Convert

After one moment when I bowed my head
And the whole world turned over and came upright,
And I came out where the old road shone white,
I walked the ways and heard what all men said,
Forests of tongues, like autumn leaves unshed,
Being not unlovable but strange and light;
Old riddles and new creeds, not in despite
But softly, as men smile about the dead.

The sages have a hundred maps to give
That trace their crawling cosmos like a tree,
They rattle reason out through many a sieve
That stores the sand and lets the gold go free:

25

And all these things are less than dust to me
Because my name is Lazarus and I live.

[From *The Ballad of St. Barbara*]

Note: The above sonnet was written on the afternoon of the day on which Chesterton was baptized into the Roman Catholic Church. The year was 1922; Chesterton was 48 years old.

The Song of the Children

The World is ours till sunset,
 Holly and fire and snow,
And the name of our dead brother
 Who loved us long ago.

The grown folk mighty and cunning,
 They write his name in gold;
But we can tell a little
 Of the million tales he told.

He taught them laws and watchwords,
 To preach and struggle and pray;
But he taught us deep in the hayfield
 The games that the angels play.

Had he stayed here for ever,
 Their world would be wise as ours—
And the king be cutting capers,
 And the priest be picking flowers.

But the dark day came: they gathered:
 On their faces we could see
They had taken and slain our brother,
 And hanged him on a tree.

[From *The Wild Knight*]

The Happy Man

To teach the grey earth like a child,
  To bid the heavens repent,
I only ask from Fate the gift
  Of one man well content.

Him will I find: though when in vain
  I search the feast and mart,
The fading flowers of liberty,
  The painted masks of art.

I only find him as the last,
  On one old hill where nod
Golgotha's ghastly trinity—
  Three persons and one god.

[From *The Wild Knight*]

A Hymn

O God of earth and altar,
  Bow down and hear our cry,
Our earthly rulers falter,
  Our people drift and die;
The walls of gold entomb us,
  The swords of scorn divide,
Take not thy thunder from us,
  But take away our pride.

From all that terror teaches,
  From lies of tongue and pen,
From all the easy speeches
  That comfort cruel men,
From sale and profanation
  Of honour and the sword,
From sleep and from damnation,
  Deliver us, good Lord.

Tie in a living tether
   The prince and priest and thrall,
Bind all our lives together,
   Smite us and save us all;
In ire and exultation
   Aflame with faith, and free,
Lift up a living nation,
   A single sword to thee.

[From *Poems*]

❧ 3 ❧

CHESTERTON AND AMERICA

INTRODUCTION

It was on New Year's Day of 1921 that Chesterton and his wife Frances
set out from Southampton on their first visit to America. They arrived
in New York City on 10 January. Chesterton was already quite famous—certainly well known in the United States—and reporters
surrounded him on the pier. According to the *New York Times*, Mrs.
Chesterton "attended to the baggage examination, opening trunks
and bags, while her husband delivered a short essay on the equality of
men and women in England since the war." A columnist for the *Chicago
Tribune* referred humorously to Chesterton's size:

> As to his arrival in America, scientific investigation proves that the
> report was greatly exaggerated that as the boat bearing him came
> into New York harbor the water rose perceptibly to the naked eye,
> and the story that he was waited on by a committee of passengers
> and begged to stand in the exact center of the vessel is also
> unfounded.

The 1921 tour took the Chestertons as far west as Omaha and
Oklahoma City. During his three months here, GKC delivered forty
lectures in twenty-six cities, including Toronto and Montreal. The
newspapers of the cities he visited announced his arrival as an important cultural event; reviewed his lectures, sometimes extensively;
often interviewed and photographed him and sometimes Mrs.
Chesterton; and at times included editorials in response to his lectures
or quoted from his many books. Gilbert and Frances left America on
12 April, and GKC's next published book was *What I Saw in America*,
several chapters of which he had written while he was here.

Chesterton made his second tour of America, from September
1930 to April 1931, in response to an invitation to give two concurrent
series of lectures at the University of Notre Dame. This time the
Chestertons were accompanied by Miss Dorothy Collins, GKC's secretary. After a brief visit to his relatives in Ottawa and speaking

engagements in Montreal and Toronto, Chesterton proceeded to Notre Dame. His lectures there, eighteen on the literature of the Victorian Age and eighteen on the history of the Victorian Age, took up most of his time from 6 October to 14 November. On the 4th of November he was awarded a Doctor of Laws degree by the university. Chesterton then embarked on an extensive speaking tour. He lectured in twenty or so cities in the East and Midwest, and in ten West Coast cities, from San Diego to Vancouver and Victoria. In all, the second trip involved forty lectures and eight debates, in addition to the Notre Dame engagement. Two of the debates were with Clarence Darrow, in New Haven and New York City; both were entitled "Will the World Return to Religion?" Chesterton took the affirmative, of course, and in a ballot that followed the debate in New York City's Mecca Temple, the audience voted more than two to one for GKC. This is a part of Henry Hazlitt's report of the debate in *The Nation:*

Mr. Chesterton's argument was like Mr. Chesterton, amiable, courteous, jolly; it was always clever, it was full of nice turns of expression, and altogether a very adroit exhibition by one of the world's ablest intellectual fencing masters and one of its most charming gentlemen. Mr. Darrow's personality, by contrast, seemed rather colorless, and certainly very dour. His attitude seemed almost surly; he slurred his words; the rise and fall of his voice was sometimes heavily melodramatic, and his argument was conducted on an amazingly low intellectual level. Ostensibly the defender of science against Mr. Chesterton, he obviously knew much less science than Mr. Chesterton did; when he essayed to answer his opponent on the views of Eddington and Jeans, it was patent that he had not the remotest conception of what the new physics was all about. His victory over Mr. Bryan at Dayton had been too cheap and easy; he remembered it not wisely but too well. His arguments are still the arguments of village atheists of the Ingersoll period; at Mecca Temple he still seemed to be trying to shock and convince yokels. Mr. Chesterton's deportment was irreproachable, but I am sure that he was secretly unhappy. He had been on the platform many times against George Bernard Shaw. This opponent could not extend his powers. He was not getting his exercise.

[From *The Nation*, 4 February 1931]

The Chestertons left America on 17 April 1931. During 1932, GKC's *Sidelights on New London and Newer York* appeared; the second part of this book contains his reflections on his later American experiences.

Selections from
What I Saw in America

I have never managed to lose my old conviction that travel narrows the
mind. At least a man must make a double effort of moral humility and
imaginative energy to prevent it from narrowing his mind. Indeed there
is something touching and even tragic about the thought of the thoughtless tourist, who might have stayed at home loving Laplanders, embrac-
ing Chinamen, and clasping Patagonians to his heart in Hampstead or
Surbiton, but for his blind and suicidal impulse to go and see what they
looked like. This is not meant for nonsense; still less is it meant for the
silliest sort of nonsense, which is cynicism. The human bond that he
feels at home is not an illusion. Man is inside all men. In a real sense any
man may be inside any men. But to travel is to leave the inside and draw
dangerously near the outside. So long as he thought of men in the
abstract, like naked toiling figures in some classic frieze, merely as those
who labour and love their children and die, he was thinking the fundamental truth about them. By going to look at their unfamiliar manners
and customs he is inviting them to disguise themselves in fantastic masks
and costumes.

[From Chapter 1]

THE officials I interviewed were very American, especially in being
very polite; for whatever may have been the mood or meaning of
Martin Chuzzlewit, I have always found Americans by far the politest
people in the world. They put in my hands a form to be filled up, to all
appearances like other forms I had filled up in other passport offices.
But in reality it was very different from any form I had ever filled up in
my life. At least it was a little like a freer form of the game called
"Confessions" which my friends and I invented in our youth; an examination paper containing questions like, "If you saw a rhinoceros in the
front garden, what would you do?" One of my friends, I remember,

wrote, "Take the pledge." But that is another story, and might bring Mr. Pussyfoot Johnson on the scene before his time.

One of the questions on the paper was, "Are you an anarchist?" To which a detached philosopher would naturally feel inclined to answer, "What the devil has that to do with you? Are you an atheist?" . . . Then there was the question, "Are you in favour of subverting the government of the United States by force?" Against this I should write, "I prefer to answer that question at the end of my tour and not at the beginning." The inquisitor, in his more than morbid curiosity, had then written down, "Are you a polygamist?" The answer to this is, "No such luck" or "Not such a fool," according to our experience of the other sex. But perhaps a better answer would be that given to W. T. Stead when he circulated the rhetorical question, "Shall I slay my brother Boer?"—the answer that ran, "Never interfere in family matters." But among many things that amused me almost to the point of treating the form thus disrespectfully, the most amusing was the thought of the ruthless outlaw who should feel compelled to treat it respectfully. I like to think of the foreign desperado, seeking to slip into America with official papers under official protection, and sitting down to write with a beautiful gravity, "I am an anarchist. I hate you all and wish to destroy you." Or, "I intend to subvert by force the government of the United States as soon as possible, sticking the long sheath-knife in my left trouser-pocket into Mr. Harding at the earliest opportunity." Or again, "Yes, I am a polygamist all right, and my forty-seven wives are accompanying me on the voyage disguised as secretaries." There seems to be a certain simplicity of mind about these answers; and it is reassuring to know that anarchists and polygamists are so pure and good that the police have only to ask them questions and they are certain to tell no lies.

Now that is the model of the sort of foreign practice, founded on foreign problems, at which a man's first impulse is naturally to laugh. Nor have I any intention of apologising for my laughter. A man is perfectly entitled to laugh at a thing because he happens to find it incomprehensible. What he has no right to do is to laugh at it as incomprehensible, and then criticise it as if he comprehended it. The very fact of its unfamiliarity and mystery ought to set him thinking about the deeper causes that make people so different from himself, and that without merely assuming that they must be inferior to himself.

[From Chapter 1]

IN a journey which I took only the year before I had occasion to have my papers passed by governments which many worthy people in the West would vaguely identify with corsairs and assassins; I have stood on the other side of Jordan, in the land ruled by a rude Arab chief, where the police looked so like brigands that one wondered what the brigands looked like. But they did not ask me whether I had come to subvert the power of the Shereef; and they did not exhibit the faintest curiosity about my personal views on the ethical basis of civil authority. These ministers of ancient Moslem despotism did not care about whether I was an anarchist; and naturally would not have minded if I had been a polygamist. The Arab chief was probably a polygamist himself. These slaves of Asiatic autocracy were content, in the old liberal fashion, to judge me by my actions; they did not inquire into my thoughts. They held their power as limited to the limitation of practice; they did not forbid me to hold a theory. It would be easy to argue here that Western democracy persecutes where even Eastern despotism tolerates or emancipates. It would be easy to develop the fancy that, as compared with the sultans of Turkey or Egypt, the American Constitution is a thing like the Spanish Inquisition.

Only the traveller who stops at that point is totally wrong; and the traveller only too often does stop at that point. He has found something to make him laugh, and he will not suffer it to make him think. And the remedy is not to unsay what he has said, not even, so to speak, to unlaugh what he has laughed, not to deny that there is something unique and curious about this American inquisition into our abstract opinions, but rather to continue the train of thought, and follow the admirable advice of Mr. H. G. Wells, who said, "It is not much good thinking of a thing unless you think it out." It is not to deny that American officialism is rather peculiar on this point, but to inquire what it really is which makes America peculiar, or which is peculiar to America. In short, it is to get some ultimate idea of what America *is;* and the answer to that question will reveal something much deeper and grander and more worthy of our intelligent interest.

[From Chapter 1]

B UT there are some things about America that a man ought to see even with his eyes shut. One is that a state that came into existence solely through its repudiation and abhorrence of the British Crown is not likely to be a respectful copy of the British Constitution. Another is that the chief mark of the Declaration of Independence is something that is not only absent from the British Constitution, but something which all our constitutionalists have invariably thanked God, with the jolliest boasting and bragging, that they had kept out of the British Constitution. It is the thing called abstraction or academic logic. It is the thing which such jolly people call theory; and which those who can practice it call thought. And the theory or thought is the very last to which English people are accustomed, either by their social structure or their traditional teaching. It is the theory of equality. It is the pure classic conception that no man must aspire to be anything more than a citizen, and that no man should endure to be anything less. It is by no means especially intelligible to an Englishman, who tends at his best to the virtues of the gentleman and at his worst to the vices of the snob. The idealism of England, or if you will the romance of England, has not been primarily the romance of the citizen. But the idealism of America, we may safely say, still revolves entirely round the citizen and his romance. The realities are quite another matter, and we shall consider in its place the question of whether the ideal will be able to shape the realities or will merely be beaten shapeless by them. The ideal is besieged by inequalities of the most towering and insane description in the industrial and economic field. It may be devoured by modern capitalism, perhaps the worst inequality that ever existed among men. Of all that we shall speak later. But citizenship is still the American ideal; there is an army of actualities opposed to that ideal; but there is no ideal opposed to that ideal. American plutocracy has never got itself respected like English aristocracy. Citizenship is the American ideal; and it has never been the English ideal.

[From Chapter 1]

I disagree with the aesthetic condemnation of the modern city with its sky-scrapers and sky-signs. I mean that which laments the loss of beauty and its sacrifice to utility. It seems to me the very reverse of the truth. Years ago, when people used to say the Salvation Army doubtless

34

had good intentions, but we must all deplore its methods, I pointed out that the very contrary is the case. Its method, the method of drums and democratic appeal, is that of the Franciscans or any other march of the Church Militant. It was precisely its aims that were dubious, with their dissenting morality and despotic finance. It is somewhat the same with things like the sky-signs in Broadway. The aesthete must not ask me to mingle my tears with his, because these things are merely useful and ugly. For I am not specially inclined to think them ugly; but I am strongly inclined to think them useless. As a matter of art for art's sake, they seem to me rather artistic. As a form of practical social work they seem to me stark stupid waste. If Mr. Bilge is rich enough to build a tower four hundred feet high and give it a crown of golden crescents and crimson stars, in order to draw attention to his manufacture of the Paradise Tooth Paste or the Seventh Heaven Cigar, I do not feel the least disposition to thank him for any serious form of social service. I have never tried the Seventh Heaven Cigar; indeed a premonition moves me towards the belief that I shall go down to the dust without trying it. I have every reason to doubt whether it does any particular good to those who smoke it, or any good to anybody except those who sell it. In short Mr. Bilge's usefulness consists in being useful to Mr. Bilge, and all the rest is illusion and sentimentalism. But because I know that Bilge is only Bilge, shall I stoop to the profanity of saying that fire is only fire? Shall I blaspheme crimson stars any more than crimson sunsets, or deny that those moons are golden any more than that this grass is green? If a child saw these coloured lights, he would dance with as much delight as at any other coloured toys; and it is the duty of every poet, and even of every critic, to dance in respectful imitation of the child. Indeed I am in a mood of so much sympathy with the fairy lights of this pantomime city, that I should be almost sorry to see social sanity and a sense of proportion return to extinguish them.

[From Chapter 3]

ONLY a very soft-headed, sentimental and rather servile generation of men could possibly be affected by advertisements at all. People who are a little more hard-headed, humorous, and intellectually independent, see the rather simple joke; and are not impressed by this or any other form of self-praise. Almost any other man in almost any other age would have seen the joke. If you had said to a man in the Stone Age, "Ugg says Ugg makes the best stone hatchets," he would have perceived a lack of detachment and disinterestedness about the testimonial. If you had said to a medieval peasant, "Robert the Bowyer proclaims, with three blasts of a horn, that he makes good bows," the peasant would have said, "Well, of course he does," and thought about something more important. It is only among people whose minds have been weakened by a sort of mesmerism that so transparent a trick as that of advertisement could ever have been tried at all.

[From Chapter 3]

NEEDLESS to say, the modern vulgarity of avarice and advertisement sprawls all over Philadelphia or Boston; but so it does over Winchester or Canterbury. But most people know that there is something else to be found in Canterbury or Winchester; many people know that it is rather more interesting; and some people know that Alfred can still walk in Winchester and that St. Thomas at Canterbury was killed but did not die. It is at least as possible for a Philadelphian to feel the presence of Penn and Franklin as for an Englishman to see the ghosts of Alfred and of Becket. Tradition does not mean a dead town; it does not mean that the living are dead but that the dead are alive. It means that it still matters what Penn did two hundred years ago or what Franklin did a hundred years ago; I never could feel in New York that it mattered what anybody did an hour ago. And these things did and do matter. Quakerism is not my favourite creed; but on that day when William Penn stood unarmed upon that spot and made his treaty with the Red Indians, his creed of humanity did have a triumph and a triumph that has not turned back. The praise given to him is not a priggish fiction of our conventional history, though such fictions have illogically curtailed it. The Nonconformists have been rather unfair to Penn even in picking their praises; and they generally forget that toleration cuts both ways and that an open mind is open on all sides. Those who deify him for consenting to bargain with the savages cannot forgive him for consenting to bargain with the Stuarts. And the same is true of the other city, yet more closely connected with the tolerant experiment of the Stuarts. The state of Maryland was the first experiment in religious freedom in human history. Lord Baltimore and his Catholics were a long march ahead of William Penn and his Quakers on what is now called the path of progress. That the first religious toleration ever granted in the world was granted by Roman Catholics is one of those little informing details with which our Victorian histories did not exactly teem. But when I went into my hotel in Baltimore and found two priests waiting to see me, I was moved in a new fashion, for I felt that I touched the end of a living chain. Nor was the impression accidental; it will always remain with me with a mixture of gratitude and grief, for they brought a message of welcome from a great American whose name I had known from childhood and whose career was drawing to its close; for it was but a few days after I left the city that I learned that Cardinal Gibbons was · dead.

[From Chapter 5]

Note: Chesterton visited Baltimore on 4–5 February 1921. Cardinal Gibbons died on Good Friday, 25 March.

I N this relative agricultural equality the Americans of the Middle West are far in advance of the English of the twentieth century. It is not their fault if they are still some centuries behind the English of the twelfth century. But the defect by which they fall short of being a true peasantry is that they do not produce their own spiritual food, in the same sense as their own material food. They do not, like some peasantries, create other kinds of culture besides the kind called agriculture. Their culture comes from the great cities; and that is where all the evil comes from.

If a man had gone across England in the Middle Ages, or even across Europe in more recent times, he would have found a culture which showed its vitality by its variety. We know the adventures of the three brothers in the old fairy tales who passed across the endless plain from city to city, and found one kingdom ruled by a wizard and another wasted by a dragon, one people living in castles of crystal and another sitting by fountains of wine. These are but legendary enlargements of the real adventures of a traveller passing from one patch of peasantry to another and finding women wearing strange head-dresses and men singing new songs.

A traveller in America would be somewhat surprised if he found the people in the city of St. Louis all wearing crowns and crusading armour in honour of their patron saint. He might even feel some faint surprise if he found all the citizens of Philadelphia clad in a composite costume, combining that of a Quaker with that of a Red Indian, in honour of the noble treaty of William Penn. Yet these are the sort of local and traditional things that would really be found giving variety to the valleys of medieval Europe. I myself felt a perfectly genuine and generous exhilaration of freedom and fresh enterprise in new places like Oklahoma. But you would hardly find in Oklahoma what was found in Oberammergau. What goes to Oklahoma is not the peasant play but the cinema. And the objection to the cinema is not so much that it goes to Oklahoma as that it does not come from Oklahoma. In other words, these people have on the economic side a much closer approach than we have to economic freedom. It is not for us, who have allowed our land to be stolen by squires and then vulgarized by sham squires, to sneer at such colonists as merely crude and prosaic. They at least have really kept something of the simplicity and, therefore, the dignity of democracy; and that democracy may yet save their country from the calamities of wealth and science.

But, while these farmers do not need to become industrial in order to become industrious, they do tend to become industrial in so far as they become intellectual. Their culture, and to some great extent their creed, do come along the railroads from the great modern urban centres, and bring with them a blast of death and a reek of rotting things. It is that influence that alone prevents the Middle West from progressing towards the Middle Ages.

[From Chapter 6]

IT happened that, when I was in America, I had just published some studies on Palestine; and I was besieged by Rabbis lamenting my "prejudice." I pointed out that they would have got hold of the wrong word, even if they had not got hold of the wrong man. As a point of personal autobiography, I do not happen to be a man who dislikes Jews; though I believe that some men do. I have had Jews among my most intimate and faithful friends since my boyhood, and I hope to have them till I die. But even if I did have a dislike of Jews, it would be illogical to call that dislike a prejudice. Prejudice is a very lucid Latin word meaning the bias which a man has before he considers a case. I might be said to be prejudiced against a Hairy Ainu because of his name, for I have never been on terms of such intimacy with him as to correct my preconceptions. But if after moving about in the modern world and meeting Jews, knowing about Jews, I came to the conclusion that I did not like Jews, my conclusion certainly would not be a prejudice. It would simply be an opinion; and one I should be perfectly entitled to hold; though as a matter of fact I do not hold it.

[From Chapter 8]

Note: The "studies on Palestine" referred to is the book *The New Jerusalem.*

NOW Prohibition, whether as a proposal in England or a pretence in America, simply means that the man who has drunk less shall have no drink, and the man who has drunk more shall have all the drink. It means that the old gentleman shall be carried home in a cab drunker than ever; but that, in order to make it quite safe for him to drink to excess, the man who drives him shall be forbidden to drink even in moderation. That is what it means; that is all it means; that is all it ever will mean. It means that often in Islam; where the luxurious and advanced drink champagne, while the poor and fanatical drink water. It means that in modern America; where the wealthy are all at this moment sipping their cocktails, and discussing how much harder labourers can be made to work if only they can be kept from festivity. This is what it means and all it means; and men are divided about it according to whether they believe in a certain transcendental concept called "justice," expressed in a more mystical paradox as the equality of men. So long as you do not believe in justice, and so long as you are rich and really confident of remaining so, you can have Prohibition and be as drunk as you choose.

[From Chapter 9]

THE world cannot keep its own ideals. The secular order cannot make secure any one of its own noble and natural conceptions of secular perfection. That will be found, as time goes on, the ultimate argument for a Church independent of the world and the secular order. What has become of all those ideal figures from the Wise Man of the Stoics to the democratic Deist of the eighteenth century? What has become of all that purely human hierarchy or chivalry, with its punctilious pattern of the good knight, its ardent ambition in the young squire? The very name of knight has come to represent the petty triumph of a profiteer, and the very word squire the petty tyranny of a landlord. What has become of all that golden liberality of the Humanists, who found on the high tablelands of the culture of Hellas the very balance of repose in beauty that is most lacking in the modern world? The very Greek language that they loved has become a mere label for stuffy and snobbish dons, and a mere cock-shy for cheap and half-educated utilitarians, who make it a symbol of superstition and reaction. We have lived to see a time when the heroic legend of the Republic and the Citizen, which seemed to Jefferson the eternal youth of the world, has begun to grow old in its turn. We cannot recover the earthly estate of knighthood, to which all the colours and complications of heraldry seemed as fresh and natural as flowers. We cannot re-enact the intellectual experiences of the Humanists, for whom the Greek grammar was like the song of a bird in spring. The more the matter is considered the clearer it will seem that these old experiences are now only alive, where they have found a lodgment in the Catholic tradition of Christendom, and made themselves friends for ever. St. Francis is the only surviving troubadour. St. Thomas More is the only surviving Humanist. St. Louis is the only surviving knight.

It would be the worst sort of insincerity, therefore, to conclude even so hazy an outline of so great and majestic a matter as the American democratic experiment, without testifying my belief that to this also the same ultimate test will come. So far as that democracy becomes or remains Catholic and Christian, that democracy will remain democratic. In so far as it does not, it will become wildly and wickedly undemocratic. Its rich will riot with a brutal indifference far beyond the feeble feudalism which retains some shadow of responsibility or at least of patronage. Its wage-slaves will either sink into heathen slavery, or seek relief in theories that are destructive not merely in method but in aim; since they are but the negations of the human appetites of property and personality. Eighteenth-century ideals, formulated in eighteenth-century language, have no longer in themselves the power to hold all those pagan passions back. Even those documents depended upon Deism; their real strength will survive in men who are still Deists. And the men who are still Deists are more than Deists. Men will more and more realise that there is no meaning in democracy if there is no meaning in anything; and that there is no meaning in anything if the universe has not a centre of significance and an authority that is the author of our rights. There is truth in every ancient fable, and there is here even something of it in the fancy that finds the symbol of the Republic in the bird that bore the bolts of Jove. Owls and bats may wander where they will in darkness, and for them as for the sceptics the universe may have no centre; kites and vultures may linger as they like over carrion, and for them as for the plutocrats existence may have no origin and no end; but it was far back in the land of legends, where instincts find their true images, that the cry went forth that freedom is an eagle, whose glory is gazing at the sun.

[From Chapter 19]

Selections from
Sidelights on New
London and Newer York

IT was not the conception of life outlined in the Declaration of Independence that was wrong; it was the thousand things that have come in since to perplex it; and many of them have come from England and from Europe. The great Revolution failed to attain those high levels of equality and luminous justice to which its first promise had pointed; not because Americans were wrong to resist a German called George the Third, but because they continued to revere a Frenchman called Calvin, a Scotchman called Macauley, an Englishman called Herbert Spencer, and all the rest of the dreary Whig and Puritan and industrial rationalism of what we call in England the Victorian Age. In this matter I am on the side of the old idealistic democrats. The vision was all right; it is the revision that is all wrong. America, instead of being the open agricultural commonwealth for which its founders hoped, has become the dumping-ground of all the most dismal ideas of decaying epochs in Europe, from Calvinism to industrialism. Even the American features which most offend a European, the extravagant exaggeration of commercial competition, or mechanical invention, or journalistic violence, are not ideas of the Revolution. They are ideas that have immigrated into America after the Revolution. For my part, I wish that Jefferson's democracy had remained immune from them.

[From Part 2, Chapter 14]

I will not say that Americans were right to overthrow the power of King George; for in fact there was no power of King George to overthrow. England was not a monarchy. England was already an aristocracy. But Americans, in my judgment, were perfectly entitled to break away from that aristocracy. An aristocracy is a system which has its advantages and disadvantages; but for those who really wish to live the democratic life even the advantages were disadvantages. And, when all is discounted from the mere cant of emancipation, it is true that a poor man leaving the English country-side for the American coast did become a free man; even if he was starved or frozen in a blizzard or eaten by a grizzly bear. He had no longer a master or a lord. At home the advantage of aristocracy was having a good squire; the disadvantage was having a bad squire. Some may even prefer a bad squire to a bear. But it is true, as far as it goes, that in breaking with aristocracy, the revolted colonies did open a democracy for those who care to be democrats.

[From Part 2, Chapter 14]

I found an exact illustration of what I really like in America. It occurred in a country town where there is a college or university in which I had just lectured. One of the professors was kind enough to say that he liked my line of argument and that it had contained one point that had not occurred to him before. A minute or two later, as I was standing waiting outside the hall, the same professor's chauffeur came up to me in exactly the same manner and said almost exactly the same thing. He said he agreed upon that particular point, but was doubtful upon some other point of controversy. There was absolutely no difference between the tone and gesture and bodily carriage of the professor and his servant. Neither was aggressive; neither was apologetic; neither thought it anything but natural to say something that had just come into his head.

That is what I like in America. That is what is nearly impossible in England. But the trouble is this: that if I say that such an incident in England would be impossible, crowds of untravelled Americans will instantly make up pictures of an arrogant aristocratic England which would be far more impossible. Many might be left with a vague idea that English chauffeurs are not admitted to lectures; or that English chauffeurs cannot read or write and are incapable of understanding lectures; or that English chauffeurs are silent out of terror of their haughty and highborn masters; or that English gentlemen strut about like Prussian Junkers, twirling military moustaches and shouting military orders to miserable chauffeurs.

Nothing of this sort could possibly happen; any more than the other thing could happen. I know exactly what would happen. It is a matter of tone; of social atmosphere; of something that can generally be better conveyed by a novelist than an essayist. Most probably the lady of the house, radiantly receiving the lecturer, might even notice the presence of the chauffeur, or the butler or the gamekeeper or the gardener or some other upper servant. And she would very probably say, with a curious sort of foggy affection in her mind, "Wiggins will take care of you. I do hope you will be comfortable." Then with a sort of running up the scale of laughter, "Wiggins went to your lecture. Wiggins reads quite a lot of books"; all with a curious warmth of pride in her tone, as if she owned the learned pig or the calculating horse or some quite exceptional animal of whom she was rather fond. And Wiggins would at first look sheepish, as if he had been caught stealing books from the library, and grin in an apologetic but speechless manner. And only afterwards when you had agreed with Wiggins about a hundred times that it was a fine day, might he begin to make fragmentary human noises, and you might learn something of what he thought of the lecture. But, anyhow, that is the difference. There is no question, in the ordinary sense, of being overbearing or brutal with such servants. One of the very first things that the small squire will be taught at the age of six is the sacred necessity of being polite to Wiggins. But he will never be the equal of Wiggins; and Wiggins will never act as if he were. That they should both comment on a strange gentleman's lecture, independently, simultaneously, spontaneously, in the same tone and at the same time—that is what does not happen in England and that is what does happen in America.

[From Part 2, Chapter 7]

THE externals of the Middle West affect an Englishman as ugly, and yet ugliness is not exactly the point. There are things in England that are quite as ugly or even uglier. Rows of red brick villas in the suburbs of a town in the Midlands are, one would suppose, as hideous as human half-wittedness could invent or endure. But they are different. They are complete; they are, in their way, compact; rounded and finished with an effect that may be prim or smug, but is not raw. The surroundings of them are neat, if it be in a niggling fashion. But American ugliness is not complete even as ugliness. It is broken off short; it is ragged at the edges; even its worthy objects have around them a sort of halo of refuse.

[From Part 2, Chapter 11]

STRANGE as it may seem, some are puzzled because I hate Americanization and do not hate America. I should have thought that I had earned some right to apply this obvious distinction to any foreign country, since I have consistently applied it to my own country. If the egoism is excusable, I am myself an Englishman (which some identify with an egoist) and I have done my best to praise and glorify a number of English things: English inns, English roads, English jokes and jokers; even to the point of praising the roads for being crooked or the humour for being Cockney; but I have invariably written, ever since I have written at all, against the cult of British Imperialism.

And when that perilous power and opportunity, which is given by wealth and worldly success, largely passed from the British Empire to the United States, I have applied exactly the same principle to the United States. I think that Imperialism is none the less Imperialism because it is spread by economic pressure or snobbish fashion rather than by conquest; indeed I have much more respect for the Empire that is spread by fighting than for the Empire that is spread by finance. . . .

The great virtue of America is that, in spite of industry and energy, in spite of progress and practical success, in spite of Edison and electricity, in spite of Ford and Fords, in spite of science and organization and enterprise and every evil work, America does really remain democratic; not perhaps in the literal sense of being a democracy, but in the moral sense of consisting of democrats. The citizens feel equal, even if they feel equally impotent. There may not be government of the people, by the people, for the people, but there is not government of the people, by the governing class, still less for the governing class. For anyone who knows anything of human history, with its heroic ideals and its prosaic disappointments, this really is and remains a remarkable achievement.

[From Part 2, Chapter 13]

Back to the Cherry Tree

IF I were an American, I should devote myself to the great labor of replanting The Cherry Tree. I am well aware that it has long been as much an American joke as an American legend. Like most English boys of my generation, I inherited the speech that Milton spoke and learned it almost entirely out of Mark Twain. But (apart from such healthy flippancy) I know that serious historians have been professing to practice Washingtonian truthfulness at the expense of Washington. With solemn eyes, putting their hands behind them, they say that they cannot tell a lie; and that there never was any cherry-tree. They even say there never was any Washington, as ideally conceived. Sometimes they suggest that his habits were such that, if he did cut down the cherry-tree, it was probably with the purpose of producing cherry-brandy. A purpose which I applaud. Anyhow *that* cannot conceivably be classed as a fault; but as one of the festive virtues of his class and generation. Some, however, feeling it inadequate to say he was drunk, have been so malignant as to say he was wealthy. They imply that his father probably had ten thousand cherry trees; and that he could easily afford to sacrifice ten in the cause of truth.

But I am not in the debunking business; and it does not concern me. In the Red Indian idiom, I am quite ready to bury the little hatchet. I am not quarrelling about the fact or fable itself; but I am interested in what is symbolized by the legend, even if it is only a legend. The first fact it stands for is the very vital fact; that the American Revolution happened long before the Industrial Revolution. The Tree of Liberty was a tree; and not a petrol-pump or a factory-chimney. If the Washingtons were rich, any number of people owned cherry-trees and were quite poor. And the next point to note is that they really owned them. The moral of the old moral tale was that little George had no right to destroy the tree, because it was not his own. That is the old and true principle of private property; which existed much more in agricultural states than it does in industrial states. The subsequent degeneration of the industrial state means simply this; that somebody did indeed do it with his little hatchet, because he had an axe to grind. He did not even want to eat the cherries; he only wanted to sell the cherries. So far from saying that he could not tell a lie, he proudly boasted that he could tell ten thousand lies to sell one cherry. He called it Salesmanship. Now under that process the child and the cherry-tree and every other natural thing has grown steadily more and more rotten. It has grown more and more rotten, as it got further away from the real ownership of cherry-trees and the old agricultural ideas of the Revolution. Thus the only real effect of Prohibition on cherry brandy is that men make sure of the brandy and are very doubtful of the cherries. It is pathetic that perhaps the only relic of poor Washington's cherry-tree is the cherry left in the cocktail.

There is a third point; to which I attach immense importance. Whether old Mrs. Washington was rich or poor, whether she was so wild and wicked as to make cherry brandy, or so mild and timid as only to make cherry pie, it is overwhelmingly probable that she made them herself. Nay, she had the superb courage to eat or drink them herself, when she had made them herself. And so long as numbers of people were themselves growing cherries and eating cherries, they were free of the huge trap in which the world is now caught; the trap that is called Trade. There was no over-production; for you can hardly produce too many cherries for little George, whatever his subsequent character. I think myself it was a good character; he was a soldier capable of defeating defeat, and a gentleman who could survive politics; and that is honor enough for any man. But that ancient anecdote does really come to us now with a new moral. The world in which wealth was counted in cherries, and consumed like cherries, was less liable to bankruptcy and despair than that in which we live; which depends on financiers buying and selling cherry orchards they have never seen and which possibly do not exist. It would therefore be an exaggeration to say that they cannot tell a lie.

Meanwhile, of course, the change from the old cherry-tree culture to the modern has brought with it a wild unreason that is almost more lawless than lying. We know what Washington's father said when his son remarked, "I did cut down the cherry-tree"; we may form our own fancies about what he would have said if his son had said, "I did not cut down the cherry-tree." But fancy altogether fails us in guessing the consequences if the son had said. "I did cut down the cherry-tree, and therefore it is still standing." Yet it is paradoxes of that description that really confront us when we try to make sense of the present economic situation. It is laboriously but lucidly explained to us that the thing which really ruins the cherry-market is cherries, and that the cherry-tree is the deadly foe of the cherry trade. The upshot of it seems to be that there are so many cherries that nobody can afford to buy any. George Washington might even have explained to his father, with precocious eloquence, that by cutting down the tree he had nobly averted a plague of over-production in the orchard. Only most of us will feel that when we reach a realm where a glut is the same as a scarcity, and more cherries mean no cherries, we have got far beyond anything so human or so logical as merely telling lies. Indeed, it will become painfully difficult to tell lies, not to mention the more normal difficulty of telling the truth; when we can hardly say anything without saying the contrary at the same time.

We ought to have known long ago, by the mere fact that our thoughts were getting into such a tangle in the world of theory, that the tangle would soon tighten into a strangling knot in the world of practice. A world in which people could argue that tribute taken from the conquered was really taken entirely from the conqueror, a world in which people could prove on paper that the rich were not much richer than the poor because a half-crown cigar cannot be cut up into half a hundred cigarettes, a world in which a score of schemes of production failed because they had succeeded in producing, a world in which there were all these inverted intellectual conceptions racking the reason and the sense of reality—all that was a world that could not last. When I say we should do better to return to the old morality of the moral tales like that of the cherry-tree and the Father of his Country, I mean that they were illuminated not only by the light of conscience, but the light of common sense. There were not only the moral conditions of truth; there were also the mental conditions of truth. They even included, in a sense, a much clearer capacity to say what was untrue. In short, little Washington, in the story, was only wrong in one essential respect. Fortunately for him, he was wrong when he chose the exact words: "Father, I cannot tell a lie." He would have been a truer type of Christian virtue if he had said, "Father, I can tell a lie"; merely adding (we may, on general grounds, hope) "but I won't." But the unlucky liars of today cannot tell a lie. You have only to look at them, trying so laboriously, in the newspapers.

[From *The Catholic Mind*, 8 April 1932]

On Abraham Lincoln

IT is recognized that Lincoln emerged from the lower grades of law and politics through an atmosphere in which the lowest tricks were regarded as only tricks of the trade. That queer, shabby figure, the "rail-splitter," with his stove-pipe hat and clumsy cotton umbrella, did undoubtedly emerge among such tricksters as being by far the most truthful. But in the world where he began he could only have been called the least tricky. It is to his credit that he shed most of these habits with a natural shame, and for no other reason. But it is clear that, at some periods, it was not only his hat and umbrella that were shabby.

But there is another paradox about Abraham Lincoln, over and above those noticed by his recent realistic biographers, and one that has always seemed to me very noticeable. He really was a hero, but he seems exactly the wrong sort of hero for all his own hero-worshippers. We should be rather surprised if a very quiet and pacific colony of Quakers in a Pennsylvanian village had no other interest in life but the glorification of the great Napoleon, the exultant and detailed description of his battles, the lyrical salute of the cannonade of Austerlitz or the cavalry charges of Wagram. We should think it odd if a company of pagan epicureans, crowned with roses and flushed with wine, had no other thought in the world but a devotion to St. Simeon Stylites, for his austerity and asceticism in standing on a pillar in the desert. It would seem curious if the young Swinburne had been the only idol of the Nonconformist Conscience, or if the Prussian militarists had thought of nothing but the Christian Socialism of Tolstoy. And yet the sort of people who incessantly sing the praises of Abraham Lincoln have got hold of a man quite as incongruous to their own conception of a hero—if ever they could turn from imagining the hero to consider the man. The sort of people who are called Puritans perpetually glorify a man who seems to have been in his youth a rather crude sort of atheist, and was famous all his life for telling dirty and profane stories. The sort of people who are generally Prohibitionists invariably invoke the name of a man who said that habitual drunkards compared favourably with most other people of his acquaintance; and who would himself, in moments of relaxation, tip up a barrel of whisky and drink the liquor through the bung-hole. The sort of people who are perpetually talking about punctuality and propriety, and the prompt performance of duty or seizure of opportunity, are always commending to us the example of a man who never turned up at his own wedding, and who made a most horrible mess of his own domestic affairs. Yes, he was a hero all right; but his hero-worshippers would not think so.

But perhaps the most curious part of the contradiction is this. Americans of his own Yankee and Puritan following are always talking about Success. Worse still, they are always talking about men who are Bound to Succeed. It seems possible that the men Bound to Succeed were those afterwards shortened into Bounders. Certainly the portraits and descriptions of such beings richly suggest the briefer description. But Lincoln was not a Bounder. Lincoln was most certainly not a man Bound to Succeed. For the greater part of his life he looked much more like a man Bound to Fail. Indeed, for that matter, a great many of his cold and uncomprehending colleagues, right up to the very end of the Civil War, thought he really was a man bound to fail. The truth is that he was a very clear and even beautiful example of the operation of the opposite principle—that God has chosen the failures of the world to confound the successes; and the true moral of his life is that of the poets and the saints. He was one of a very rare and very valuable race, whose representatives appear from time to time in history. He was one of the Failures who happen to succeed.

What I mean is this: that, if ninety-nine out of a hundred of the people who specially praise Lincoln to-day had met him at almost any time of his life till within a few years of his death, they would have avoided him as they avoid the drunkard, the lunatic, the impecunious poet, the habitual criminal, and the man who is always borrowing money. This, of course, is even more true of General Grant than of President Lincoln; and it is a queer irony that the great Puritan and commercial power of the North should have been saved by two such men. But, though Lincoln was never an habitual drunkard like Grant, he had about him in all his early days the same savour of unsuccess. The philanthropists and social reformers who now worship his name would have regarded him as belonging to the type which they think "unemployable"; a scallywag, a drifter and dreamer, a man who would come to no good. His casualness, his coarseness, his habit of taking up this and that and not making it pay, his changes of trade and dwelling-place—all these would have sufficed to make him seem from the first fated to failure. But, whatever his weaknesses or even his vices, they would not have been so fatal to his chances as his own supreme virtue. The one great virtue of Abraham Lincoln would have seemed alone sufficient to cut him off from all hope of success in modern civilization.

For this great man had one secret vice far more unpopular among his followers than the habit of drinking. He had the habit of thinking. We might almost call it the habit of secret thinking, a dark consolation like that of secret drinking; for during his early days he must have practiced it unappreciated, and it has been said that he worked out the propositions of Euclid as a relief after having been nagged by his wife. This habit of thinking was not the thoughtless thing commonly called free-thinking, though he may have picked up a little of that in his less enlightened days. It was real thinking, which means knowing exactly where to draw the line—a logic which is often mistaken for compromise.

The great glory of Lincoln is that, almost alone among politicians, he really knew what he thought about politics. He really thought slavery was bad, but he really thought the disruption of America was worse. It is perfectly possible for an intelligent person to disagree with him on either or both of these points. But he was an intelligent person when he stated them in that way, and put them in that order. In short, he had a native love of Truth; and, like every man with such a love, he had a natural hatred of mere Tendency. He had no use for progress, for evolution, for going with the stream, for letting the spirit of the age lead him onward. He knew exactly what he thought, not only about the perfection, but the proportion of truth; not only about the direction, but the distance. He was not always right; but he always tried to be reasonable, and that in exactly the sense which his special admirers have never understood from that day to this. He tried to be reasonable. It is not surprising that his life was a martyrdom, and that he died murdered.

[From *Come to Think of It*]

On Myself on Abraham Lincoln

AN American critic, apparently of the Baptist persuasion, has uttered a furious denunciation of me for my celebrated slander on Abraham Lincoln. And this is odd, as the poet said; because I was under the strong impression that I had written a eulogy on Abraham Lincoln. It so happens that I have a particular enthusiasm for Lincoln; and I endeavoured to state the real reasons for admiring him, and the real things in which he was admirable. But apparently all the things that I think admirable the Baptist critic thinks abominable, and *vice versa*. So deep are the moral divisions in this happy age of the union of all creeds and nations.

I will start with one simple and yet curious example. I said that Lincoln had the sort of mind that does not really bother about Progress or the spirit of the age. Whether or no this be a fact, I need hardly say that it was meant as a compliment. I meant that he thought for himself and had independent and indestructible convictions, unaltered by fashion and cant. But the American critic actually regards my remark as a mortal insult to his ideal Lincoln. He declares passionately that Lincoln *was* affected by Progress. He affirms, trembling with indignation, that Lincoln *was* controlled by the spirit of the age. Most extraordinary of all, he actually quotes in favour of Lincoln something that Lincoln said against himself: when he modestly observed that "he had not controlled events, but been controlled by them." It is perfectly possible that Lincoln said this, in a humorous sort of humility and self-disparagement; but I do not see why, because he disparaged himself, his almost idolatrous adorer is bound to disparage him. Certainly I do not see why the critic should disparage him in so damaging a style as this. I am pretty sure that Lincoln would not have been controlled by events, or even by the spirit of the age, where *ideas* were concerned. I do not believe he would have admitted that Slavery was right, if the South had won the War and the slave States had prospered ten times more than the free.

The next point that I should like to have cleared up is this. The critic is very much horrified at my suggesting that Lincoln was any more tolerant or liberal than the critic himself on the subject of strong drink. He owns that Lincoln once lifted a whisky barrel and took what he (the critic) delicately calls "a sip." Unless I am much mistaken in Abe, he had rather too good a sense of humour to take a sip. But that is a trivial matter, and I will leave on one side all charges of intemperance against Abe; all the more readily because I never brought any. The case is very different touching charges of intemperance against Grant. And it is here that I wish to understand clearly on what basis I am expected to argue. For the Baptist critic repeatedly reviles me for daring to suggest such things about so historic a hero as the great Northern conqueror of the South. Am I to understand that the critic contradicts flatly all the accepted evidence that Grant, that great soldier, certainly did drink whisky rather well than wisely? Or am I to understand that, even if he did, historians are to hide it forever, because he was a General and a President, and the country has gone Prohibitionist? I never said anything else against Grant except that he drank rather freely; because I willingly admit that there is not much else to be said. Nor do I consider it a very horrible charge against him. Nor did Abraham Lincoln. Does the critic deny the words of Lincoln himself, who went so far as to say that habitual drunkards compare well with other people in many or most important respects? If the critic is shocked at my words, he must be much more shocked at Lincoln's. I shudder to think what he would say of some remarks of my friend Mr. Christopher Hollis, in a paragraph beginning "The fascinating question of when General Grant was drunk and when sober," and proceeding to say that he was probably sober at Appomattox, but almost certainly drunk at Shiloh; that he afterwards, on reaching the Presidency, took some sort of teetotal pledge; and concluding with the words, "It is enough to add that he was a very good General and a very bad President."

Such playfulness, however, is not for the Baptist critic, nor for me when I am criticizing him. I do not think drunkenness a commendable quality; but I do not think it the one specially and supremely damnable one. And that is where we come to the real difference between this American critic and myself. And that difference becomes clearer when we reach the third of his complaints against me. I stated my strong impression, from what I have read of the life of Lincoln, that he was emphatically not the type of the mere self-made man who sticks to one trade and succeeds; that there was a great deal in him of the erratic genius who either succeeds as a genius or fails at everything; that there was in him not a little of the unworldly weaknesses of the artist or the loafer, as shown in many such strange incidents as his absence from his own wedding. I do not claim to be an expert on the details of his biography, but some of these facts are universally known; some I found in a recent and responsible American Life of Lincoln; and the critic had better fight it out with the American biographer rather than with me.

But the point of the thing is this: that I thought it was a compliment to consider Lincoln unworldly; but the critic, in his heart, really thinks it a compliment to consider him worldly. That is where there is a real difference between his moral philosophy and mine. If the words "worldly" and "unworldly" do not convey the same meaning to him as to me, or if they seem far-fetched in relation to what I said, I will willingly substitute the words "success" and "failure." When I say that Lincoln was a man who easily might have been a failure, very nearly was a failure, and in some ways actually remains a failure, I mean it as in the case of poets or martyrs. But the critic cannot bear to think that his hero was not a success, and bound to be a success, and satisfied with being a success; as in the case of magnates and millionaires. He cannot bear to think that his hero was not a Go-getter, a Booster, a Best-Seller, a Bright Salesman, and a Man Born to Succeed. I can only say that it is not my impression of Lincoln that he was like that.

The important thing to realize here, much more important than his essay or mine, is that we really are becoming divided in moral ideals. I am sure that my critic is quite sincere in his hero-worship; just as I am quite sincere in mine. What is to me extraordinary beyond words is the implied system of tests which he applies to a hero. He wishes to show that Lincoln was more heroic than I had represented him; and the following seem to be the essential qualities that go to constitute a truly heroic figure. First, he must be a teetotaller; or, as I should say, he must be a Moslem rather than a Christian on the moral problem of wine. Second, he must take very seriously the business of getting on in this world, prospering in his profession and obtaining the solid rewards this world has to give. Third, he must worship Progress or the Spirit of the Age; which can only mean (so far as I can make any sense of it) that he must allow his own conscience and conviction to be twisted into any shapes that the pressure of the present state of politics and society may tend to produce. I do not think any of these things especially admirable; I do not think any of them even reasonably arguable; and I do not think any of them any more characteristic of Lincoln than of Lee or Bayard or Joan of Arc, or any hero or heroine in history.

[From *Come to Think of It*]

❧ 4 ❧

ON LYING IN BED

L YING in bed would be an altogether perfect and supreme experience if only one had a coloured pencil long enough to draw on the
ceiling. This, however, is not generally a part of the domestic apparatus
on the premises. I think myself that the thing might be managed with
several pails of Aspinall and a broom. Only if one worked in a really
sweeping and masterly way, and laid on the colour in great washes, it
might drip down again on one's face in floods of rich and mingled colour
like some strange fairy rain; and that would have its disadvantages. I am
afraid it would be necessary to stick to black and white in this form of
artistic composition. To that purpose, indeed, the white ceiling would
be of the greatest possible use; in fact it is the only use I think of a white
ceiling being put to.

But for the beautiful experiment of lying in bed I might never have
discovered it. For years I have been looking for some blank spaces in a
modern house to draw on. Paper is much too small for any really
allegorical design; as Cyrano de Bergerac says: "Il me faut des géants."
But when I tried to find these fine clear spaces in the modern rooms such
as we all live in I was continually disappointed. I found an endless
pattern and complication of small objects hung like a curtain of fine
links between me and my desire. I examined the walls; I found them to
my surprise to be already covered with wallpaper, and I found the
wallpaper to be already covered with very uninteresting images, all
bearing a ridiculous resemblance to each other. I could not understand
why one arbitrary symbol (a symbol apparently entirely devoid of any
religious or philosophical significance) should thus be sprinkled all over
my nice walls like a sort of small-pox. The Bible must be referring to
wallpapers, I think, when it says "Use not vain repetitions, as the
Gentiles do." I found the Turkey carpet a mass of unmeaning colours,
rather like the Turkish Empire, or like the sweetmeat called Turkish
Delight. I do not exactly know what Turkish Delight really is; but I
suppose it is Macedonian Massacres. Everywhere that I went forlornly,
with my pencil or my paint brush, I found that others had unaccount-

ably been before me, spoiling the walls, the curtains, and the furniture with their childish and barbaric designs.

Nowhere did I find a really clear space for sketching until this occasion when I prolonged beyond the proper limit the process of lying on my back in bed. Then the light of that white heaven broke upon my vision, that breadth of mere white which is indeed almost the definition of Paradise, since it means purity and also means freedom. But alas! like all heavens now that it is seen it is found to be unattainable; it looks more austere and more distant than the blue sky outside the window. For my proposal to paint on it with the bristly end of a broom has been discouraged—never mind by whom; by a person debarred from all political rights—and even my minor proposal to put the other end of the broom into the kitchen fire and turn it into charcoal has not been conceded. Yet I am certain that it was from persons in my position that all the original inspiration came for covering the ceilings of palaces and cathedrals with a riot of fallen angels or victorious gods. I am sure that it was only because Michelangelo was engaged in the ancient and honourable occupation of lying bed that he ever realized how the roof of the Sistine Chapel might be made into an awful imitation of a divine drama that could only be acted in the heavens.

The tone now commonly taken towards the practice of lying in bed is hypocritical and unhealthy. Of all the marks of modernity that seem to mean a kind of decadence, there is none more menacing and dangerous than the exaltation of very small and secondary matters of conduct at the expense of very great and primary ones, at the expense of eternal ties and tragic human morality. If there is one thing worse than the modern weakening of major morals it is the modern strengthening of minor morals. Thus it is considered more withering to accuse a man of bad taste than of bad ethics. Cleanliness is not next to godliness nowadays, for cleanliness is made an essential and godliness is regarded as an offence. A playwright can attack the institution of marriage so long as he does not misrepresent the manners of society, and I have met Ibsenite pessimists who thought it wrong to take beer but right to take prussic acid. Especially this is so in matters of hygiene; notably such matters as lying in bed. Instead of being regarded, as it ought to be, as a matter of personal convenience and adjustment, it has come to be regarded by many as if it were a part of essential morals to get up early in the morning. It is upon the whole part of practical wisdom; but there is nothing good about it or bad about its opposite.

Misers get up early in the morning; and burglars, I am informed, get up the night before. It is the great peril of our society that all its mechanism may grow more fixed while its spirit grows more fickle. A man's minor actions and arrangements ought to be free, flexible, creative; the things that should be unchangeable are his principles, his ideals. But with us the reverse is true; our views change constantly; but our lunch does not change. Now, I should like men to have strong and rooted conceptions, but as for their lunch, let them have it sometimes in the garden, sometimes in bed, sometimes on the roof, sometimes in the top of a tree. Let them argue from the same first principles, but let them do it in a bed, or a boat, or a balloon. This alarming growth of good habits really means a too great emphasis on those virtues which mere custom can ensure, it means too little emphasis on those virtues which custom can never quite ensure, sudden and splendid virtues of inspired pity or of inspired candour. If ever that abrupt appeal is made to us we may fail. A man can get used to getting up at five o'clock in the morning. A man cannot very well get used to being burnt for his opinions; the first experiment is commonly fatal. Let us pay a little more attention to these possibilities of the heroic and the unexpected. I dare say that when I get out of this bed I shall do some deed of an almost terrible virtue.

For those who study the great art of lying in bed there is one emphatic caution to be added. Even for those who can do their work in bed (like journalists), still more for those whose work cannot be done in bed (as, for example, the professional harpooners of whales), it is obvious that the indulgence must be very occasional. But that is not the caution I mean. The caution is this: if you do lie in bed, be sure you do it without any reason or justification at all. I do not speak, of course, of the seriously sick. But if a healthy man lies in bed, let him do it without a rag of excuse; then he will get up a healthy man. If he does it for some secondary hygienic reason, if he has some scientific explanation, he may get up a hypochondriac.

[From *Tremendous Trifles*]

❦ 5 ❧

REASON, PROGRESS, EDUCATION

The Rev. Leo Hetzler of Rochester, New York, a noted authority on Chesterton, described in a lecture how Chesterton upheld—during an age of doubt and scepticism—the primacy of reason, defending the mind's grasp of first principles and the reasoning powers of the intellect. There was, according to Father Hetzler, a general attack on reason and certitude during the first part of the present century. One critic rebuked GKC for maintaining the need for a fixed moral code and argued for an evolutionary ethics. An Oxford student wrote, in response to a Chesterton essay, that any belief in an objective and unchanging truth would be adverse to democracy and freedom of thought. The student said: "True religion is a life, not a creed, and knows no dogmas. It deals with conduct and behavior, and not necessarily with knowledge or belief." The novelist Arnold Bennett stated that in his opinion it was impossible for a young man with a first-class mind to accept any form of dogma.

Chesterton was not deterred by such assertions. To begin with, he stated that in discussions of basic and ultimate questions it is wrong to regard as "impartial" only those persons who refuse to have principles or convictions, and it is likewise wrong to condemn as "prejudiced" those persons who have come to definite intellectual conclusions. Father Hetzler explained the rational basis of Chesterton's thinking, which was founded on the philosophy of Saint Thomas Aquinas and included such clear principles as that the human mind can know reality, that contradictories cannot exist, and that individuation and generalization are both possible. This philosophy is the primal, common-sense one that gives due recognition to both existing reality and the operation of the mind.

Chesterton respected the convictions of those who disagreed with him, especially the really sincere thinkers who honestly believed in their socialism or atheism, for example. But he disliked the sceptics who dismissed the tenets of sincere men. In his lecture Father Hetzler noted one main social reason why GKC was opposed to scepticism: unless citizens argued out their problems from definite philosophical convictions, democracy would degenerate into a tyranny of fads and tastes.

Chesterton also regarded "evolutionary progressive" thinking—which considered truth and moral norms as relative and changing—as equally opposed to democracy, since such a frame of thought would favor the powerful and the ruthless. Father Hetzler concluded his presentation by stating that Chesterton contended that to have freedom, social justice, and democracy, one cannot validly maintain with the sceptic that truths are uncertain or unknowable, nor with the pragmatist that they are relative, nor with the progressive that they are evolving in unknown directions. To retain the old liberal ideals of the self-governing state, the equality of men, and religious liberty, one must affirm that there are certain beliefs that are undeniably true and timeless.

[Notes from Rev. Hetzler's lecture to the Rochester Chesterton Society, 27 May 1976]

Essay Excerpts

THE idea of logic is so entirely lost in this phase of philosophical history, that even those who invoke it do so rather as the Athenians once invoked the Unknown God, or the men of the Dark Ages retained a dim respect for Virgil as a conjuror. The very people who say, "be logical," will generally be found to be quite illogical in their own notion of logic. . . .

Let us begin with a trifle that does not matter in the least. . . . Some journalist the other day shook the foundation of the universe and the British Empire by raising the question of whether a girl ought to smoke a cigar. But what I noted about him, and about the hundred eager correspondents who pursued this great theme, was that they wrote again and again some such sentence as this: "If you like a girl to smoke a cigarette, why can't you be logical and like her to smoke a cigar?" Now I do not care an ounce of shag whether she smokes a cigarette or a cigar or a corn-cob pipe or a hubble-bubble, or whether she smokes three cigars at once, or whether she is an Anti-Tobacco crank. But it is none the less true that when a man writes that sentence telling us to "be logical," he shows that he has never even heard of the nature of logic. He might just as well write: "You like the look of a horse; why won't you be logical and like the look of a hippopotamus?" The only answer is, "Well, I don't," and it is not illogical, because it does not in any way invade the realm of logic. A man has a perfect right to say that he likes the look of one thing and does not like the look of another thing; or even that he likes the look of a smaller thing, but does not like the look of a larger but somewhat similar thing. It is all a question of liking; and not in the least a question of logic. There is no logical compulsion upon him whatever to go on from the smaller to the larger and like them both. . . .

It is not logical, because it has not been deduced from any premises; it has simply been stated without reference to any premises.

And that is what is the matter with the modern man who says, "be logical." He cannot take his own advice, and therefore he cannot state his own first principles. But though his logic is nonsense as he states it, it does refer to some first principles if he could only state them. It all depends on the *reason* for approving of cigarettes or cigars or girls or any other strange creatures. What he really means, at the back of his muddled modernistic mind, is something like this: "If I approve of Jennifer smoking a cigarette because Jennifer can jolly well do anything she likes, and does, *then* it is illogical in me to object to her liking a cigar; or for that matter an opium pipe or a pint of laudanum or a bottle of prussic acid." And this statement would really be quite logical, because the logical reason is given. Or if he said, "It is my first principle that women may do anything that men can do; *therefore* I am bound in logic to pass the cigars to my daughter as much as to my son," then that also is perfectly reasonable as the application of a stated principle. But to say that a man is bound in logic to like a cigar as much as a cigarette whether in his own mouth or that of his maiden aunt or his maternal grandmother, is stark staring unreason; and shows that the speaker is entirely illogical in dealing with the two ideas of liking and logic.

[From *All Is Grist*]

THE vice of the modern notion of mental progress is that it is always something concerned with the breaking of bonds, the effacing of boundaries, the casting away of dogmas. But if there be such a thing as mental growth, it must mean the growth into more and more definite convictions, into more and more dogmas. The human brain is a machine for coming to conclusions; if it cannot come to conclusions it is rusty. When we hear of a man too clever to believe, we are hearing of something having almost the character of a contradiction in terms. It is like hearing of a nail that was too good to hold down a carpet; or a bolt that was too strong to keep a door shut. Man can hardly be defined, after the fashion of Carlyle, as an animal who makes tools; ants and beavers and many other animals make tools, in the sense that they make an apparatus. Man can be defined as an animal that makes dogmas. As he piles doctrine on doctrine and conclusion on conclusion in the formation of some tremendous scheme of philosophy and religion, he is, in the only legitimate sense of which the expression is capable, becoming more and more human. When he drops one doctrine after another in a refined scepticism, when he declines to tie himself to a system, when he says that he has outgrown definitions, when he says that he disbelieves in finality, when, in his own imagination, he sits as God, holding no form of creed but contemplating all, then he is by that very process sinking slowly backwards into the vagueness of the vagrant animals and the unconsciousness of the grass. Trees have no dogmas. Turnips are singularly broad-minded.

[From *Heretics*]

I have never understood why there is supposed to be something crabbed or antique about a syllogism; still less can I understand what anybody means by talking as if induction had somehow taken the place of deduction. The whole point of deduction is that true premises produce a true conclusion. What is called induction seems simply to mean collecting a larger number of true premises, or perhaps, in some physical matters, taking rather more trouble to see that they are true. It may be a fact that a modern man can get more out of a great many premises, concerning microbes or asteroids than a medieval man could get out of a very few premises about salamanders and unicorns. But the process of deduction from the data is the same for the modern mind as for the medieval mind; and what is pompously called induction is simply collecting more of the data. And Aristotle or Aquinas, or anybody in his five wits, would of course agree that the conclusion could only be true if the premises were true; and that the more true premises there were the better. It was the misfortune of medieval culture that there were not enough true premises, owing to the rather ruder conditions of travel or experiment. But however perfect were the conditions of travel or experiment, they could only produce premises; it would still be necessary to deduce conclusions. But many modern people talk as if what they call induction were some magic way of reaching a conclusion, without using any of those horrid old syllogisms. But induction does not lead us to a conclusion. Induction only leads us to a deduction. Unless the last three syllogistic steps are all right, the conclusion is all wrong. Thus the great nineteenth century men of science, whom I was brought up to revere ("accepting the conclusions of science," it was always called), went out and closely inspected the air and the earth, the chemicals and the gases, doubtless more closely than Aristotle or Aquinas, and then came back and embodied their final conclusion in a syllogism. "All matter is made of microscopic little knobs which are indivisible. My body is made of matter. Therefore my body is made of microscopic little knobs which are indivisible." They were not wrong in the form of their reasoning; because it is the only way to reason. In this world there is nothing except a syllogism—and a fallacy. But of course these modern men knew, as the medieval men knew, that their conclusions would not be true unless their premises were true. And that is where the trouble began. For the men of science, or their sons and nephews, went out and took another look at the knobby nature of matter; and were surprised to find that it was not knobby at all. So they came back and completed the process with their syllogism; "All matter is made of whirling protons and electrons. My body is made of matter. Therefore my body is made of whirling protons and electrons." And that again is a good syllogism; though they may have to look at matter once or twice more, before we know whether it is a true premise and a true conclusion. But in the final process of truth there is nothing else except a good syllogism. The only other thing is a bad syllogism; as in the familiar fashionable shape; "All matter is made of protons and electrons. I should very much like to think that mind is much the same as matter. So I will announce, through the microphone or the megaphone, that my mind is made of protons and electrons." But that is not induction; it is only a very bad blunder in deduction. That is not another or new way of thinking; it is only ceasing to think.

[From *St. Thomas Aquinas*]

IN all the current controversies people begin at the wrong end as readily as at the right end; never stopping to consider which is really the end. A little while ago an intellectual weekly started an argument among the intellectuals about whether Man has improved the earth he lives on; whether nature as a whole was better for the presence of Man.

Nobody seemed to notice that this is assuming that the end of Man is to grow more grass or improve the breed of rattlesnakes, apart from any theory about the origin or object of these things. A man may serve God and be good to mankind for that reason or a man may serve mankind and be good to other things to preserve the standard of mankind; but it is very hard to prove exactly how far he is bound to make the jungle thicker or encourage very tall giraffes. Here again the common sense of mankind, even working unconsciously, has always stated the matter the other way round. All sane men have assumed that, while a man may be right to feel benevolently towards the jungle, he is also right to treat it as something that may be put to his use, and something which he may refuse to assist indefinitely for its own sake at his own expense. A man should be kind to a giraffe; he should if necessary feed it; he may very properly stroke it or pat it on the head, even if he has to procure a ladder for these good offices. He is perfectly right to pat a giraffe; there is no objection to his patting a palm-tree. But he is not bound to regard a man as something created for the good of a palm-tree. Nor is he bound to answer the question, with any burden on his conscience: "If there were no men, would there be more palm-trees?" I only give this as one example out of many, that have caught my eye lately, of the fact that even thoughtful people seem to have forgotten how to think.

There are a great many other examples of putting the cart before the horse or the means before the end. One very common form of the blunder is to make modern conditions an absolute end and then try to fit human necessities to that end, as if they were only a means. Thus people say, "Home life is not suited to the business life of to-day." Which is as if they said "Heads are not suited to the sort of hats now in fashion." Then they might go round cutting off people's heads to meet the shortage or shrinkage of hats; and calling it the Hat Problem.

[From *Generally Speaking*]

THERE lies on the table before me . . . an invitation to join a movement for Peace and Progress Throughout the World, which a number of men more distinguished than myself seem to have already joined. And I cannot help feeling a faint curiosity, in reading the terms of such appeals, about whether these distinguished men and their friends ever have sat down suddenly and said, "I am in a rut, I know, but if I would make the least effort . . ." For it seems to me that what is the matter with the modern world, distinguished men and all, is that they have allowed their minds to be completely cluttered up with a lumber of language, some of it the legacy of old blunders, some of it suited to old conditions which no longer exist. There are any number of phrases which when they were used the first time may have meant something, and which are now used for the millionth time because they mean nothing. I will take one example out of a thousand, an example which happens to occur in the idealistic document of which I have spoken. I mean the expression about being ready to welcome "men of every race and creed."

Now the modern tragedy of man is that he does not stop and start when he has used these words, and gaze at them with a wild surmise, and cry distractedly, "My God! what am I saying?" For he really does not know what he is saying. He is classing together two things as if they were obviously in the same class, when they have obviously never been in the same category. This does not mean that a man may not feel fraternity or charity for men of every race and creed, as he may for men with every sort of heaven and hat, or with every type of truthfulness and trousers, or with every variety of saintly self-sacrifice and taste in tobacco. But the things have nothing particular to do with each other; there is no sort of reason why they should go together; and the phrase is based on the assumption that they must always go together. Race and creed are linked in the language, like pots and pans, or sticks and straws, or boots and shoes, or any other recognized groupings of things of the same type. But they are no more things of the same type than adenoids and algebra.

[From *Come to Think of It*]

EVERY one of the popular modern phrases and ideals is a dodge in order to shirk the problem of what is good. We are fond of talking about "liberty"; that, as we talk of it, is a dodge to avoid discussing what is good. We are fond of talking about "progress"; that is a dodge to avoid discussing what is good. We are fond of talking about "education"; that is a dodge to avoid discussing what is good. The modern man says, "Let us leave all these arbitrary standards and embrace liberty." This is, logically rendered, "Let us not decide what is good, but let it be considered good not to decide it." He says, "Away with your old moral formulae; I am for progress." This, logically stated, means, "Let us not settle what is good; but let us settle whether we are getting more of it." He says, "Neither in religion nor morality, my friend, lies the hope of the race, but in education." This, clearly expressed, means, "We cannot decide what is good, but let us give it to our children."

[From *Heretics*]

THE case of the general talk of "progress" is, indeed, an extreme one. As enunciated to-day "progress" is simply a comparative of which we have not settled the superlative. We meet every ideal of religion, patriotism, beauty, or brute pleasure with the alternative ideal of progress—that is to say, we meet every proposal of getting something that we know about, with an alternative proposal of getting a great deal more of nobody knows what. Progress, properly understood, has, indeed, a most dignified and legitimate meaning. But as used in opposition to precise moral ideals, it is ludicrous. So far from it being the truth that the ideal of progress is to be set against that of ethical or religious finality, the reverse is the truth. Nobody has any business to use the word "progress" unless he has a definite creed and a cast-iron code of morals. Nobody can be progressive without being doctrinal; I might almost say that nobody can be progressive without being infallible—at any rate, without believing in some infallibility. For progress by its very name indicates a direction; and the moment we are in the least doubtful about the direction, we become in the same degree doubtful about the progress. . . .

I do not, therefore, say that the word "progress" is unmeaning; I say it is unmeaning without the previous definition of a moral doctrine, and that it can only be applied to groups of persons who hold that doctrine in common. Progress is not an illegitimate word, but it is logically evident that it is illegitimate for us. It is a sacred word, a word which could only rightly be used by rigid believers and in the ages of faith.

[From *Heretics*]

IT is sometimes said that the devotees of a doctrinal religion, who are so often depicted as donkeys, are . . . wearing blinkers. The word is not wisely chosen by the critics; and in one sense is much more applicable to the critic himself. The man who teaches authoritative answers to ultimate questions, even if he only says that Mumbo Jumbo made the world out of a pumpkin, may be dogmatizing or persecuting or tyranically laying down the law about everything, but he is not blinking anything. He is not wearing blinkers, which implies deliberately limiting the field of his own vision. His vision may be in our view an illusion; but if it is very vivid to him, we cannot blame him for describing it; and anyhow he is describing the whole of it. If there is such a thing in the world as a donkey deliberately wearing blinkers, it is the enlightened educationist who is always making a nervous effort to keep out of his task of imparting knowledge any reference to the things that men from the beginning of the world have most wanted to know. Nor are these things mere hole-and-corner objects of a special curiosity. Whether or no they can ever be known, they are not only worth knowing, but they are the simplest and most elementary sort of knowledge. It is a good thing that children should fully realize that there is an objective world outside them, as solid as the lamp-post out in the street. But even when we make the lamp-post quite objective, it is not unnatural to ask what is its object. A naturalist, noting the common objects of the street, may observe many facts and put them down in a note-book. A bicyclist may bump into a lamp-post; a tramp may lean against a lamp-post; a drunkard may embrace a lamp-post or even in a lighter moment try to climb a lamp-post. But it is not a strange or specialist sort of knowledge to note about a lamp-post that it has a lamp.

Now secular education really means that everybody shall make a point of looking down on the pavement, lest by some fatal chance somebody should look up at the lamp. The lamp of faith that did in fact illuminate the street for the mass of mankind in most ages of history, was not only a wandering fire seen floating in the air by visionaries; it was also for most people the explanation of the post.

[From *The Spice of Life*]

NOW against the specialist, against the man who studies only art or electricity, or the violin, or the thumbscrew or what not, there is only one really important argument, and that, for some reason or other, is never offered. People say that specialists are inhuman; but that is unjust. People say an expert is not a man; but that is unkind and untrue. The real difficulty about the specialist or expert is much more singular and fascinating. The trouble with the expert is never that he is not a man; it is always that wherever he is not an expert he is too much of an ordinary man. Wherever he is not exceptionally learned he is quite casually ignorant. This is the great fallacy in the case of what is called the impartiality of men of science. If scientific men had no idea beyond their scientific work it might be all very well—that is to say, all very well for everybody except them. But the truth is that, beyond their scientific ideas, they have not the absence of ideas but the presence of the most vulgar and sentimental ideas that happen to be common to their social clique. If a biologist had no views on art and morals it might be all very well. The truth is that a biologist has all the wrong views of art and morals that happen to be going about in the smart set of his time.

[From *William Blake*]

SCIENCE enormously emphasizes the unique status of Man. It makes him much more obviously the lord of creation, the measure of all things, the image of God. What it does not do is to give any guarantee whatever that this magician will use his powers well, that he will advance *pari passu* in moral as in material things. Put those two facts together, and you find yourself facing the two dogmas of the Creation and the Fall.

[From *America*, 12 November 1927]

The Fallacy of Success

THERE has appeared in our time a particular class of books and articles which I sincerely and solemnly think may be called the silliest ever known among men. They are much more wild than the wildest romances of chivalry and much more dull than the dullest religious tract. Moreover, the romances of chivalry were at least about chivalry; the religious tracts are about religion. But these things are about nothing; they are about what is called Success. On every bookstall, in every magazine, you may find works telling people how to succeed. They are books showing men how to succeed in everything; they are written by men who cannot even succeed in writing books. To begin with, of course, there is no such thing as Success. Or, if you like to put it so, there is nothing that is not successful. That a thing is successful merely means that it is; a millionaire is successful in being a millionaire and a donkey in being a donkey. Any live man has succeeded in living; any dead man may have succeeded in committing suicide. But, passing over the bad logic and bad philosophy in the phrase, we may take it, as these writers do, in the ordinary sense of success in obtaining money or worldly position. These writers do not profess to tell the ordinary man how he may succeed in his trade or speculation—how, if he is a builder, he may succeed as a builder; how, if he is a stockbroker, he may succeed as a stockbroker. They profess to show him how, if he is a grocer, he may become a sporting yachtsman; how, if he is a tenth-rate journalist, he may become a peer; and how, if he is a German Jew, he may become an Anglo-Saxon. This is a definite and business-like proposal, and I really think that the people who buy these books (if any people do buy them) have a moral, if not a legal, right to ask for their money back. Nobody would dare to publish a book about electricity which literally told one nothing about electricity; no one would dare to publish an article on botany which showed that the writer did not know which end of a plant grew in the earth. Yet our modern world is full of books about Success and successful people which literally contain no kind of idea, and scarcely any kind of verbal sense.

It is perfectly obvious that in any decent occupation (such as bricklaying or writing books) there are only two ways (in any special sense) of succeeding. One is by doing very good work, the other is by cheating. Both are much too simple to require any literary explanation. If you are in for the high jump, either jump higher than any one else, or manage somehow to pretend that you have done so. If you want to succeed at whist, either be a good whist-player, or play with marked cards. You may want a book about jumping; you may want a book about whist; you may want a book about cheating at whist. But you cannot want a book about Success. Especially you cannot want a book about Success such as those which you can now find scattered by the hundred about the book-market. You may want to jump or to play cards; but you do not want to read wandering statements to the effect that jumping is jumping, or that games are won by winners. If these writers, for instance, said anything about success in jumping it would be something like this: "The jumper must have a clear aim before him. He must desire definitely to jump higher than the other men who are in for the same competition. He must let no feeble feelings of mercy (sneaked from the sickening Little Englanders and Pro-Boers) prevent him from trying to *do his best.* He must remember that a competition in jumping is distinctly competitive, and that, as Darwin has gloriously demonstrated, THE WEAKEST GO TO THE WALL." That is the kind of thing the book would say, and very useful it would be, no doubt, if read out in a low and tense voice to a young man just about to take the high jump. Or suppose that in the course of his intellectual rambles the philosopher of Success dropped in upon our other case, that of playing cards, his bracing advice would run—"In playing cards it is very necessary to avoid the mistake (commonly made by maudlin humanitarians and Free Traders) of permitting your opponent to win the game. You must have grit and snap and *go in to win.* The days of idealism and superstition are over. We live in a time of science and hard common sense, and it has now been definitely proved that in any game where two are playing IF ONE DOES NOT WIN THE OTHER WILL." It is all very stirring, of course; but I confess that if I were playing cards I would rather have some decent little book which told me the rules of the game. Beyond the rules of the game it is all a question either of talent or dishonesty; and I will undertake to provide either one or the other—which, it is not for me to say.

Turning over a popular magazine, I find a queer and amusing example. There is an article called "The Instinct that Makes People Rich." It is decorated in front with a formidable portrait of Lord Rothschild. There are many definite methods, honest and dishonest, which make people rich; the only "instinct" I know of which does it is that instinct which theological Christianity crudely describes as "the sin of avarice." That, however, is beside the present point. I wish to quote the following exquisite paragraphs as a piece of typical advice as to how to succeed. It is so practical; it leaves so little doubt about what should be our next step—

"The name of Vanderbilt is synonymous with wealth gained by modern enterprise. 'Cornelius,' the founder of the family, was the first of the great American magnates of commerce. He started as the son of a poor farmer; he ended as a millionaire twenty times over.

"He had the money-making instinct. He seized his opportunities, the opportunities that were given by the application of the steam-engine to ocean traffic, and by the birth of railway locomotion in the wealthy but undeveloped United States of America, and consequently he amassed an immense fortune.

"Now it is, of course, obvious that we cannot all follow exactly in the footsteps of this great railway monarch. The precise opportunities that fell to him do not occur to us. Circumstances have changed. But, although this is so, still, in our own sphere and in our own circumstances, we *can* follow his general methods; we can seize those opportunities that are given us, and give ourselves a very fair chance of attaining riches."

In such strange utterances we see quite clearly what is really at the bottom of all these articles and books. It is not mere business; it is not even mere cynicism. It is mysticism; the horrible mysticism of money. The writer of that passage did not really have the remotest notion of how Vanderbilt made his money, or of how anybody else is to make his. He does, indeed, conclude his remarks by advocating some scheme; but it has nothing in the world to do with Vanderbilt. He merely wished to prostrate himself before the mystery of a millionaire. For when we really worship anything, we love not only its clearness but its obscurity. We exult in its very invisibility. Thus, for instance, when a man is in love with a woman he takes special pleasure in the fact that a woman is unreasonable. Thus, again, the very pious poet, celebrating his Creator, takes pleasure in saying that God moves in a mysterious way. Now, the writer of the paragraph which I have quoted does not seem to have had anything to do with a god, and I should not think (judging by his extreme unpracticality) that he had ever been really in love with a woman. But the thing he does worship—Vanderbilt—he treats in exactly this mystical manner. He really revels in the fact his deity Vanderbilt is keeping a secret from him. And it fills his soul with a sort of transport of cunning, an ecstasy of priestcraft, that he should pretend to be telling to the multitudes that terrible secret which he does not know.

Speaking about the instinct that makes people rich, the same writer remarks—

"In olden days its existence was fully understood. The Greeks enshrined it in the story of Midas, of the 'Golden Touch.' Here was a man who turned everything he laid his hands upon into gold. His life was a progress amidst riches. Out of everything that came in his way he created the precious metal. 'A foolish legend,' said the wiseacres of the Victorian age. 'A truth,' say we of today. We all know of such men. We are ever meeting or reading about such persons who turn everything they touch into gold. Success dogs their very footsteps. Their life's pathway leads unerringly upwards. They cannot fail."

Unfortunately, however, Midas could fail; he did. His path did not lead unerringly upward. He starved because whenever he touched a biscuit or a ham sandwich it turned into gold. That was the whole point of the story, though the writer has to suppress it delicately, writing so near to a portrait of Lord Rothschild. The old fables of mankind are, indeed, unfathomably wise; but we must not have them expurgated in the interests of Mr. Vanderbilt. We must not have King Midas represented as an example of success; he was a failure of an unusually painful kind. Also, he had the ears of an ass. Also (like most other prominent and wealthy persons) he endeavoured to conceal the fact. It was his barber (if I remember right) who had to be treated on a confidential footing with regard to this peculiarity; and his barber, instead of behaving like a go-ahead person of the Succeed-at-all-costs school and trying to blackmail King Midas, went away and whispered this splendid piece of society scandal to the reeds, who enjoyed it enormously. It is said that they also whispered it as the winds swayed them to and fro. I look reverently at the portrait of Lord Rothschild; I read reverently about the exploits of Mr. Vanderbilt. I know that I cannot turn everything I touch to gold; but then I also know that I have never tried, having a preference for other substances, such as grass, and good wine. I know that these people have certainly succeeded in something; that they have certainly overcome somebody; I know that they are kings in a sense that no men were ever kings before; that they create markets and bestride continents. Yet it always seems to me that there is some small domestic fact that they are hiding, and I have sometimes thought I heard upon the wind the laughter and whisper of the reeds.

At least, let us hope that we shall all live to see these absurd books about Success covered with a proper derision and neglect. They do not teach people to be successful, but they do teach people to be snobbish; they do spread a sort of evil poetry of worldliness. The Puritans are always denouncing books that inflame lust; what shall we say of books that inflame the viler passions of avarice and pride? A hundred years ago we had the ideal of the Industrious Apprentice; boys were told that by thrift and work they would all become Lord Mayors. This was fallacious, but it was manly, and had a minimum of moral truth. In our society, temperance will not help a poor man to enrich himself, but it may help him to respect himself. Good work will not make him a rich man, but good work may make him a good workman. The Industrious Apprentice rose by virtues few and narrow indeed, but still virtues. But what shall we say of the gospel preached to the new Industrious Apprentice; the Apprentice who rises not by his virtues, but avowedly by his vices?

[From *All Things Considered*]

On Business Education

A long time ago I pointed out the fallacy of crying out for a practical man. I noted, what should be obvious enough, that when a problem is really bad and basic, we should rather wail and pray and cry aloud for an unpractical man. The practical man only knows the machine in practice; just as many a man can drive a motor-car who could not mend it, still less design it. The more serious is the trouble, the more probable it is that some knowledge of scientific theory will be required; and though the theorist will be called unpractical, he will probably be also indispensable. What is generally meant by a business man is a man who knows the way in which our particular sort of modern business does generally work. It does not follow that he is imaginative enough to suggest something else, when it obviously does not work. And (unless I very much misread the signs of the modern transition) we are soon coming to a time when everybody will be looking for somebody who can suggest something else.

I am glad to see that what I applied to the unpractical reformer has been applied, by an unimpeachably practical man, to the unpractical instructor. Mr. John C. Parker, a hundred-per-cent American, a highly successful engineer, the vigorous agent of a company named after Edison—in short, a man with all the unquestioned stigmata of a Regular Guy, rigorous and energetic in the application of science to business, has recently astonished his friends by delivering an address with the truly admirable title, "Wanted—An Unpractical Education." I have only read his remarks in an indirect form, but they seem to me quite excellent remarks. "My complaint would be rather that training youth to earn a living is not education at all; second, that a specific training may keep the youngster from earning the best kind of living; and third, that it can't be done in school anyhow." Or, again, "I would infinitely prefer that education fit him for happiness and decency in poverty, than for wealth acquired through the sacrifice of himself and his character." These are almost startlingly sensible counsels; though what they would look like side by side with those shiny and strenuous advertisements inscribed "You Can Add Ten Thousand Dollars to Your Salary," or "This Man Trebled his Turnover in Two Weeks," it is not my province to conjecture.

But this extraordinary affair called Business Education, which has begun to be supported in England after having long subsisted in America, has another aspect perhaps not so easy to explain. When I say that we want to train the citizen and not the city man, or the equivocal "something in the city," I mean even more than Mr. Parker's just and rational ideal of "the fitting of students to live richly and fully and contribute most broadly to the welfare of the social group who have paid for their education." Being myself a senile survival of the old republican idealism (I use the adjective to express the American political principle, not the American political party) I mean something else, as well as the mere social enjoyment of culture. I mean that to train a citizen is to train a critic. The whole point of education is that it should give a man abstract and eternal standards, by which he can judge material and fugitive conditions. If the citizen is to be a reformer, he must start with some ideal which he does not obtain merely by gazing reverently at the unreformed institutions. And if anyone asks, as so many are asking: "What is the use of my son learning all about ancient Athens and remote China and medieval guilds and monasteries, and all sorts of dead or distant things, when he is going to be a superior scientific plumber in Pimlico?" the answer is obvious enough. "The use of it is that he may have some power of comparison, which will not only prevent him from supposing that Pimlico covers the whole planet, but also enable him, while doing full credit to the beauties and virtues of Pimlico, to point out that, here and there, as revealed by alternative experiments, even Pimlico may conceal somewhere a defect."

Now, the nuisance of all this notion of Business Education, of a training for certain trades, whether of plumber or plutocrat, is that they will *prevent* the intelligence being sufficiently active to criticize trade and business properly. They begin by stuffing the child, not with the sense of justice by which he can judge the world, but with the sense of inevitable doom or dedication by which he must accept that particular very worldly aspect of the world. Even while he is a baby he is a bank-clerk, and accepts the principles of banking which Mr. Joseph Finsbury so kindly explained to the banker. Even in the nursery he is an actuary or an accountant; he lisps in numbers and the numbers come. But he cannot *criticize* the principles of banking, or entertain the intellectual fancy that the modern world is made to turn too much on a Pythagorean worship of numbers. But that is because he has never heard of the Pythagorean philosophy; or, indeed, of any other philosophy. He has never been taught to think, but only to count. He lives in a cold temple of abstract calculation, of which the pillars are columns of figures. But he has no basic sense of Comparative Religion (in the true sense of that tiresome phrase), by which he may discover whether he is in the right temple, or distinguish one temple from another. This is bad enough when we are dealing with the normal sense of number and quantity, the eternal foundations of rational and permanent commerce; which are in themselves as pure and abstract as Pythagoras. It becomes both preposterous and perilous when we are dealing with the mere scramble of speculation and economic illusion which is called business in America and elsewhere; with all its degrading publicity, with all its more dangerous secrecy. To begin a boy's training by teaching him to admire these things, and then call it Business Education, is exactly like teaching him to worship Baal and Baphomet, and then calling it Religious Education. And much of what is called commercial training is really of this character. Stevenson, with the assistance of Lloyd Osbourne (himself an American), gives a very vivid and amusing sketch of it in *The Wrecker*. His American hero very justly resents being laughed at merely because he leaves the *u* out of "colour"; but adds that his critics might have had a better case had they known that his father "had paid large sums to have him brought up in a gambling-hall."

Anyhow, that is what is the matter with Business Education; that it narrows the mind; whereas the whole object of education is to broaden the mind; and especially to broaden it so as to enable it to criticize and condemn such narrowness. Everybody ought to learn first a general view of the history of man, of the nature of man, and (as I, for one, should add) of the nature of God. This may enable him to consider the rights and wrongs of slavery in a slave community, of cannibalism in a cannibal community, or of commerce in a commercial community. If he is immediately initiated into the mysteries of these institutions themselves, if he is sworn in infancy to take them as seriously as they take themselves, if he becomes a trader not only before he becomes a traveller, but even before he becomes a true citizen of his own town, he will never be able to denounce those institutions—or even to improve them. Such a state will never have the ideas or imagination to reform itself; and hustle and bustle and business activity will have resulted in the dead fixity of a fossil.

[From *All Is Grist*]

On Experience

IT will be remarked that Experience, which was once claimed by the aged, is now claimed exclusively by the young. There used to be a system of morals and metaphysics that was specially known as the Experience Philosophy; but those who advanced it were grim rationalists and utilitarians who were already old in years, or, more commonly, old before their time. We all know that Experience now stands rather for the philosophy of those who claim to be young long after their time. But they preach something that may, in a sense, be called an Experience Philosophy, though some of the experiences seem to me the reverse of philosophical. So far as I can make it out, it consists of two dogmas: first, that there is no such thing as right or wrong; and secondly, that they themselves have a right to experience. How they manage to have any rights if there is no such thing as right I do not know; nor do they. But perhaps the philosophy was best summed up in a phrase I saw recently in a very interesting and important American magazine, quoted from one of the more wild and fanciful of the American critics. I have not the text before me, but the substance of the remark was this. The critic demanded indignantly to know how many ordinary American novelists had any Experiences outside those of earning their bread, pottering about in a farm or frame-house, helping to mind the baby, and so on. The question struck me as striking at the very root of all the rot and corruption and imbecility of the times.

On the face of it, of course, the whole question is rather a joke; only that these gay pleasure-seekers and revellers in the joy of life have seldom been known to see a joke. We might politely inquire exactly how much Experience is needed to equip a novelist to write novels? How many marks does he get for being vamped or for being intoxicated; and which are the particular discreditable acts by which he can get credits? How many liaisons give him this singular rank as a literary liaison officer; and how many double lives does it take to constitute Life? Is it only after his fourth divorce that he may write his first novel? For my part, I do not see why the same principle should not be applied to all the other Ten Commandments as well as to that particular Commandment. It should surely be obvious that, if love affairs are necessary to the writing of this particular sort of love story, then it follows that crime is necessary to the writing of any kind of crime story. I have myself made arrangements (on paper) for no fewer than fifty-two murders in my time; they took the form of short stories; and I shall expose myself to the withering contempt of the young sages of Experience when I confess that I am not really a murderer, and have never yet committed an actual murder. And what about all the other forms of criminal Experience? Must a writer be a forger, and manufacture other men's names before he is allowed to make his own? Must there be a journalistic apprenticeship in picking pockets as well as in picking brains; and have we to look to the establishment of an Academy of Anarchy, with the power of conferring degrees? Novelists might proudly print after their names the letters indicating the degrees they had taken; such as F.Y.B., meaning "Five Years for Burglary," or T.N.H., for "Twice Nearly Hanged." Altogether it may be said that writers do not rob, but it may be fortunate that robbers do not write. It is possible that the wild and wicked criminal might, after all, make almost as good a novelist as the novelist.

It would also be easy enough to attack the fallacy upon the facts. Everybody who has any real experience knows that good writing would not necessarily come from people with many experiences. Some of the art which is closest to life has been produced under marked limitations of living. Its prestige has generally lasted longer than the splash made by sensational social figures. Jane Austen has already survived George Sand. Even the most modern critic, if he is really a critic, will admit that Jane Austen is really realistic, in a sense in which George Sand is only romantic. She was, indeed, a flaming, fashionable figure created entirely by the Romantic movement; but Jane Austen did not belong to any movement; she does not move, but she stays. And, though I do not agree with the too common depreciation of Byron, it is true that all his somewhat excessive Experience, in the new or juvenile sense, has not prevented people feeling him to be the very reverse of realistic, and in some ways strangely unreal.

But there is, of course, a much deeper objection to the whole of this new sort of Experience Philosophy, which is quite sufficiently exposed in the very examples I quoted from the magazine. There are certainly all sorts of experiences, some great and some small. But the small ones are those which the critic imagines to be great, and the great ones are those that he contemptuously dismisses as small. There are no more universal affairs than those which he imagines to be little and local. There are no events more tremendous than those which he regards as trivial. There are no experiences more exciting than those which he dully imagines to be dull. To take his own example, a literary man who cannot see that a baby is marvellous could not see that anything was marvellous. He has certainly no earthly logical reason for regarding a movie vamp as marvellous. The movie vamp is only what happens to the baby when it goes wrong; but, from a really imaginative and intellectual standpoint, there is nothing marvellous about either of them, except what is already marvellous in the mere existence of the baby. But this sort of moralist or immoralist has a queer, half-baked prejudice to the effect that there is no good in anything until it has gone bad. It is supposed to be a part of Experience for the woman to be a vamp, but not for the woman to be a mother; although it stares us all in the face, as a stark fact of common sense, that child-bearing really is an experience, and a highly realistic experience, while the other sort of experiment may not really be an experience at all. It may be in the exact sense mere play-acting; and, as the game is now played, the main preoccupation is to prevent its ending with an addition to the cast of characters. Whatever happens, it must not be the means of bringing on the scene a new, breathing, thinking, conscious creature like a baby. That would not be Life.

Now, if there is one thing of which I have been certain since my boyhood, and grow more certain as I advance in age, it is that nothing is poetical if plain daylight is not poetical; and no monster should amaze us if the normal man does not amaze. All this talk of waiting for experiences in order to write is simply a confession of incapacity to experience anything. It is a confession of never having felt the big facts in such experiences as babyhood and the baby. A paralytic of this deaf-and-dumb description imagines he can be healed in strange waters or after strange wanderings; and announces himself ready to drink poisons, that they may stimulate him like drugs. But it is futile for him to suppose that this sort of quackery will teach him how to be a writer, for he has been from the first admittedly blind to everything that is worth writing about. He will find nothing in the wilderness but the broken shards or ruins of what should have been sacred in his own home; and if he can really make nothing of the second he will certainly make nothing of the first. The whole theory rests on a ridiculous confusion by which it is supposed that certain primary principles or relations will become interesting when they are damaged, but are bound to be depressing when they are intact. None of those who are perpetually suggesting this view ever states it thus plainly; for they are incapable of making plain statements, just as they are incapable of feeling plain things. But the point they have to prove, if they really want their Experience Philosophy accepted by those who do not care for catchwords, is that the high perils, pleasures, and creative joys of life do not occur on the high road of life, but only in certain crooked and rambling by-paths made entirely by people who have lost their way. As yet they have not even begun to prove it; and in any case, and in every sense, it could be disproved by a baby.

[From *All Is Grist*]

The Revival of Philosophy—Why?

THE best reason for a revival of philosophy is that unless a man has a philosophy certain horrible things will happen to him. He will be practical; he will be progressive; he will cultivate efficiency; he will trust in evolution; he will do the work that lies nearest; he will devote himself to deeds, not words. Thus struck down by blow after blow of blind stupidity and random fate, he will stagger on to a miserable death with no comfort but a series of catchwords; such as those which I have catalogued above. Those things are simply substitutes for thoughts. In some cases they are the tags and tail-ends of somebody else's thinking. That means that a man who refuses to have his own philosophy will not even have the advantages of a brute beast, and be left to his own instincts. He will only have the used-up scraps of somebody else's philosophy; which the beasts do not have to inherit; hence their happiness. Men have always one of two things: either a complete and conscious philosophy or the unconscious acceptance of the broken bits of some incomplete and shattered and often discredited philosophy. Such broken bits are the phrases I have quoted: efficiency and evolution and the rest. The idea of being "practical," standing all by itself, is all that remains of a Pragmatism that cannot stand at all. It is impossible to be practical without a Pragma. And what would happen if you went up to the next practical man you met and said to the poor dear old duffer, "Where is your Pragma?" Doing the work that is nearest is obvious nonsense; yet it has been repeated in many albums. In nine cases out of ten it would mean doing the work that we are least fitted to do, such as cleaning the windows or clouting the policeman over the head. "Deeds, not words" is itself an excellent example of "Words, not thoughts." It is a deed to throw a pebble into a pond and a word that sends a prisoner to the gallows. But there are certainly very futile words; and this sort of journalistic philosophy and popular science almost entirely consists of them.

Some people fear that philosophy will bore or bewilder them; because they think it is not only a string of long words, but a tangle of complicated notions. These people miss the whole point of the modern situation. These are exactly the evils that exist already; mostly for want of a philosophy. The politicians and the papers are always using long words. It is not a complete consolation that they use them wrong. The political and social relations are already hopelessly complicated. They are far more complicated than any page of medieval metaphysics; the only difference is that the medievalist could trace out the tangle and follow the complications; and the moderns cannot. The chief practical things of today, like finance and political corruption, are frightfully complicated. We are content to tolerate them because we are content to misunderstand them, not to understand them. The business world needs metaphysics—to simplify it.

I know these words will be received with scorn, and with gruff reassertion that this is no time for nonsense and paradox; and that what is really wanted is a practical man to go in and clear up the mess. And a practical man will doubtless appear, one of the unending succession of practical men; and he will doubtless go in, and perhaps clear up a few millions for himself and leave the mess more bewildering than before; as each of the other practical men has done. The reason is perfectly simple. This sort of rather crude and unconscious person always adds to the confusion; because he himself has two or three different motives at the same moment, and does not distinguish between them. A man has, already entangled hopelessly in his own mind, (1) a hearty and human desire for money, (2) a somewhat priggish and superficial desire to be progressing, or going the way the world is going, (3) a dislike of being thought too old to keep up with the young people, (4) a certain amount of vague but genuine patriotism or public spirit, (5) a misunderstanding of a mistake made by Mr. H. G. Wells, in the form of a book on Evolution. When a man has all these things in his head, and does not even attempt to sort them out, he is called by common consent and acclamation a practical man. But the practical man cannot be expected to improve the impracticable muddle; for he cannot clear up the muddle in his own mind, let alone in his own highly complex community and civilisation. For some strange reason, it is the custom to say of this sort of practical man that "he knows his own mind." Of course this is exactly what he does not know. He may in a few fortunate cases know what he wants, as does a dog or a baby of two years old; but even then he does not know why he wants it. And it is the why and the how that have to be considered when we are tracing out the way in which some culture or tradition has got into a tangle. What we need, as the ancients understood, is not a politician who is a business man, but a king who is a philosopher.

I apologise for the word "king," which is not strictly necessary to the sense; but I suggest that it would be one of the functions of the philosopher to pause upon such words, and determine their importance and unimportance. The Roman Republic and all its citizens had to the last a horror of the word "king." It was in consequence of this that they invented and imposed on us the word "Emperor." The great Republicans who founded America also had a horror of the word "king"; which has therefore reappeared with the special qualification of a Steel King, an Oil King, a Pork King, or other similar monarchs made of similar materials. The business of the philosopher is not necessarily to condemn the innovation or to deny the distinction. But it is his duty to ask himself exactly what it is that he or others dislike in the word "king." If what he dislikes is a man wearing the spotted fur of a small animal called the ermine, or a man having once had a metal ring placed on the top of his head by a clergyman, he will decide one way. If what he dislikes is a man having vast or irresponsible powers over other men, he may decide another. If what he dislikes is such fur or such power being handed on from father to son, he will enquire whether this ever occurs under commercial conditions today. But, anyhow, he will have the habit of testing the thing by the thought; by the idea which he likes or dislikes; and not merely by the sound of a syllable or the look of four letters beginning with a "K."

Philosophy is merely thought that has been thought out. It is often a great bore. But man has no alternative, except between being influenced by thought that has been thought out and being influenced by thought that has not been thought out. The latter is what we commonly call culture and enlightenment today. But man is always influenced by thought of some kind, his own or somebody else's; that of somebody he trusts or that of somebody he never heard of, thought at first, second or third hand; thought from exploded legends or unverified rumours; but always something with the shadow of a system of values and a reason for preference. A man does test everything by something. The question here is whether he has ever tested the test.

I will take one example out of a thousand that might be taken. What is the attitude of an ordinary man on being told of an extraordinary event: a miracle? I mean the sort of thing that is loosely called supernatural, but should more properly be called preternatural. For the word supernatural applies only to what is higher than man; and a good many modern miracles look as if they came from what is considerably lower. Anyhow, what do modern men say when apparently confronted with something that cannot, in the cant phrase, be naturally explained? Well, most modern men immediately talk nonsense. When such a thing is currently mentioned, in novels or newspapers or magazine stories, the first comment is always something like, "But my dear fellow, this is the twentieth century!" It is worth having a little training in philosophy if only to avoid looking so ghastly a fool as that. It has on the whole rather less sense or meaning than saying, "But my dear fellow, this is Tuesday afternoon." If miracles cannot happen, they cannot happen in the twentieth century or in the twelfth. If they can happen, nobody can prove that there is a time when they cannot happen. The best that can be said for the sceptic is that he cannot say what he means, and therefore, whatever else he means, he cannot mean what he says. But if he only means that miracles can be *believed* in the twelfth century, but cannot be believed in the twentieth, then he is wrong again, both in theory and in fact. He is wrong in theory, because an intelligent recognition of possibilities does not depend on a date but on a philosophy. An atheist could disbelieve in the first century and a mystic could continue to believe in the twenty-first century. And he is wrong, in fact, because there is every sign of there being a great deal of mysticism and miracle in the twenty-first century; and there is quite certainly an increasing mass of it in the twentieth.

But I have only taken that first superficial repartee because there is a significance in the mere fact that it comes first; and its very superficiality reveals something of the subconsciousness. It is almost an automatic repartee; and automatic words are of some importance in psychology. Let us not be too severe on the worthy gentleman who informs his dear fellow that it is the twentieth century. In the mysterious depths of his being even that enormous ass does actually mean something. The point is that he cannot really explain what he means; and *that* is the argument for a better education in philosophy. What he really means is something like this, "There is a theory of this mysterious universe to which more and more people were in fact inclined during the second half of the eighteenth and the first half of the nineteenth centuries; and up to that point at least, this theory did grow with the growing inventions and discoveries of science to which we owe our present social organisation—or disorganisation. That theory maintains that cause and effect have from the first operated in an uninterrupted sequence like a fixed fate; and that there is no will behind or within that fate; so that it must work itself out in the absence of such a will, as a machine must run down in the absence of a man. There were more people in the nineteenth century than in the ninth who happened to hold this particular theory of the universe. I myself happened to hold it; and therefore I obviously cannot believe in miracles." That is perfectly good sense; but so is the counter-statement; "I do not happen to hold it; and therefore I obviously can believe in miracles."

The advantage of an elementary philosophic habit is that it permits a man, for instance, to understand a statement like this, "Whether there can or can not be exceptions to a process depends on the nature of that process." The disadvantage of not having it is that a man will turn impatiently even from so simple a truism; and call it metaphysical gibberish. He will then go off and say: "One can't have such things in the twentieth century"; which really is gibberish. Yet the former statement could surely be explained to him in sufficiently simple terms. If a man sees a river run downhill day after day and year after year, he is justified in reckoning, we might say in betting, that it will do so till he dies. But he is not justified in saying that it cannot run uphill, until he really knows why it runs downhill. To say it does so by gravitation answers the physical but not the philosophical question. It only repeats that there is a repetition; it does not touch the deeper question of whether that repetition could be altered by anything outside it. And that depends on whether there *is* anything outside it. For instance, suppose that a man had only seen the river in a dream. He might have seen it in a hundred dreams, always repeating itself and always running downhill. But that would not prevent the hundredth dream being different and the river climbing the mountain; because the dream is a dream, and there *is* something outside it. Mere repetition does not prove reality or inevitability. We must know the nature of the thing and the cause of the repetition. If the nature of the thing is a Creation, and the cause of the thing a Creator, in other words if the repetition itself is only the repetition of something willed by a person, then it is *not* impossible for the same person to will a different thing. If a man is a fool for believing in a Creator, then he is a fool for believing in a miracle; but not otherwise. Otherwise, he is simply a philosopher who is consistent in his philosophy.

A modern man is quite free to choose either philosophy. But what is actually the matter with the modern man is that he does not know even his own philosophy; but only his own phraseology. He can only answer the next spiritual message produced by a spiritualist, or the next cure attested by doctors at Lourdes, by repeating what are generally nothing but phrases; or are, at their best, prejudices.

Thus, when so brilliant a man as Mr. H. G. Wells says that such supernatural ideas have become impossible "for intelligent people," he is (for that instant) not talking like an intelligent person. In other words, he is not talking like a philosopher; because he is not even saying what he means. What he means is, not "impossible for intelligent men," but, "impossible for intelligent monists," or, "impossible for intelligent determinists." But it is not a negation of *intelligence* to hold any coherent and logical conception of so mysterious a world. It is not a negation of intelligence to think that all experience is a dream. It is not unintelligent to think it a delusion, as some Buddhists do; let alone to think it a product of creative will, as Christians do. We are always being told that men must no longer be so sharply divided into their different religions. As an immediate step in progress, it is much more urgent that they should be more clearly and more sharply divided into their different philosophies.

[From *The Common Man*]

❦ 6 ❧

THE LITTLE BIRDS
WHO WON'T SING

O N my last morning on the Flemish coast, when I knew that in a
few hours I should be in England, my eye fell upon one of the
details of Gothic carving of which Flanders is full. I do not know
whether the thing was old, though it was certainly knocked about and
indecipherable, but at least it was certainly in the style and tradition of
the early Middle Ages. It seemed to represent men bending themselves
(not to say twisting themselves) to certain primary employments. Some
seemed to be sailors tugging at ropes; others, I think, were reaping;
others were energetically pouring something into something else. This
is entirely characteristic of the pictures and carvings of the early thirteenth century, perhaps the most purely vigorous time in all history.
The great Greeks preferred to carve their gods and heroes doing nothing. Splendid and philosophic as their composure is there is always
about it something that marks the master of many slaves. But if there
was one thing the early medievals liked it was representing people doing
something—hunting or hawking, or rowing boats, or treading grapes,
or making shoes, or cooking something in a pot. "Quicquid agunt
homines votum timor ira voluptas." (I quote from memory.) The Middle Ages is full of that spirit in all its monuments and manuscripts.
Chaucer retains it in his jolly insistence on everybody's type of trade
and toil. It was the earliest and youngest resurrection of Europe, the
time when social order was strengthening, but had not yet become
oppressive; the time when religious faiths were strong, but had not yet
been exasperated. For this reason the whole effect of Greek and Gothic
carving is different. The figures in the Elgin marbles, though often
rearing their steeds for an instant in the air, seem frozen for ever at that
perfect instant. But a mass of medieval carving seems actually a sort of
bustle or hubbub in stone. Sometimes one cannot help feeling that the
groups actually move and mix, and the whole front of a great cathedral
has the hum of a huge hive.

But about these particular figures there was a peculiarity of which I could not be sure. Those of them that had any heads had very curious heads, and it seemed to me that they had their mouths open. Whether or no this really meant anything or was an accident of nascent art I do not know; but in the course of wondering I recalled to my mind the fact that singing was connected with many of the tasks there suggested, that there were songs for reapers reaping and songs for sailors hauling ropes. I was still thinking about this small problem when I walked along the pier at Ostend; and I heard some sailors uttering a measured shout as they laboured, and I remembered that sailors still sing in chorus while they work, and even sing different songs according to what part of their work they are doing. And a little afterwards, when my sea journey was over, the sight of men working in the English fields reminded me again that there are still songs for harvest and for many agricultural routines. And I suddenly wondered why if this were so it should be quite unknown for any modern trade to have a ritual poetry. How did people come to chant rude poems while pulling certain ropes or gathering certain fruit, and why did nobody do anything of the kind while producing any of the modern things? Why is a modern newspaper never printed by people singing in chorus? Why do shopmen seldom, if ever, sing?

If reapers sing while reaping, why should not auditors sing while auditing and bankers while banking? If there are songs for all the separate things that have to be done in a boat, why are there not songs for all the separate things that have to be done in a bank? As the train from Dover flew through the Kentish gardens, I tried to write a few songs suitable for commercial gentlemen. Thus, the work of bank clerks when casting up columns might begin with a thundering chorus in praise of Simple Addition.

"Up my lads, and lift the ledgers, sleep and ease are o'er.
  Hear the Stars of Morning shouting: 'Two and Two are Four.'
Though the creeds and realms are reeling, though the sophists
    roar,
  Though we weep and pawn our watches, Two and Two are
    Four."

And then, of course, we should need another song for times of financial crisis and courage, a song with a more fierce and panic-stricken metre, like the rushing of horses in the night:

"There's a run upon the Bank—
    Stand away!
For the Manager's a crank and the Secretary drank, and the Upper

> Tooting Bank
> Turns to bay!
> Stand close: there is a run
> On the Bank.
> Of our ship, our royal one, let the ringing legend run,
> that she fired every gun
> Ere she sank."

And as I came into the cloud of London I met a friend of mine who actually is in a bank, and submitted these suggestions in rhyme to him for use among his colleagues. But he was not very hopeful about the matter. It was not (he assured me) that he underrated the verses, or in any sense lamented their lack of polish. No; it was rather, he felt, an indefinable something in the very atmosphere of the society in which we live that makes it spiritually difficult to sing in banks. And I think he must be right; though the matter is very mysterious. I may observe here that I think there must be some mistake in the calculations of the Socialists. They put down all our distress not to a moral tone, but to the chaos of private enterprise. Now, banks are private; but post offices are Socialistic: therefore I naturally expected that the post office would fall into the collectivist idea of a chorus. Judge of my surprise when the lady in my local post office (whom I urged to sing) dismissed the idea with far more coldness than the bank clerk had done. She seemed, indeed, to be in a considerably greater state of depression than he. Should anyone suppose that this was the effect of the verses themselves, it is only fair to say that the specimen verse of the Post Office Hymn ran thus:

> "O'er London our letters are shaken like snow,
> Our wires o'er the world like the thunderbolts go.
> The news that may marry a maiden in Sark,
> Or kill an old lady in Finsbury Park."
> *Chorus (with a swing of joy and energy):*
> "Or kill an old lady in Finsbury Park."

And the more I thought about the matter the more painfully certain it seemed that the most important and typical modern things could not be done with a chorus. One could not, for instance, be a great financier and sing; because the essence of being a great financier is that you keep quiet. You could not even in many modern circles be a public man and sing; because in those circles the essence of being a public man is that you do nearly everything in private. Nobody would imagine a chorus of money-lenders. Everyone knows the story of the solicitors' corps of volunteers who, when the Colonel on the battlefield cried "Charge!" all said simultaneously, "Six-and eightpence." Men can sing while charging in a military, but hardly in a legal sense. And at the end of my reflections I had really got no further than the subconscious feeling of my friend the bank clerk—that there is something spiritually suffocating about our life; not about our laws merely, but about our life. Bank clerks are without songs not because they are poor, but because they are sad. Sailors are much poorer. As I passed homewards I passed a little tin building of some religious sort, which was shaken with shouting as a trumpet is torn with its own tongue. *They* were singing anyhow; and I had for an instant a fancy I had often had before: that with us the super-human is the only place where you can find the human. Human nature is hunted, and has fled into sanctuary.

[From *Tremendous Trifles*]

❧ 7 ❧

EXCERPTS FROM *ORTHODOXY*

Remarks by Karl G. Schmude:
For our time, perhaps the most pertinent quality of *Orthodoxy* is its unswervingly objective approach to truth. Though Chesterton undoubtedly responded to his own deeply felt need for an explanation of life, he did not conduct his research along those lines. He did not derive his philosophy from his own inner experience, as if this were an infallible response to objective reality; above all did he avoid being guided uncritically by what Sir Arnold Lunn has called a "Fif," a "funny internal feeling," which Lunn considered the most common basis for contemporary thought and behaviour. Chesterton grounded his thought in experience outside himself, relating it to circumstances and standards that are universally recognizable. Hence, his philosophy was not a personal philosophy in the sense that it was unique to him and incommunicable. "God and humanity made it," he said, "and it made me."

[From Karl G. Schmude, *The Man Who Was Chesterton*]

THE only possible excuse for this book is that it is an answer to a challenge. Even a bad shot is dignified when he accepts a duel. When some time ago I published a series of hasty but sincere papers, under the name of "Heretics," several critics for whose intellect I have a warm respect (I may mention specially Mr. G. S. Street) said that it was all very well for me to tell everybody to affirm his cosmic theory, but that I had carefully avoided supporting my precepts with example. "I will begin to worry about my philosophy," said Mr. Street, "when Mr. Chesterton has given us his." It was perhaps an incautious suggestion to make to a person only too ready to write books upon the feeblest provocation. But after all, though Mr. Street has inspired and created this book, he need not read it. If he does read it, he will find that in its pages I have attempted in a vague and personal way, in a set of mental pictures rather than in a series of deductions, to state the philosophy in which I have come to believe, I will not call it my philosophy; for I did not make it. God and humanity made it; and it made me.

I have often had a fancy for writing a romance about an English yachtsman who slightly miscalculated his course and discovered England under the impression that it was a new island in the South Seas. I always find, however, that I am either too busy or too lazy to write this fine work, so I may as well give it away for the purposes of philosophical illustration. There will probably be a general impression that the man who landed (armed to the teeth and talking by signs) to plant the British flag on that barbaric temple which turned out to be the Pavilion at Brighton, felt rather a fool. I am not here concerned to deny that he looked a fool. But if you imagine that he felt a fool, or at any rate that the sense of folly was his sole or his dominant emotion, then you have not studied with sufficient delicacy the rich romantic nature of the hero of this tale. His mistake was really a most enviable mistake; and he knew it, if he was the man I take him for. What could be more delightful than to have in the same few minutes all the fascinating terrors of going abroad combined with all the humane security of coming home again? What could be better than to have all the fun of discovering South Africa without the disgusting necessity of landing there? What could be more glorious than to brace one's self up to discover New South Wales and then realize, with a gush of happy tears, that it was really old South Wales. This at least seems to me the main problem for philosophers, and is in a manner the main problem of this book. How can we contrive to be at once astonished at the world and yet at home in it? How can this queer cosmic town, with its many-legged citizens, with its monstrous and ancient lamps, how can this world give us at once the fascination of a strange town and the comfort and honour of being our own town?

To show that a faith or a philosophy is true from every standpoint would be too big an undertaking even for a much bigger book than this; it is necessary to follow one path of argument; and this is the path that I here propose to follow. I wish to set forth my faith as particularly answering this double spiritual need, the need for that mixture of the familiar and the unfamiliar which Christendom has rightly named romance. For the very word "romance" has in it the mystery and ancient meaning of Rome. Any one setting out to dispute anything ought always to begin by saying what he does not dispute. Beyond stating what he proposes to prove he should always state what he does not propose to prove. The thing I do not propose to prove, the thing I propose to take as common ground between myself and any average reader, is this desirability of an active and imaginative life, picturesque and full of a poetical curiosity, a life such as western man at any rate always seems to have desired. If a man says that extinction is better than existence or blank existence better than variety and adventure, then he is not one of the ordinary people to whom I am talking. If a man prefers nothing I can give him nothing. But nearly all people I have ever met in this western society in which I live would agree to the general proposition that we need this life of practical romance; the combination of something that is strange with something that is secure. We need so to view the world as to combine an idea of wonder and an idea of welcome. We need to be happy in this wonderland without once being merely comfortable. It is *this* achievement of my creed that I shall chiefly pursue in these pages.

But I have a peculiar reason for mentioning the man in a yacht, who discovered England. For I am that man in a yacht. I discovered England. I do not see how this book can avoid being egotistical; and I do not quite see (to tell the truth) how it can avoid being dull. Dulness will, however, free me from the charge which I most lament; the charge of being flippant. Mere light sophistry is the thing that I happen to despise most of all things, and it is perhaps a wholesome fact that this is the thing of which I am generally accused. I know nothing so contemptible as a mere paradox; a mere ingenious defence of the indefensible. If it were true (as has been said) that Mr. Bernard Shaw lived upon paradox, then he ought to be a mere common millionaire; for a man of his mental activity could invent a sophistry every six minutes. It is as easy as lying; because it is lying. The truth is, of course, that Mr. Shaw is cruelly hampered by the fact that he cannot tell any lie unless he thinks it is the truth. I find myself under the same intolerable bondage. I never in my life said anything merely because I thought it funny; though of course, I have had ordinary human vainglory, and may have thought it funny because I had said it. It is one thing to describe an interview with a gorgon or a griffin, a creature who does not exist. It is another thing to discover that the rhinoceros does exist and then take pleasure in the fact that he looks as if he didn't. One searches for truth, but it may be that one pursues instinctively the more extraordinary truths. And I offer this book with the heartiest sentiments to all the jolly people who hate what I write, and regard it (very justly, for all I know) as a piece of poor clowning or a single tiresome joke.

For if this book is a joke it is a joke against me. I am the man who with the utmost daring discovered what had been discovered before. If there is an element of farce in what follows, the farce is at my own expense; for this book explains how I fancied I was the first to set foot in Brighton and then found I was the last. It recounts my elephantine adventures in pursuit of the obvious. No one can think my case more ludicrous than I think it myself; no reader can accuse me here of trying to make a fool of him: I am the fool of this story, and no rebel shall hurl me from my throne. I freely confess all the idiotic ambitions of the end of the nineteenth century. I did, like all other solemn little boys, try to be in advance of the age. Like them I tried to be some ten minutes in advance of the truth. And I found that I was eighteen hundred years behind it. I did strain my voice with a painfully juvenile exaggeration in uttering my truths. And I was punished in the fittest and funniest way, for I have kept my truths: but I have discovered, not that they were not truths, but simply that they were not mine. When I fancied that I stood alone I was really in the ridiculous position of being backed up by all Christendom. It may be, Heaven forgive me, that I did try to be original; but I only succeeded in inventing all by myself an inferior copy of the existing traditions of civilized religion. The man from the yacht thought he was the first to find England; I thought I was the first to find Europe. I did try to found a heresy of my own; and when I had put the last touches to it, I discovered that it was orthodoxy.

It may be that somebody will be entertained by the account of this happy fiasco. It might amuse a friend or an enemy to read how I gradually learnt from the truth of some stray legend or from the falsehood of some dominant philosophy, things that I might have learnt from my catechism—if I had ever learnt it. There may or may not be some entertainment in reading how I found at last in an anarchist club or a Babylonian temple what I might have found in the nearest parish church. If any one is entertained by learning how the flowers of the field or the phrases in an omnibus, the accidents of politics or the pains of youth came together in a certain order to produce a certain conviction of Christian orthodoxy, he may possibly read this book. But there is in everything a reasonable division of labour. I have written the book, and nothing on earth would induce me to read it.

I add one purely pedantic note which comes, as a note naturally should, at the beginning of the book. These essays are concerned only to discuss the actual fact that the central Christian theology (sufficiently summarized in the Apostles' Creed) is the best root of energy and sound ethics. They are not intended to discuss the very fascinating but quite different question of what is the present seat of authority for the proclamation of that creed. When the word "orthodoxy" is used here it means the Apostles' Creed, as understood by everybody calling himself Christian until a very short time ago and the general historic conduct of those who held such a creed. I have been forced by mere space to confine myself to what I have got from this creed; I do not touch the matter much disputed among modern Christians, of where we ourselves got it. This is not an ecclesiastical treatise but a sort of slovenly autobiography. But if anyone wants my opinions about the actual nature of the authority, Mr. G. S. Street has only to throw me another challenge, and I will write him another book.

[From Chapter 1]

MYSTICISM keeps men sane. As long as you have mystery you have health; when you destroy mystery you create morbidity. The ordinary man has always been sane because the ordinary man has always been a mystic. He has permitted the twilight. He has always had one foot in earth and the other in fairyland. He has always left himself free to doubt his gods; but (unlike the agnostic of to-day) free also to believe in them. He has always cared more for truth than for consistency. If he saw two truths that seemed to contradict each other, he would take the two truths and the contradiction along with them. His spiritual sight is stereoscopic, like his physical sight: he sees two different pictures at once and yet sees all the better for that. Thus he has always believed that there was such a thing as fate, but such a thing as free will also. Thus he believed that children were indeed the kingdom of heaven, but nevertheless ought to be obedient to the kingdom of earth. He admired youth because it was young and age because it was not. It is exactly this balance of apparent contradictions that has been the whole buoyancy of the healthy man. The whole secret of mysticism is this: that man can understand everything by the help of what he does not understand. The morbid logician seeks to make everything lucid, and succeeds in making everything mysterious. The mystic allows one thing to be mysterious, and everything else becomes lucid. The determinist makes the theory of causation quite clear, and then finds that he cannot say "if you please" to the housemaid. The Christian permits free will to remain a sacred mystery; but because of this his relations with the housemaid become of a sparkling and crystal clearness. He puts the seed of dogma in a central darkness; but it branches forth in all directions with abounding natural health. As we have taken the circle as the symbol of reason and madness, we may very well take the cross as the symbol at once of mystery and of health. Buddhism is centripetal, but Christianity is centrifugal: it breaks out. For the circle is perfect and infinite in its nature; but it is fixed for ever in size; it can never be larger or smaller. But the cross, though it has at its heart a collision and a contradiction, can extend its four arms for ever without altering its shape. Because it has a paradox in its centre it can grow without changing. The circle returns upon itself and is bound. The cross opens its arms to the four winds; it is a signpost for free travellers.

[From Chapter 2]

THE sages, it is often said, can see no answer to the riddle of religion. But the trouble with our sages is not that they cannot see the answer; it is that they cannot even see the riddle. They are like children so stupid as to notice nothing paradoxical in the playful assertion that a door is not a door. The modern latitudinarians speak, for instance, about authority in religion not only as if there were no reason for it, but as if there had never been any reason for it. Apart from seeing its philosophical basis, they cannot even see its historical cause. Religious authority has often, doubtless, been oppressive or unreasonable; just as every legal system (and especially our present one) has been callous and full of a cruel apathy. It is rational to attack the police; nay, it is glorious. But the modern critics of religious authority are like men who should attack the police without ever having heard of burglars. For there is a great and possible peril to the human mind: a peril as practical as burglary. Against it religious authority was reared, rightly or wrongly, as a barrier. And against it something certainly must be reared as a barrier, if our race is to avoid ruin.

That peril is that the human intellect is free to destroy itself. Just as one generation could prevent the very existence of the next generation, by all entering a monastery or jumping into the sea, so one set of thinkers can in some degree prevent further thinking by teaching the next generation that there is no validity in any human thought. It is idle to talk always of the alternative of reason and faith. It is an act of faith to assert that our thoughts have any relation to reality at all. If you are merely a sceptic, you must sooner or later ask yourself the question, "Why should *anything* go right; even observation and deduction? Why should not good logic be as misleading as bad logic? They are both movements in the brain of a bewildered ape?" The young sceptic says, "I have a right to think for myself." But the old sceptic, the complete sceptic, says, "I have no right to think for myself. I have no right to think at all."

There is a thought that stops thought. That is the only thought that ought to be stopped. That is the ultimate evil against which all religious authority was aimed. It only appears at the end of decadent ages like our own: and already Mr. H. G. Wells has raised its ruinous banner; he has written a delicate piece of scepticism called "Doubts of the Instrument." In this he questions the brain itself, and endeavours to remove all reality from all his own assertions, past, present, and to come. But it was against this remote ruin that all the military systems in religion were originally ranked and ruled. The creeds and the crusades, the hierarchies and the horrible persecutions were not organized, as is ignorantly said, for the suppression of reason. They were organized for the difficult defence of reason. Man, by a blind instinct, knew that if once things were wildly questioned, reason could be questioned first. The authority of priests to absolve, the authority of popes to define the authority, even of inquisitors to terrify: these were all only dark defences erected round one central authority, more undemonstrable, more supernatural than all—the authority of a man to think. We know now that this is so; we have no excuse for not knowing it. For we can hear scepticism crashing through the old ring of authorities, and at the same moment we can see reason swaying upon her throne. In so far as religion is gone, reason is going. For they are both of the same primary and authoritative kind. They are both methods of proof which cannot themselves be proved. And in the act of destroying the idea of Divine authority we have largely destroyed the idea of that human authority by which we do a long-division sum. With a long and sustained tug we have attempted to pull the mitre off pontifical man; and his head has come off with it.

[From Chapter 3]

I am concerned with a certain way of looking at life, which was created in me by the fairy tales, but has since been meekly ratified by the mere facts.

It might be stated this way. There are certain sequences or developments (cases of one thing following another), which are, in the true sense of the word, reasonable. They are, in the true sense of the word, necessary. Such are mathematical and merely logical sequences. We in fairyland (who are the most reasonable of all creatures) admit that reason and that necessity. For instance, if the Ugly Sisters are older than Cinderella, it is (in an iron and awful sense) *necessary* that Cinderella is younger than the Ugly Sisters. There is no getting out of it. Haeckel may talk as much fatalism about that fact as he pleases: it really must be. If Jack is the son of a miller, a miller is the father of Jack. Cold reason decrees it from her awful throne: and we in fairyland submit. If the three brothers all ride horses, there are six animals and eighteen legs involved: that is true rationalism, and fairyland is full of it. But as I put my head over the hedge of the elves and began to take notice of the natural world, I observed an extraordinary thing. I observed that learned men in spectacles were talking of the actual things that happened—dawn and death and so on—as if *they* were rational and inevitable. They talked as if the fact that trees bear fruit were just as *necessary* as the fact that two and one trees make three. But it is not. There is an enormous difference by the test of fairyland; which is the test of the imagination. You cannot *imagine* two and one not making three. But you can easily imagine trees not growing fruit; you can imagine them growing golden candlesticks or tigers hanging on by the tail. These men in spectacles spoke much of a man named Newton, who was hit by an apple, and who discovered a law. But they could not be got to see the distinction between a true law, a law of reason, and the mere fact of apples falling. If the apple hit Newton's nose, Newton's nose hit the apple. That is a true necessity: because we cannot conceive the one occurring without the other. But we can quite well conceive the apple not falling on his nose; we can fancy it flying ardently through the air to hit some other nose, of which it had a more definite dislike. We have always in our fairy tales kept this sharp distinction between the science of mental relations, in which there really are laws, and the science of physical facts, in which there are no laws, but only weird repetitions. We believe in bodily miracles, but not in mental impossibilities. We believe that a Bean-stalk climbed up to Heaven; but that does not at all confuse our convictions on the philosophical question of how many beans make five.

Here is the peculiar perfection of tone and truth in the nursery tales. The man of science says, "Cut the stalk, and the apple will fall"; but he says it calmly, as if the one idea really led up to the other. The witch in the fairy tale says, "Blow the horn, and the ogre's castle will fall"; but she does not say it as if it were something in which the effect obviously arose out of the cause. Doubtless she has given the advice to many champions, and has seen many castles fall, but she does not lose either her wonder or her reason. She does not muddle her head until it imagines a necessary mental connection between a horn and a falling tower. But the scientific men do muddle their heads, until they imagine a necessary mental connection between an apple leaving the tree and an apple reaching the ground. They do really talk as if they had found not only a set of marvelous facts, but a truth connecting those facts. They do talk as if the connection of two strange things physically connected them philosophically. They feel that because one incomprehensible thing constantly follows another incomprehensible thing the two together somehow make up a comprehensible thing. Two black riddles make a white answer.

In fairyland we avoid the word "law"; but in the land of science they are singularly fond of it. Thus they will call some interesting conjecture about how forgotten folks pronounced the alphabet, Grimm's Law. But Grimm's Law is far less intellectual than Grimm's Fairy Tales. The tales are, at any rate, certainly tales; while the law is not a law. A law implies that we know the nature of the generalisation and enactment; not merely that we have noticed some of the effects. If there is a law that pick-pockets shall go to prison, it implies that there is an imaginable mental connection between the idea of prison and the idea of picking pockets. And we know what the idea is. We can say why we take liberty from a man who takes liberties. But we cannot say why an egg can turn into a chicken any more than we can say why a bear could turn into a fairy prince. As *ideas,* the egg and the chicken are further off from each other than the bear and the prince; for no egg in itself suggests a chicken, whereas some princes do suggest bears. Granted, then, that certain transformations do happen, it is essential that we should regard them in the philosophic manner of fairy tales, not in the unphilosophic manner of science and the "Laws of Nature." When we are asked why eggs turn to birds or fruits fall in autumn, we must answer exactly as the fairy godmother would answer if Cinderella asked her why mice turned to horses or her clothes fell from her at twelve o'clock. We must answer that it is *magic.* It is not a "law," for we do not understand its general formula. It is not a necessity, for though we can count on it happening practically, we have no right to say that it must always happen. It is no argument for unalterable law (as Huxley fancied) that we count on the ordinary course of things. We do not count on it; we bet on it. We risk the remote possibility of a miracle as we do that of a poisoned pancake or a world-destroying comet. We leave it out of account, not because it is a miracle, and therefore an impossibility, but because it is a miracle, and therefore an exception. All the terms used in the science books, "law," "necessity," "order," "tendency," and so on, are really unintellectual, because they assume an inner synthesis, which we do not possess. The only words that ever satisfied me as describing Nature are the terms used in the fairy books, "charm," "spell," "enchantment." They express the arbitrariness of the fact and its mystery. A tree grows fruit because it is a *magic* tree. Water runs downhill because it is be-witched. The sun shines because it is bewitched.

[From Chapter 4]

THERE were, then, these two first feelings, indefensible and indis-putable. The world was a shock, but it was not merely shocking; existence was a surprise, but it was a pleasant surprise. In fact, all my first views were exactly uttered in a riddle that stuck in my brain from boyhood. The question was, "What did the first frog say?" And the answer was, "Lord, how you made me jump!" That says succinctly all that I am saying. God made the frog jump; but the frog prefers jumping. But when these things are settled there enters the second great principle of the fairy philosophy.

Any one can see it who will simply read "Grimm's Fairy Tales" or the fine collection of Mr. Andrew Lang. For the pleasure of pedantry I will call it the Doctrine of Conditional Joy. Touchstone talked of much virtue in an "if"; according to elfin ethics all virtue is in an "if." The note of the fairy utterance always is, "You may live in a palace of gold and sapphire, *if* you do not say the word 'cow' "; or "You may live happily with the King's daughter, *if* you do not show her an onion." The vision always hangs upon a veto. All the dizzy and colossal things conceded depend upon one small thing withheld. All the wild and whirling things that are let loose depend upon one thing that is forbid-den. . . . In the fairy tale an incomprehensible happiness rests upon an incomprehensible condition. A box is opened, and all evils fly out. A word is forgotten, and cities perish. A lamp is lit, and love flies away. A flower is plucked, and human lives are forfeited. An apple is eaten, and the hope of God is gone.

.   .   .   .   .   .

I have explained that the fairy tales founded in me two convictions; first, that this world is a wild and startling place, which might have been quite different, but which is quite delightful; second, that before this wildness and delight one may well be modest and submit to the queerest limitations of so queer a kindness. But I found the whole modern world running like a high tide against both my tendernesses; and the shock of that collision created two sudden and spontaneous sentiments, which I have had ever since and which, crude as they were, have since hardened into convictions.

First, I found the whole modern world talking scientific fatalism; saying that everything is as it must always have been, being unfolded without fault from the beginning. The leaf on the tree is green because it could never have been anything else. Now, the fairy-tale philosopher is glad that the leaf is green precisely because it might have been scarlet. He feels as if it had turned green an instant before he looked at it. He is pleased that snow is white on the strictly reasonable ground that it might have been black. Every colour has in it a bold quality as of choice; the red of garden roses is not only decisive but dramatic, like suddenly spilt blood. He feels that something has been *done*. But the great determinists of the nineteenth century were strongly against this native feeling that something had happened an instant before. In fact, according to them, nothing ever really had happened since the beginning of the world. Nothing ever had happened since existence had happened; and even about the date of that they were not very sure.

The modern world as I found it was solid for modern Calvinism, for the necessity of things being as they are. But when I came to ask them I found they had really no proof of this unavoidable repetition in things except the fact that the things were repeated. Now, the mere repetition made the things to me rather more weird than more rational. It was as if, having seen a curiously shaped nose in the street and dismissed it as an accident, I had then seen six other noses of the same astonishing shape. I should have fancied for a moment that it must be some local secret society. So one elephant having a trunk was odd; but all elephants having trunks looked like a plot. I speak here only of an emotion, and of an emotion at once stubborn and subtle. But the repetition in Nature seemed sometimes to be an excited repetition, like that of an angry schoolmaster saying the same thing over and over again. The grass seemed signalling to me with all its fingers at once; the crowded stars seemed bent upon being understood. The sun would make me see him if he rose a thousand times. The recurrences of the universe rose to the maddening rhythm of an incantation, and I began to see an idea.

All the towering materialism which dominates the modern mind rests ultimately upon one assumption; a false assumption. It is supposed that if a thing goes on repeating itself it is probably dead; a piece of clockwork. People feel that if the universe was personal it would vary; if the sun were alive it would dance. This is a fallacy even in relation to known fact. For the variation in human affairs is generally brought into them, not by life, but by death; by the dying down or breaking off of their strength or desire. A man varies his movements because of some slight element of failure or fatigue. He gets into an omnibus because he is tired of walking; or he walks because he is tired of sitting still. But if his life and joy were so gigantic that he never tired of going to Islington, he might go to Islington as regularly as the Thames goes to Sheerness. The very speed and ecstacy of his life would have the stillness of death. The sun rises every morning. I do not rise every morning; but the variation is due not to my activity, but to my inaction. Now, to put the matter in a popular phrase, it might be true that the sun rises regularly because he never gets tired of rising. His routine might be due, not to a lifelessness, but to a rush of life. The thing I mean can be seen, for instance, in children, when they find some game or joke that they specially enjoy. A child kicks his legs rhythmically through excess, not absence, of life. Because children have abounding vitality, because they are in spirit fierce and free, therefore they want things repeated and unchanged. They always say, "Do it again"; and the grown-up person does it again until he is nearly dead. For grown-up people are not strong enough to exult in monotony. But perhaps God is strong enough to exult in monotony. It is possible that God says every morning, "Do it again" to the sun; and every evening, "Do it again" to the moon. It may not be automatic necessity that makes all daisies alike; it may be that God makes every daisy separately, but has never got tired of making them. It may be that He has the eternal appetite of infancy; for we have sinned and grown old, and our Father is younger than we. The repetition in Nature may not be a mere recurrence; it may be a theatrical *encore*. Heaven may *encore* the bird who laid an egg. If the human being conceives and brings forth a human child instead of bringing forth a fish, or a bat, or a griffin, the reason may not be that we are fixed in an animal fate without life or purpose. It may be that our little tragedy has touched the gods, that they admire it from their starry galleries, and that at the end of every human drama man is called again and again before the curtain. Repetition may go on for millions of years, by mere choice, and at any instant it may stop. Man may stand on the earth generation after generation, and yet each birth be his positively last appearance.

This was my first conviction; made by the shock of my childish emotions meeting the modern creed in mid-career. I had always vaguely felt facts to be miracles in the sense that they are wonderful: now I began to think them miracles in the stricter sense that they were *wilful*. I mean that they were, or might be, repeated exercises of some will. In short, I had always believed that the world involved magic: now I thought that perhaps it involved a magician. And this pointed to a profound emotion always present and sub-conscious; that this world of ours has some purpose; and if there is a purpose, there is a person. I had always felt life first as a story: and if there is a story there is a story-teller.

But modern thought also hit my second human tradition. It went against the fairy feeling about strict limits and conditions. The one thing it loved to talk about was expansion and largeness. Herbert Spencer would have been greatly annoyed if any one had called him an imperialist, and therefore it is highly regrettable that nobody did. But he was an imperialist of the lowest type. He popularized this contemptible notion that the size of the solar system ought to over-awe the spiritual dogma of man. Why should a man surrender his dignity to the solar system any more than to a whale? If mere size proves that man is not the image of God, then a whale may be the image of God; a somewhat formless image; what one might call an impressionist portrait. It is quite futile to argue that man is small compared to the cosmos; for man was always small compared to the nearest tree. But Herbert Spencer, in his headlong imperialism, would insist that we had in some way been conquered and annexed by the astronomical universe. He spoke about men and their ideals exactly as the most insolent Unionist talks about the Irish and their ideals. He turned mankind into a small nationality. And his evil influence can be seen even in the most spirited and honourable of later scientific authors; notably in the early romances of Mr. H. G. Wells. Many moralists have in an exaggerated way represented the earth as wicked. But Mr. Wells and his school made the heavens wicked. We should lift up our eyes to the stars from whence would come our ruin.

But the expansion of which I speak was much more evil than all this. I have remarked that the materialist, like the madman, is in prison; in the prison of one thought. These people seemed to think it singularly inspiring to keep on saying that the prison was very large. The size of this scientific universe gave one no novelty, no relief. The cosmos went on for ever, but not in its wildest constellation could there be anything really interesting; anything, for instance, such as forgiveness or free will. The grandeur or infinity of the secret of its cosmos added nothing to it. It was like telling a prisoner in Reading gaol that he would be glad to hear that the gaol now covered half the country. The warder would have nothing to show the man except more and more long corridors of stone lit by ghastly lights and empty of all that is human. So these expanders of the universe had nothing to show us except more and more infinite corridors of space lit by ghastly suns and empty of all that is divine.

In fairyland there had been a real law; a law that could be broken, for the definition of a law is something that can be broken. But the machinery of this cosmic prison was something that could not be broken; for we ourselves were only a part of its machinery. We were either unable to do things or we were destined to do them. The idea of the mystical condition quite disappeared; one can neither have the firmness of keeping laws nor the fun of breaking them. The largeness of this universe had nothing of that freshness and airy outbreak which we have praised in the universe of the poet. This modern universe is literally an empire; that is, it was vast, but it is not free. One went into larger and larger windowless rooms, rooms big with Babylonian perspective; but one never found the smallest window or a whisper of outer air.

Their infernal parallels seemed to expand with distance; but for me all good things come to a point, swords for instance. So finding the boast of the big cosmos so unsatisfactory to my emotions I began to argue about it a little; and I soon found that the whole attitude was even shallower than could have been expected. According to these people the cosmos was one thing since it had one unbroken rule. Only (they would say) while it is one thing it is also the only thing there is. Why, then, should one worry particularly to call it large? There is nothing to compare it with. It would be just as sensible to call it small. A man may say, "I like this vast cosmos, with its throng of stars and its crowd of varied creatures." But if it comes to that why should not a man say, "I like this cosy little cosmos, with its decent number of stars and as neat a provision of live stock as I wish to see"? One is as good as the other; they are both mere sentiments. It is mere sentiment to rejoice that the sun is larger than the earth; it is quite as sane a sentiment to rejoice that the sun is no larger than it is. A man chooses to have an emotion about the largeness of the world: why should he not choose to have an emotion about its smallness?

It happened that I had that emotion. When one is fond of anything one addresses it by diminutives, even if it is an elephant or a life-guardsman. The reason is, that anything, however huge, that can be conceived of as complete, can be conceived of as small. If military moustaches did not suggest a sword or tusks a tail, then the object would be vast because it would be immeasurable. But the moment you can imagine a guardsman you can imagine a small guardsman. The moment you really see an elephant you can call it "Tiny." If you can make a statue of a thing you can make a statuette of it. These people professed that the universe was one coherent thing; but they were not fond of the universe. But I was frightfully fond of the universe and wanted to address it by a diminutive. I often did so; and it never seemed to mind. Actually and in truth I did feel that these dim dogmas of vitality were better expressed by calling the world small than by calling it large.

For about infinity there was a sort of carelessness which was the reverse of the fierce and pious care which I felt touching the pricelessness and the peril of life. They showed only a dreary waste; but I felt a sort of sacred thrift. For economy is far more romantic than extravagance. To them stars were an unending income of halfpence; but I felt about the golden sun and the silver moon as a schoolboy feels if he has one sovereign and one shilling.

These subconscious convictions are best hit off by the colour and tone of certain tales. Thus I have said that stories of magic alone can express my sense that life is not only a pleasure but a kind of eccentric privilege. I may express this other feeling of cosmic cosiness by allusion to another book always read in boyhood, "Robinson Crusoe," which I read about this time, and which owes its eternal vivacity to the fact that it celebrates the poetry of limits, nay, even the wild romance of prudence. Crusoe is a man on a small rock with a few comforts just snatched from the sea: the best thing in the book is simply the list of things saved from the wreck. The greatest of poems is an inventory. Every kitchen tool becomes ideal because Crusoe might have dropped it in the sea. It is a good exercise, in empty or ugly hours of the day, to look at anything, the coal-scuttle or the book-case, and think how happy one could be to have brought it out of the sinking ship on to the solitary island. But it is a better exercise still to remember how all things have had this hairbreadth escape: everything has been saved from a wreck. Every man has had one horrible adventure: as a hidden untimely birth he had not been, as infants that never see the light. Men spoke much in my boyhood of restricted or ruined men of genius: and it was common to say that many a man was a Great Might-Have-Been. To me it is a more solid and startling fact that any man in the street is a Great Might-Not-Have-Been.

But I really felt (the fancy may seem foolish) as if all the order and number of things were the romantic remnant of Crusoe's ship. That there are two sexes and one sun, was like the fact that there were two guns and one axe. It was poignantly urgent that none should be lost; but somehow, it was rather fun that none could be added. The trees and the planets seemed like things saved from the wreck: and when I saw the Matterhorn I was glad that it had not been overlooked in the confusion. I felt economical about the stars as if they were sapphires (they are called so in Milton's Eden): I hoarded the hills. For the universe is a single jewel, and while it is a natural cant to talk of a jewel as peerless and priceless, of this jewel it is literally true. This cosmos is indeed without peer and without price: for there cannot be another one.

Thus ends, in unavoidable inadequacy, the attempt to utter the unutterable things. These are my ultimate attitudes towards life; the soils for the seeds of doctrine. These in some dark way I thought before I could write, and felt before I could think: that we may proceed more easily afterwards, I will roughly recapitulate them now. I felt in my bones; first, that this world does not explain itself. It may be a miracle with a supernatural explanation; it may be a conjuring trick, with a natural explanation. But the explanation of the conjuring trick, if it is to satisfy me, will have to be better than the natural explanations I have heard. The thing is magic, true or false. Second, I came to feel as if magic must have a meaning, and meaning must have some one to mean it. There was something personal in the world, as in a work of art; whatever it meant it meant violently. Third, I thought this purpose beautiful in its old design, in spite of its defects, such as dragons. Fourth, that the proper form of thanks to it is some form of humility and restraint: we should thank God for beer and Burgundy by not drinking too much of them. We owed, also, an obedience to whatever made us. And last, and strangest, there had come into my mind a vague and vast impression that in some way all good was a remnant to be stored and held sacred out of some primordial ruin. Man had saved his good as Crusoe saved his goods: he had saved them from a wreck. All this I felt and the age gave me no encouragement to feel it. And all this time I had not even thought of Christian theology.

[From Chapter 4]

A S I read and re-read all the non-Christian or anti-Christian accounts of the faith, from Huxley to Bradlaugh, a slow and awful impression grew gradually but graphically upon my mind—the impression that Christianity must be a most extraordinary thing. For not only (as I understood) had Christianity the most flaming vices, but it had apparently a mystical talent for combining vices which seemed inconsistent with each other. It was attacked on all sides and for all contradictory reasons. No sooner had one rationalist demonstrated that it was too far to the east than another demonstrated with equal clearness that it was much too far to the west. No sooner had my indignation died down at its angular and aggressive squareness than I was called up again to notice and condemn its enervating and sensual roundness. In case any reader has not come across the thing I mean, I will give such instances as I remember at random of this self-contradiction in the sceptical attack. I give four or five of them; there are fifty more.

Thus, for instance, I was much moved by the eloquent attack on Christianity as a thing of inhuman gloom; for I thought (and still think) sincere pessimism the unpardonable sin. Insincere pessimism is a social accomplishment, rather agreeable than otherwise; and fortunately nearly all pessimism is insincere. But if Christianity was, as these people said, a thing purely pessimistic and opposed to life, then I was quite prepared to blow up St. Paul's Cathedral. But the extraordinary thing is this. They did prove to me in Chapter I. (to my complete satisfaction) that Christianity was too pessimistic; and then, in Chapter II., they began to prove to me that it was a great deal too optimistic. One accusation against Christianity was that it prevented men, by morbid tears and terrors, from seeking joy and liberty in the bosom of Nature. But another accusation was that it comforted men with a fictitious providence, and put them in a pink-and-white nursery. One great agnostic asked why Nature was not beautiful enough, and why it was hard to be free. Another great agnostic objected that Christian optimism, "the garment of make-believe woven by pious hands," hid from us the fact that Nature was ugly, and that it was impossible to be free. One rationalist had hardly done calling Christianity a nightmare before another began to call it a fool's paradise. This puzzled me; the charges seemed inconsistent. Christianity could not at once be the black mask on a white world, and also the white mask on a black world. The state of the Christian could not be at once so comfortable that he was a coward to cling to it, and so uncomfortable that he was a fool to stand it. If it falsified human vision it must falsify it one way or another; it could not wear both green and rose-coloured spectacles. I rolled on my tongue with a terrible joy, as did all young men of that time, the taunts which Swinburne hurled at the dreariness of the creed—

"Thou hast conquered, O pale Galilean, the world has
    grown gray with Thy breath."

But when I read the same poet's accounts of paganism (as in "Atalanta"), I gathered that the world was, if possible, more gray before the Galilean breathed on it than afterwards. The poet maintained, indeed, in the abstract, that life itself was pitch dark. And yet, somehow, Christianity had darkened it. The very man who denounced Christianity for pessimism was himself a pessimist. I thought there must be something wrong. And it did for one wild moment cross my mind that, perhaps, those might not be the very best judges of the relation of religion to happiness who, by their own account, had neither one nor the other.

It must be understood that I did not conclude hastily that the accusations were false or the accusers fools. I simply deduced that Christianity must be something even weirder and wickeder than they made out. A thing might have these two opposite vices; but it must be a rather queer thing if it did. A man might be too fat in one place and too thin in another; but he would be an odd shape. At this point my thoughts were only of the odd shape of the Christian religion; I did not allege any odd shape in the rationalistic mind.

Here is another case of the same kind. I felt that a strong case against Christianity lay in the charge that there is something timid, monkish, and unmanly about all that is called "Christian," especially in its attitude towards resistance and fighting. The great sceptics of the nineteenth century were largely virile. Bradlaugh in an expansive way, Huxley, in a reticent way, were decidedly men. In comparison, it did seem tenable that there was something weak and over patient about Christian counsels. The Gospel paradox about the other cheek, the fact that priests never fought, a hundred things made plausible the accusation that Christianity was an attempt to make a man too like a sheep. I read it and believed it, and if I had read nothing different, I should have gone on believing it. But I read something very different. I turned the next page in my agnostic manual, and my brain turned upside down. Now I found that I was to hate Christianity not for fighting too little, but for fighting too much. Christianity, it seemed, was the mother of wars. Christianity had deluged the world with blood. I had got thoroughly angry with the Christian, because he never was angry. And now I was told to be angry with him because his anger had been the most huge and horrible thing in human history; because his anger had soaked the earth and smoked to the sun. The very people who reproached Christianity with the meekness and non-resistance of the monasteries were the very people who reproached it also with the violence and valour of the Crusades. It was the fault of poor old Christianity (somehow or other) both that Edward the Confessor did not fight and that Richard Coeur de Lion did. The Quakers (we were told) were the only characteristic Christians; and yet the massacres of Cromwell and Alva were characteristic Christian crimes. What could it all mean? What was this Christianity which always forbade war and always produced wars? What could be the nature of the thing which one could abuse first because it would not fight, and second because it was always fighting? In what world of riddles was born this monstrous murder and this monstrous meekness? The shape of Christianity grew a queerer shape every instant.

I take a third case; the strangest of all, because it involves the one real objection to the faith. The one real objection to the Christian religion is simply that it is one religion. The world is a big place, full of very different kinds of people. Christianity (it may reasonably be said) is one thing confined to one kind of people; it began in Palestine, it has practically stopped with Europe. I was duly impressed with this argument in my youth, and I was much drawn towards the doctrine often preached in Ethical Societies—I mean the doctrine that there is one great unconscious church of all humanity founded on the omnipresence of the human conscience. Creeds, it was said, divided men; but at least morals united them. The soul might seek the strangest and most remote lands and ages and still find essential ethical common sense. It might find Confucius under Eastern trees, and he would be writing "Thou shalt not steal." It might decipher the darkest hieroglyphic on the most primeval desert, and the meaning when deciphered would be "Little boys should tell the truth." I believed this doctrine of the brotherhood of all men in the possession of a moral sense, and I believe it still—with other things. And I was thoroughly annoyed with Christianity for suggesting (as I supposed) that whole ages and empires of men had utterly escaped this light of justice and reason. But then I found an astonishing thing. I found that the very people who said that mankind was one church from Plato to Emerson were the very people who said that morality had changed altogether, and that what was right in one age was wrong in another. If I asked, say, for an altar, I was told that we needed none, for men our brothers gave us clear oracles and one creed in their universal customs and ideals. But if I mildly pointed out that one of men's universal customs was to have an altar, then my agnostic teachers turned clean round and told me that men had always been in darkness and the superstitions of savages. I found it was their daily taunt against Christianity that it was the light of one people and had left all others to die in the dark. But I also found that it was their special boast for themselves that science and progress were the discovery of one people, and that all other peoples had died in the dark. Their chief insult to Christianity was actually their chief compliment to themselves, and there seemed to be a strange unfairness about all their relative insistence on the two things. When considering some pagan or agnostic, we were to remember that all men had one religion; when considering some mystic or spiritualist, we were only to consider what absurd religions some men had. We could trust the ethics of Epictetus, because ethics had never changed. We must not trust the ethics of Bossuet, because ethics had changed. They changed in two hundred years, but not in two thousand.

This began to be alarming. It looked not so much as if Christianity was bad enough to include any vices, but rather as if any stick was good enough to beat Christianity with. What again could this astonishing thing be like which people were so anxious to contradict, that in doing so they did not mind contradicting themselves? I saw the same thing on every side. I can give no further space to this discussion of it in detail; but lest anyone supposes that I have unfairly selected three accidental cases I will run briefly through a few others. Thus, certain sceptics wrote that the great crime of Christianity had been its attack on the family; it had dragged women to the loneliness and contemplation of the cloister, away from their homes and their children. But, then, other sceptics (slightly more advanced) said that the great crime of Christianity was forcing the family and marriage upon us; that it doomed women to the drudgery of their homes and children, and forbade them loneliness and contemplation. The charge was actually reversed. Or, again, certain phrases in the Epistles or the marriage service, were said by the anti-Christians to show contempt for woman's intellect. But I found that the anti-Christians themselves had a contempt for woman's intellect; for it was their great sneer at the Church on the Continent that "only women" went to it. Or again, Christianity was reproached with its naked and hungry habits; with its sackcloth and dried peas. But the next minute Christianity was being reproached with its pomp and its ritualism; its shrines of porphyry and its robes of gold. It was abused for being too plain and for being too coloured. Again Christianity had always been accused of restraining sexuality too much, when Bradlaugh the Malthusian discovered that it restrained it too little. It is often accused in the same breath of prim respectability and of religious extravagance. Between the covers of the same atheistic pamphlet I have found the faith rebuked for its disunion, "One thinks one thing, and one another," and rebuked also for its union, "It is difference of opinion that prevents the world from going to the dogs." In the same conversation a freethinker, a friend of mine, blamed Christianity for despising Jews, and then despised it himself for being Jewish.

I wished to be quite fair then, and I wish to be quite fair now; and I did not conclude that the attack on Christianity was all wrong. I only concluded that if Christianity was wrong, it was very wrong indeed. Such hostile horrors might be combined in one thing, but that thing must be very strange and solitary. There are men who are misers, and also spendthrifts; but they are rare. There are men sensual and also ascetic; but they are rare. But if this mass of mad contradictions really existed, quakerish and bloodthirsty, too gorgeous and too thread-bare, austere, yet pandering preposterously to the lust of the eye, the enemy of women and their foolish refuge, a solemn pessimist and a silly optimist, if this evil existed, then there was in this evil something quite supreme and unique. For I found in my rationalist teachers no explanation of such exceptional corruption. Christianity (theoretically speaking) was in their eyes only one of the ordinary myths and errors of mortals. *They* gave me no key to this twisted and unnatural badness. Such a paradox of evil rose to the stature of the supernatural. It was, indeed, almost as supernatural as the infallibility of the Pope. An historic institution, which never went right, is really quite as much of a miracle as an institution that cannot go wrong. The only explanation which immediately occurred to my mind was that Christianity did not come from heaven, but from hell. Really, if Jesus of Nazareth was not Christ, He must have been Antichrist.

And then in a quiet hour a strange thought struck me like a still thunderbolt. There had suddenly come into my mind another explanation. Suppose we heard an unknown man spoken of by many men. Suppose we were puzzled to hear that some men said he was too tall and some too short; some objected to his fatness, some lamented his leanness; some thought him too dark, and some too fair. One explanation (as has been already admitted) would be that he might be an odd shape. But there is another explanation. He might be the right shape. Outrageously tall men might feel him to be short. Very short men might feel him to be tall. Old bucks who are growing stout might consider him insufficiently filled out; old beaux who were growing thin might feel that he expanded beyond the narrow lines of elegance. Perhaps Swedes (who have pale hair like tow) called him a dark man, while negroes considered him distinctly blonde. Perhaps (in short) this extraordinary thing is really the ordinary thing; at least the normal thing, the centre. Perhaps, after all, it is Christianity that is sane and all its critics that are mad—in various ways. I tested this idea by asking myself whether there was about any of the accusers anything morbid that might explain the accusation. I was startled to find that this key fitted a lock. For instance, it was certainly odd that the modern world charged Christianity at once with bodily austerity and with artistic pomp. But then it was also odd, very odd, that the modern world itself combined extreme bodily luxury with an extreme absence of artistic pomp. The modern man thought Becket's robes too rich and his meals too poor. But then the modern man was really exceptional in history; no man before ever ate such elaborate dinners in such ugly clothes. The modern man found the church too simple exactly where modern life is too complex; he found the church too gorgeous exactly where modern life is too dingy. The man who disliked the plain fasts and feasts was mad on *entrées*. The man who disliked vestments wore a pair of preposterous trousers. And surely if there was any insanity involved in the matter at all it was in the trousers, not in the simply falling robe. If there was any insanity at all, it was in the extravagant *entrées*, not in the bread and wine.

I went over all the cases, and I found the key fitted so far. The fact that Swinburne was irritated at the unhappiness of Christians and yet more irritated at their happiness was easily explained. It was no longer a complication of diseases in Christianity, but a complication of diseases in Swinburne. The restraint of Christians saddened him simply because he was more hedonist than a healthy man should be. The faith of Christians angered him because he was more pessimist than a healthy man should be. In the same way the Malthusians by instinct attacked Christianity; not because there is anything especially anti-Malthusian about Christianity, but because there is something a little anti-human about Malthusianism.

Nevertheless it could not, I felt, be quite true that Christianity was merely sensible and stood in the middle. There was really an element in it of emphasis and even frenzy which had justified the secularists in their superficial criticism. It might be wise, I began more and more to think that it was wise, but it was not merely worldly wise; it was not merely temperate and respectable. Its fierce crusaders and meek saints might balance each other; still, the crusaders were very fierce and the saints were very meek, meek beyond all decency. Now, it was just at this point of the speculation that I remembered my thoughts about the martyr and the suicide. In that matter there had been this combination between two almost insane positions which yet somehow amounted to sanity. This was just such another contradiction; and this I had already found to be true. This was exactly one of the paradoxes in which sceptics found the creed wrong; and in this I had found it right. Madly as Christians might love the martyr or hate the suicide, they never felt these passions more madly than I had felt them long before I dreamed of Christianity. Then the most difficult and interesting part of the mental process opened, and I began to trace this idea darkly through all the enormous thoughts of our theology. The idea was that which I had outlined touching the optimist and the pessimist; that we want not an amalgam or compromise, but both things at the top of their energy; love and wrath both burning. Here I shall only trace it in relation to ethics. But I need not remind the reader that the idea of this combination is indeed central in orthodox theology. For orthodox theology has specially insisted that Christ was not a being apart from God and man, like an elf, nor yet a being half human and half not, like a centaur, but both things at once and both things thoroughly, very man and very God. Now let me trace this notion as I found it.

All sane men can see that sanity is some kind of equilibrium; that one may be mad and eat too much, or mad and eat too little. . . . . But granted that we have all to keep balance, the real interest comes in with the question of how that balance can be kept. That was the problem which Paganism tried to solve: that was the problem which I think Christianity solved and solved in a very strange way.

Paganism declared that virtue was in a balance; Christianity declared it was in a conflict: the collision of two passions apparently opposite. Of course they were not really inconsistent; but they were such that it was hard to hold simultaneously. Let us follow for a moment the clue of the martyr and the suicide; and take the case of courage. No quality has ever so much addled the brains and tangled the definitions of merely rational sages. Courage is almost a contradiction in terms. It means a strong desire to live taking the form of a readiness to die. "He that will lose his life, the same shall save it," is not a piece of mysticism for saints and heroes. It is a piece of everyday advice for sailors and mountaineers. It might be printed in an Alpine guide or a drill book. This paradox is the whole principle of courage; even of quite earthly or quite brutal courage. A man cut off by the sea may save his life if he will risk it on the precipice. He can only get away from death by continually stepping within an inch of it. A soldier surrounded by enemies, if he is to cut his way out, needs to combine a strong desire for living with a strange carelessness about dying. He must not merely cling to life, for then he will be a coward, and will not escape. He must not merely wait for death, for then he will be a suicide, and will not escape. He must seek his life in a spirit of furious indifference to it; he must desire life like water and yet drink death like wine. No philosopher, I fancy, has ever expressed this romantic riddle with adequate lucidity, and I certainly have not done so. But Christianity has done more; it has marked the limits of it in the awful graves of the suicide and the hero, showing the distance between him who dies for the sake of living and him who dies for the sake of dying. And it has held up ever since above the European lances the banner of the mystery of chivalry: the Christian courage, which is a disdain of death; not the Chinese courage, which is a disdain of life.

And now I began to find that this duplex passion was the Christian key to ethics everywhere. Everywhere the creed made a moderation out of the still crash of two impetuous emotions. Take, for instance, the matter of modesty, of the balance between mere pride and mere prostration. The average pagan, like the average agnostic, would merely say that he was content with himself, but not insolently self-satisfied, that there were many better and many worse, that his deserts were limited, but he would see that he got them. In short, he would walk with his head in the air; but not necessarily with his nose in the air. This is a manly and rational position, but it is open to the objection we noted against the compromise between optimism and pessimism—the "resignation" of Matthew Arnold. Being a mixture of two things, it is a dilution of two things; neither is present in its full strength or contributes its full colour. This proper pride does not lift the heart like the tongue of trumpets; you cannot go clad in crimson and gold for this. On the other hand, this mild rationalist modesty does not cleanse the soul with fire and make it clear like crystal; it does not (like a strict and searching humility) make a man as a little child, who can sit at the feet of the grass. It does not make him look up and see marvels; for Alice must grow small if she is to be Alice in Wonderland. Thus it loses both the poetry of being proud and the poetry of being humble. Christianity sought by this same strange expedient to save both of them.

It separated the two ideas and then exaggerated them both. In one way Man was to be haughtier than he had ever been before; in another way he was to be humbler than he had ever been before. In so far as I am Man I am the chief of creatures. In so far as I am *a* man I am the chief of sinners. All humility that had meant pessimism, that had meant man taking a vague or mean view of his whole destiny—all that was to go. We were to hear no more the wail of Ecclesiastes that humility had no pre-eminence over the brute, or the awful cry of Homer that man was only the saddest of all the beasts of the field. Man was a statue of God walking about the garden. Man had pre-eminence over all the brutes; man was only sad because he was not a beast, but a broken god. The Greeks had spoken of men creeping on the earth, as if clinging to it. Now Man was to tread on the earth as if to subdue it. Christianity thus held a thought of the dignity of man that could only be expressed in crowns rayed like the sun and fans of peacock plumage. Yet at the same time it could hold a thought about the abject smallness of man that could only be expressed in fasting and fantastic submission, in the gray ashes of St. Dominic and the white snows of St. Bernard. When one came to think of *one's self*, there was vista and void enough for any amount of bleak abnegation and bitter truth. There the realistic gentleman could let himself go—as long as he let himself go at himself. There was an open playground for the happy pessimist. Let him say anything against himself short of blaspheming the original aim of his being; let him call himself a fool and even a damned fool (though that is Calvinistic); but he must not say that fools are not worth saving. He must not say that a man, *quâ* man, can be valueless. Here, again in short, Christians got over the difficulty of combining furious opposites, by keeping them both, and keeping them both furious. The Church was positive on both points. One can hardly think too little of one's self. One can hardly think too much of one's soul.

Take another case: the complicated question of charity, which some highly uncharitable idealists seem to think quite easy. Charity is a paradox, like modesty and courage. Stated baldly, charity certainly means one of two things—pardoning unpardonable acts, or loving unlovable people. But if we ask ourselves (as we did in the case of pride) what a sensible pagan would feel about such a subject, we shall probably be beginning at the bottom of it. A sensible pagan would say that there were some people one could forgive, and some one couldn't: a slave who stole wine could be laughed at; a slave who betrayed his benefactor could be killed, and cursed even after he was killed. In so far as the act was pardonable, the man was pardonable. That again is rational, and even refreshing; but it is a dilution. It leaves no place for a pure horror of injustice, such as that which is a great beauty in the innocent. And it leaves no place for a mere tenderness for men as men, such as is the whole fascination of the charitable. Christianity came in here as before. It came in startlingly with a sword, and clove one thing from another. It divided the crime from the criminal. The criminal we must forgive unto seventy times seven. The crime we must not forgive at all. It was not enough that slaves who stole wine inspired partly anger and partly kindness. We must be much more angry with theft than before, and yet much kinder to thieves than before. There was room for wrath and love to run wild. And the more I considered Christianity, the more I found that while it had established a rule and order, the chief aim of that order was to give room for good things to run wild.

. . . . .

ST. Francis, in praising all good, could be a more shouting optimist than Walt Whitman. St. Jerome, in denouncing all evil, could paint the world blacker than Schopenhauer. Both passions were free because both were kept in their place. The optimist could pour out all the praise he liked on the gay music of the march, the golden trumpets, and the purple banners going into battle. But he must not call the fight needless. The pessimist might draw as darkly as he chose the sickening marches or the sanguine wounds. But he must not call the fight hopeless. So it was with all the other moral problems, with pride, with protest, and with compassion. By defining its main doctrine, the Church not only kept seemingly inconsistent things side by side, but, what was more, allowed them to break out in a sort of artistic violence otherwise possible only to anarchists. Meekness grew more dramatic than madness. . . .

Thus, the double charges of the secularists, though throwing nothing but darkness and confusion on themselves, throw a real light on the faith. It *is* true that the historic Church has at once emphasised celibacy and emphasised the family; has at once (if one may put it so) been fiercely for having children and fiercely for not having children. It has kept them side by side like two strong colours, red and white, like the red and white upon the shield of St. George. It has always had a healthy hatred of pink. It hates that combination of two colours which is the feeble expedient of the philosophers. It hates that evolution of black into white which is tantamount to a dirty gray. In fact, the whole theory of the Church on virginity might be symbolized in the statement that white is a colour: not merely the absence of a colour. All that I am urging here can be expressed by saying that Christianity sought in most of these cases to keep two colours coexistent but pure. It is not a mixture like russet or purple; it is rather like a shot silk, for a shot silk is always at right angles, and is in the pattern of the cross.

. . . . .

C HRISTIAN doctrine detected the oddities of life. It not only discovered the law, but it foresaw the exceptions. Those underrate Christianity who say that it discovered mercy; any one might discover mercy. In fact every one did. But to discover a plan for being merciful and also severe—*that* was to anticipate a strange need of human nature. For no one wants to be forgiven for a big sin as if it were a little one. Any one might say that we should be neither quite miserable nor quite happy. But to find out how far one *may* be quite miserable without making it impossible to be quite happy—that was a discovery in psychology. Any one might say, "Neither swagger nor grovel"; and it would have been a limit. But to say, "Here you can swagger and there you can grovel"—that was an emancipation.

This was the big fact about Christian ethics; the discovery of the new balance. Paganism had been like a pillar of marble, upright because proportioned with symmetry. Christianity was like a huge and ragged and romantic rock, which, though it sways on its pedestal at a touch, yet, because its exaggerated excrescences exactly balance each other, it is enthroned there for a thousand years. In a Gothic cathedral the columns were all different, but they were all necessary. Every support seemed an accidental and fantastic support; every buttress was a flying buttress. So in Christendom apparent accidents balanced. Becket wore a hair shirt under his gold and crimson, and there is much to be said for the combination; for Becket got the benefit of the hair shirt while the people in the street got the benefit of the crimson and gold. It is at least better than the manner of the modern millionaire, who has the black and the drab outwardly for others, and the gold next his heart. But the balance was not always in one man's body as in Becket's; the balance was often distributed over the whole body of Christendom. Because a man prayed and fasted on the Northern snows, flowers could be flung at his festival in the Southern cities; and because fanatics drank water on the sands of Syria, men could still drink cider in the orchards of England. This is what makes Christendom at once so much more perplexing and so much more interesting than the Pagan empire. . . .

Last and most important, it is exactly this which explains what is so inexplicable to all the modern critics of the history of Christianity. I mean the monstrous wars about small points of theology, the earthquakes of emotion about a gesture or a word. It was only a matter of an inch; but an inch is everything when you are balancing. The Church could not afford to swerve a hair's breadth on some things if she was to continue her great and daring experiment of the irregular equilibrium. Once let one idea become less powerful and some other idea would become too powerful. It was no flock of sheep the Christian shepherd was leading, but a herd of bulls and tigers, of terrible ideals and devouring doctrines, each one of them strong enough to turn to a false religion and lay waste the world. Remember that the Church went in specifically for dangerous ideas; she was a lion tamer. The idea of birth through a Holy Spirit, of the death of a divine being, of the forgiveness of sins, or the fulfillment of prophecies, are ideas which, any one can see, need but a touch to turn them into something blasphemous or ferocious. The smallest link was let drop by the artificers of the Mediterranean, and the lion of ancestral pessimism burst this chain in the forgotten forests of the north. Of these theological equalisations I have to speak afterwards. Here it is enough to notice that if some small mistake were made in doctrine, huge blunders might be made in human happiness. A sentence phrased wrong about the nature of symbolism would have broken all the best statues in Europe. A slip in the definitions might stop all the dances; might wither all the Christmas trees or break all the Easter eggs. Doctrine had to be defined within strict limits, even in order that man might enjoy general human liberties. The Church had to be careful, if only that the world might be careless.

This is the thrilling romance of Orthodoxy. People have fallen into a foolish habit of speaking of orthodoxy as something heavy, humdrum, and safe. There never was anything so perilous or so exciting as orthodoxy. It was sanity: and to be sane is more dramatic than to be mad. It was the equilibrium of a man behind madly rushing horses, seeming to stoop this way and to sway that, yet in every attitude having the grace of statuary and the accuracy of arithmetic. The Church in its early days went fierce and fast with any warhorse; yet it is utterly unhistoric to say that she merely went mad along one idea, like a vulgar fanaticism. She swerved to left and right, so exactly as to avoid enormous obstacles. She left on one hand the huge bulk of Arianism, buttressed by all the worldly powers to make Christianity too worldly. The next instant she was swerving to avoid an orientalism, which would have made it too unworldly. The orthodox Church never took the tame course or accepted the conventions; the orthodox Church was never respectable. It would have been easier to have accepted the earthly power of the Arians. It would have been easy, in the Calvinistic seventeenth century, to fall into the bottomless pit of predestination. It is easy to be a madman: it is easy to be a heretic. It is always easy to let the age have its head; the difficult thing is to keep one's own. It is always easy to be a modernist; as it is easy to be a snob. To have fallen into any of those open traps of error and exaggeration which fashion after fashion and sect after sect set along the historic path of Christendom—that would indeed have been simple. It is always simple to fall; there are an infinity of angles at which one falls, only one at which one stands. To have fallen into any one of the fads from Gnosticism to Christian Science would indeed have been obvious and tame. But to have avoided them all has been one whirling adventure; and in my vision the heavenly chariot flies thundering through the ages, the dull heresies sprawling and prostrate, the wild truth reeling but erect.

[From Chapter 6]

Remarks by A. L. Maycock:
Chesterton was one of the few great English men of letters to whom the Christian religion was an all-embracing philosophy to which nothing could be irrelevant. Leaving aside his purely emphemeral journalism it can be said of him that, in the whole range and variety of his literary expression, he was never concerned with anything less than the ultimate meaning and purpose of life. . . .
There was plenty of good Christian apologetic being produced in Edwardian England, but it made little impact on the ordinary reading public because it was written, naturally and properly enough, in the

language of theology and had a specifically 'religious' flavour and intention. Most of it was essentially defensive, and Chesterton from the first struck an entirely different note. Here, writing regularly in the secular press on all kinds of topics, was a Christian apologist who possessed a great skill in debate, an exuberant wit, a keener understanding of the minds of his opponents than they had themselves, and a sound equipment as a practical theologian—an apologist, too, who was by no means content with a strategy of defence. On the contrary, he was concerned to show, as the starting-point of his counter-offensive, that Christianity provided the only sane explanation of the universe and that the Christian life, so far from being a stuffy, outmoded system of vetos and restrictions, was a great adventure in possession of the truth that can alone make a man free. He was further concerned to show that the articles of orthodox Christian belief had an immediate and most practical relevance to the whole ordering of human life. . . .

Comparatively little of his work was in the strict sense theological. What mattered—what gave the power and the special character to all that he had to say—was the belief, illustrated in every book that he ever wrote, that a sane and true theology is the necessary framework of any satisfactory way of life. He first found that theology summarized in the granite formulae of the Nicene Creed. And during the early years of this century he was the only important English writer—the only writer, that is, of anything like the same genius or with anything approaching the same appeal—whose work was informed through and through by a belief in Christian orthodoxy.

[From A. L. Maycock, *The Man Who Was Orthodox*]

❦ 8 ❧

MARRIAGE, FAMILY, WOMAN

Essay Excerpts

VERY few people ever state properly the strong argument in favour of marrying for love or against marrying for money. The argument is not that all lovers are heros and heroines, nor is it that all dukes are profligates or all millionaires cads. The argument is this, that the differences between a man and a woman are at the best so obstinate and exasperating that they practically cannot be got over unless there is an atmosphere of exaggerated tenderness and mutual interest. To put the matter in one metaphor, the sexes are two stubborn pieces of iron; if they are to be welded together, it must be while they are red-hot. Every woman has to find out that her husband is a selfish beast, because every man is a selfish beast by the standard of a woman. But let her find out the beast while they are both still in the story of "Beauty and the Beast." Every man has to find out that his wife is cross—that is to say, sensitive to the point of madness: for every woman is mad by the masculine standard. But let him find out that she is mad while her madness is more worth considering than anyone else's sanity.

[From *The Common Man*]

SUPPOSING it to be conceded that humanity has acted at least not unnaturally in dividing itself into two halves, respectively typifying the ideals of special talent and of general sanity (since they are genuinely difficult to combine completely in one mind), it is not difficult to see why the line of cleavage has followed the line of sex, or why the female became the emblem of the universal and the male of the special and superior. Two gigantic facts of nature fixed it thus: first, that the woman who frequently fulfilled her functions literally could not be specially prominent in experiment and adventure; and second, that the same natural operation surrounded her with very young children, who require to be taught not so much anything as everything. Babies need not to be taught a trade, but to be introduced to a world. To put the matter shortly, woman is generally shut up in a house with a human being at the time when he asks all the questions that there are, and some that there aren't. It would be odd if she retained any of the narrowness of a specialist. Now if anyone says that this duty of general enlightenment (even when freed from modern rules and hours, and exercised more spontaneously by a more protected person) is in itself too exacting and oppressive, I can understand the view. I can only answer that our race has thought it worth while to cast this burden on women in order to keep common-sense in the world. But when people begin to talk about this domestic duty as not merely difficult but trivial and dreary, I simply give up the question. For I cannot with the utmost energy of imagination conceive what they mean. When domesticity, for instance, is called drudgery, all the difficulty arises from a double meaning in the word. If drudgery only means dreadfully hard work, I admit the woman drudges in the home, as a man might drudge at the Cathedral of Amiens or drudge behind a gun at Trafalgar. But if it means that the hard work is more heavy because it is trifling, colorless and of small import to the soul, then as I say, I give it up; I do not know what the words mean. To be Queen Elizabeth within a definite area, deciding sales, banquets, labors and holidays; to be Whitely within a certain area, providing toys, boots, sheets, cakes, and books; to be Aristotle within a certain area, teaching morals, manners, theology, and hygiene; I can understand how this might exhaust the mind, but I cannot imagine how it could narrow it. How can it be a large career to tell other people's children about the Rule of Three, and a small career to tell one's own children about the universe? How can it be broad to be the same thing to everyone, and narrow to be everything to someone? No; a woman's function is laborious, but because it is gigantic, not because it is minute. I will pity Mrs. Jones for the hugeness of her task; I will never pity her for its smallness.

[From *What's Wrong with the World*]

I am puzzled . . . when I hear, as we often hear just now, somebody saying that he was formerly opposed to Female Suffrage but was converted to it by the courage and patriotism shown by women in nursing and similar war work. Really, I do not wish to be superior in my turn, when I can only express my wonder in a question. But from what benighted dens can these people have crawled, that they did not know that women are brave? What horrible sort of women have they known all their lives? Where do they come from? Or, what is a still more apposite question, where do they think they come from? Do they think they fell from the moon, or were really found under cabbage-leaves, or brought over the sea by storks? . . . Should we any of us be here at all if women were not brave? Are we not all trophies of that war and triumph? Does not every man stand on the earth like a graven statue as the monument of the valour of a woman?

[From *Fancies versus Fads*]

NOTHING can ever overcome that one enormous sex superiority, that even the male child is born closer to his mother than to his father. No one, staring at that frightful female privilege, can quite believe in the equality of the sexes. Here and there we read of a girl brought up like a tom-boy; but every boy is brought up like a tame girl. The flesh and spirit of femininity surround him from the first like the four walls of a house; and even the vaguest or most brutal man has been womanized by being born. Man that is born of woman has short days and full of misery; but nobody can picture the obscenity and bestial tragedy that would belong to such a monster as man that was born of a man.

[From *What's Wrong with the World*]

"BUT the cold fact remains: imprudent marriages do lead to long unhappiness and disappointment—you've got used to your drinks and things—I shan't be pretty much longer—"

"Imprudent marriages!" roared Michael. "And pray where on earth or heaven are there any prudent marriages? Might as well talk about prudent suicides. You and I have dawdled round each other long enough, and are we any safer than Smith and Mary Gray, who met last night? You never know a husband till you marry him. Unhappy! of course you'll be unhappy. Who the devil are you that you shouldn't be unhappy, like the mother that bore you? Disappointed! of course we'll be disappointed. I, for one, don't expect till I die to be so good a man as I am at this minute, for just now I'm fifty thousand feet high—a tower with all the trumpets shouting."

"You see all this," said Rosamund, with a grand sincerity in her solid face, "and do you really want to marry me?"

"My darling, what else is there to do?" reasoned the Irishman. "What other occupation is there for an active man on this earth, except to marry you?"

[From *Manalive*]

Marriage and the Modern Mind

I have been requested to write something about Marriage and the Modern Mind. It would perhaps be more appropriate to write about Marriage and the Modern Absence of Mind. In much of their current conduct, those who call themselves "modern" seem to have abandoned the use of reason; they have sunk back into their own subconsciousness, perhaps under the influence of the psychology now most fashionable in the drawing-room; and it is an understatement to say that they act more automatically than the animals. Wives and husbands seem to leave home more in the manner of somnambulists.

If anybody thinks I exaggerate the mindlessness of modern comment on this matter, I am content to refer him to the inscription under a large photograph of a languishing lady, in the newspaper now before me. It states that the lady has covered herself with glory as the inventor of "Companionate Divorce." It goes on to state, in her own words, that she will marry her husband again if he asks her again; and that she has been living with him ever since she was divorced from him. If mortal muddle-headedness can go deeper than that, in this vale of tears, I should like to see it. The newspaper picture and paragraph I can actually see; and stupidity so stupendous as that has never been known in human history before. The first thing to say about marriage and the modern mind, therefore, is that it is natural enough that people with no mind should want to have no marriage.

But there is another simple yet curious illustration of modern stupidity in the matter. And that is that, while I have known thousands of people arguing about marriage, some furiously against it, sometimes rather feebly in favour of it, I have never known any one of the disputants begin by asking what marriage is. They nibble at it with negative criticism; they chip pieces off it and exhibit them as specimens, called "hard cases"; they treat every example of the rule as an exception to the rule; but they never look at the rule. They never ask, even in the name of history or human curiosity, what the thing is, or why it is, or why the overwhelming mass of mankind believes that it must be. Let us begin with the alphabet, as one does with infants.

Marriage, humanly considered, rests upon a fact of human nature, which we may call a fact of natural history. All the higher animals require much longer parental protection than do the lower; the baby elephant is a baby much longer than the baby jellyfish. But even beyond this natural tutelage, man needs something quite unique in nature. Man alone needs education. I know that animals train their young in particular tricks; as cats teach kittens to catch mice. But this is a very limited and rudimentary education. It is what the hustling millionaires call Business Education; that is, it is not education at all. Even at that, I doubt whether any pupil presenting himself for Matriculation or entrance into Standard VI, would now be accepted if flaunting the stubborn boast of a capacity to catch mice. Education is a complex and many-sided culture to meet a complex and many-sided world; and the animals, especially the lower animals, do not require it. It is said that the herring lays thousands of eggs in a day. But, though evidently untouched by the stunt of Birth-Control, in other ways the herring is highly modern. The mother herring has no need to remember her own children, and certainly therefore, no need to remember her own mate. But then the duties of a young herring, just entering upon life, are very simple and largely instinctive; they come, like a modern religion, from within. A herring does not have to be taught to take a bath, for he never takes anything else. He does not have to be trained to take off a hat to a lady herring, for he never puts on a hat, or any other Puritanical disguise to hamper the Greek grace of his movements. Consequently his father and mother have no common task or responsibility; and they can safely model their union upon the boldest and most advanced of the new novels and plays. Doubtless the female herring does say to the male herring, "True marriage must be free from the dogmas of priests; it must be a thing of one exquisite moment." Doubtless the male herring does say to the female herring, "When Love has died in the heart, Marriage is a mockery in the home."

This philosophy, common among the lower forms of life, is obviously of no use among the higher. This way of talking, however suitable for herrings, or even for rats and rabbits, who are said to be so prolific, does not meet the case of the creature endowed with reason. The young of the human species, if they are to reach the full possibilities of the human culture, so various, so laborious, so elaborate, must be under the protection of responsible persons through very long periods of mental and moral growth. I know there are some who grow merely impatient and irrational at this point; and say they could do just as well without education. But they lie; for they could not even express that opinion, if they had not laboriously learnt one particular language in which to talk nonsense. The moment we have realised this, we understand why the relations of the sexes normally remain static; and in most cases, permanent. For though, taking this argument alone, there would be a case for the father and mother parting when the children were mature, the number of people who at the age of fifty really wish to bolt with the typist or be abducted by the chauffeur is less than is now frequently supposed.

Well, even if the family held together as long as that, it would be better than nothing; but in fact even such belated divorce is based on bad psychology. All the modern licence is based on bad psychology; because it is based on the latest psychology. And that is like knowing the last proposition in Euclid without knowing the first. It is the first elements of psychology that the people called "modern" do not know. One of the things they cannot comprehend is the thing called "atmosphere"; as they show by shrieking with derision when anybody demands "a religious atmosphere" in the schools. The atmosphere of something safe and settled can only exist where people see it in the future as well as in the past. Children know exactly what is meant by having really come home; and the happier of them keep something of the feeling as they grow up. But they cannot keep the feeling for ten minutes, if there is an assumption that Papa is only waiting for Tommy's twenty-first birthday to carry the typist off to Trouville; or that the chauffeur actually has the car at the door, that Mrs. Brown may go off the moment Miss Brown has "come out."

That is, in practical experience, the basic idea of marriage; that the founding of a family must be on a firm foundation; that the rearing of the immature must be protected by something patient and enduring. It is the common conclusion of all mankind; and all common sense is on its side. A small minority of what may be called the idle Intelligentsia have, just recently and in our corner of the world, criticised this idea of Marriage in the name of what they call the Modern Mind. The first obvious or apparent question is how they deal with the practical problem of children. The first apparent answer is that they do not deal with it at all.

At best, they propose to get rid of babies, or the problem of babies, in one of three typically modern ways. One is to say that there shall be no babies. This suggestion may be addressed to the individual; but it is addressed to every individual. Another is that the father should instantly send the babies, especially if they are boys, to a distant and inaccessible school, with bounds like a prison, that the babies may become men, in a manner that is considered impossible in the society of their own father. But this is rapidly ceasing to be a Modern method; and even the Moderns have found that it is rather behind the times. The third way, which is unimpeachably Modern, is to imitate Rousseau, who left his baby on the doorstep of the Foundling Hospital. It is true that, among the Moderns, it is generally nothing so human or traditional as the Foundling Hospital. The baby is to be left on the doorstep of the State Department for Education and Universal Social Adjustment. In short, these people mean, with various degrees of vagueness, that the place of the Family can now be taken by the State.

The difficulty of the first method, and so far, of the second and third, is that they may be carried out. The suggestion is made to everybody in the hope that it will not be accepted by everybody; it is offered to all in the hope that it may not be accepted by all. If *nobody* has any children, everybody can still be satisfied by Birth-Control methods and justified by Birth-Control arguments. Even the reformers do not want this; but they cannot offer any objection to any individual—or every individual. In somewhat the same way, Rousseau may act as an individual and not as a social philosopher; but he could not prevent all the other individuals acting as individuals. And if all the babies born in the world were left on the doorstep of the Foundling Hospital, the Hospital, and the doorstep, would have to be considerably enlarged. Now something like this is what has really happened, in the vague and drifting centralization of our time. The Hospital has been enlarged into the School and then into the State; not the guardian of some abnormal children, but the guardian of all normal children. Modern mothers and fathers, of the emancipated sort, could not do their quick-change acts of bewildering divorce and scattered polygamy, if they did not believe in a big benevolent Grandmother, who could ultimately take over ten million children by very grandmotherly legislation.

The modern notion about the State is a delusion. It is not founded on the history of real States, but entirely on reading about unreal or ideal States, like the Utopias of Mr. Wells. The real State, though a necessary human combination, always has been and always will be, far too large, loose, clumsy, indirect and even insecure, to be the "home" of the human young who are to be trained in the human tradition. If mankind had not been organized into families, it would never have had the organic power to be organized into commonwealths. Human culture is handed down in the customs of countless households; it is the only way in which human culture can remain human. The households are right to confess a common loyalty or federation under some king or republic. But the king cannot be the nurse in every nursery; or even the government become the governess in every schoolroom. Look at the real story of States, modern as well as ancient, and you will see a dissolving view of distant and uncontrollable things, making up most of the politics of the earth. Take the most populous centre. China is now called a Republic. In consequence it is ruled by five contending armies and is much less settled than when it was an Empire. What has preserved China has been its domestic religion. South America, like all Latin lands, is full of domestic graces and gaieties; but it is governed by a series of revolutions. We ourselves may be governed by a Dictator; or by a General Strike; or by a banker living in New York. Government grows more elusive every day. But the traditions of humanity support humanity; and the central one is this tradition of Marriage. And the essential of it is that a free man and a free woman choose to found on earth the only voluntary state; the only state which creates and which loves its citizens. So long as these real responsible beings stand together, they can survive all the vast changes, deadlocks and disappointments which make up mere political history. But if they fail each other, it is as certain as death that "the State" will fail them.

[From *Sidelights on New London and Newer York*]

The Drift from Domesticity

IN the matter of reforming things, as distinct from deforming them, there is one plain and simple principle, a principle which will probably be called a paradox. There exists a certain institution or a law; let us call it, for the sake of simplicity, a fence or gate erected across a road. The more modern type of reformer goes gayly up to it and says: "I don't see the use of this; let us clear it away." To which the more intelligent type of reformer will do well to answer: "If you don't see the use of it, I certainly won't let you clear it away. Go away and think. Then, when you can come back and tell me that you *do* see the use of it, I may allow you to destroy it."

This paradox rests on the most elementary common-sense. The gate or fence did not grow there. It was not set up by somnambulists, who built it in their sleep. It is highly improbable that it was put there by escaped lunatics, who were for some reason loose in the street. Some person had some reason for thinking it would be a good thing for somebody. And until we know what the reason was, we really cannot judge whether the reason was reasonable. It is extremely probable that we have overlooked some whole aspect of the question, if something set up by human beings like ourselves seems to be entirely meaningless and mysterious.

There are reformers who get over this difficulty by assuming that all their fathers were fools; but if that be so, we can only say that folly appears to be a hereditary disease. But the truth is that nobody has any business to destroy a social institution until he has really seen it as an historical institution. If he knows how it arose, and what purposes it was supposed to serve, he may really be able to say that they were bad purposes, or that they have since become bad purposes, or that they are purposes which are no longer served. But if he simply stares at the thing as a senseless monstrosity that has somehow sprung up in his path, it is he and not the traditionalist who is suffering from an illusion.

Among the traditions that are being thus attacked, not intelligently but most unintelligently, is the fundamental human creation called the Household or the Home. That is a typical thing which men attack, not because they can see through it, but because they cannot see it at all. They beat at it blindly, in a fashion entirely haphazard and opportunist; and many of them would pull it down without even pausing to ask why it was ever put up. It is true that only a few of them would avow this object in so many words. That only proves how very blind and blundering they are. But they have fallen into a habit of mere drift and gradual detachment from family life, something that is often merely accidental and devoid of any definite theory at all. It seems to be largely founded on individual irritation, an irritation which varies with the individual. We are merely told that in this or that case a particular temperament was tormented by a particular environment; but nobody even explained how the evil arose, let alone whether the evil is really escaped. We are told that in this or that family Grandmamma talked a great deal of nonsense, which God knows is true; or that it was very difficult to have intimate intellectual relations with Uncle Gregory without telling him he was a fool; which is indeed the case. But nobody seriously considers the remedy, or even the malady; or whether the existing individualistic dissolution is a remedy at all.

Much of this business began with the influence of Ibsen, a very powerful dramatist and an exceedingly feeble philosopher. I suppose that Nora of "The Doll's House" was intended to be an inconsequent person; but certainly her most inconsequent action was her last. She complained that she was not yet fit to look after children and then proceeded to get as far as possible from the children that she might study them more closely.

There is one simple test and type of this neglect of scientific thinking and the sense of a social rule; the neglect which has now left us with nothing but a welter of exceptions. I have read hundreds and thousands of times, in all the novels and newspapers of our epoch, certain phrases about the just right of the young to liberty, about the unjust claim of the elders to control, about the conception that all souls must be free or all citizens equal, about the absurdity of authority or the degradation of obedience. I am not arguing those matters directly at the moment. But what strikes me as astounding, in a logical sense, is that not one of these myriad novelists and newspaper-men ever seem to think of asking the next and most obvious question.

It never seems to occur to them to inquire what becomes of the opposite obligation. If the child is free from the first to disregard the parent, why is not the parent free from the first to disregard the child? If Mr. Jones Senior and Mr. Jones Junior are only two free and equal citizens, why should one citizen sponge on another citizen for the first fifteen years of his life? Why should the elder Mr. Jones be expected to feed, clothe and shelter out of his own pocket another person who is entirely free of any obligations to him? If the bright young thing cannot be asked to tolerate her grandmother, who has become something of a bore, why should the grandmother or the mother have tolerated the bright young thing at a period of her life when she was by no means bright? Why did they laboriously look after her at a time when her contributions to the conversation were seldom epigrammatic and not often intelligible? Why should Jones Senior stand drinks and free meals to anybody so unpleasant as Jones Junior in the immature phases of his existence? Why should he not throw the baby out of the window; or at any rate kick the boy out of doors? It is obvious that we are dealing with a real relation, which may be equality, but is certainly not similarity.

Some social reformers try to evade this difficulty, I know, by some vague notions about the State or an abstraction called Education eliminating the parental function. But this, like many notions of solid scientific persons, is a wild illusion of the nature of mere moonshine. It is based on that strange new superstition, the idea of infinite resources of organization. It is as if officials grew like grass or bred like rabbits. There is supposed to be an endless supply of salaried persons, and of salaries for them; and they are to undertake all that human beings naturally do for themselves, including the care of children. But men cannot live by taking in each other's baby-linen. They cannot provide a tutor for each citizen; who is to tutor the tutors? Men cannot be educated by machinery; and though there might be a Robot bricklayer or scavenger there will never be a Robot schoolmaster or governess. The actual effect of this theory is that one harassed person has to look after a hundred children, instead of one normal person looking after a normal number of them. Normally that normal person is urged by a natural force, which costs nothing and does not require a salary: the force of natural affection for his young, which exists even among the animals. If you cut off that natural force, and substitute a paid bureaucracy, you are like a fool who should pay men to turn the wheel of his mill, because he refused to use wind or water which he could get for nothing. You are like a lunatic who should carefully water his garden with a watering-can, while holding up an umbrella to keep off the rain.

It is now necessary to recite these truisms; for only by doing so can we begin to get a glimpse of that *reason* for the existence of the family which I began this essay by demanding. They were all familiar to our fathers, who believed in the links of kinship and also in the links of logic.

Today our logic consists mostly of missing links, and our family largely of absent members. But anyhow, this is the right end at which to begin any such inquiry; and *not* at the tail end or the fag end of some private muddle by which Dick has become discontented or Susan has gone off on her own. If Dick or Susan wish to destroy the family because they do not see the use of it, I say as I said in the beginning: if they do not see the use of it, they had much better preserve it. They have no business even to think of destroying it until they have seen the use of it.

But it has other uses, besides the obvious fact that it means a necessary social work being done for love when it cannot be done for money; and (one might almost dare to hint) presumably to be repaid with love, since it is never repaid in money. On that simple side of the matter the general situation is easy to record. The existing and general system of society, subject in our own age and industrial culture to very gross abuses and painful problems, is nevertheless a normal one. It is the idea that a commonwealth is made up of a number of small kingdoms, of which a man and a woman become the king and queen and in which they exercise a reasonable authority, subject to the common sense of the commonwealth, until those under their care grow up to found similar kingdoms and exercise similar authority. This is the social structure of mankind, far older than all its records and more universal than any of its religions; and all attempts to alter it are mere talk and tomfoolery.

But the other advantage of the small group is now not so much neglected as simply not realized. Here again we have some extraordinary delusions spread all over the literature and journalism of our time. Those delusions now exist in such a degree that we may say, for all practical purposes, that when a thing has been stated about a thousand times as obviously true, it is almost certain to be obviously false. One such statement may be specially noted here. There is undoubtedly something to be said against domesticity and in favor of the general drift towards life in hotels, clubs, colleges, communal settlements and the rest; or for a social life organized on the plan of the great commercial systems of our time. But the truly extraordinary suggestion is often made that this escape from the home is an escape into greater freedom. The change is actually offered as favorable to liberty.

To anybody who can think, of course, it is exactly the opposite. The domestic division of human society is not perfect, being human. It does not achieve complete liberty, a thing somewhat difficult to do or even to define. But it is a mere matter of arithmetic that it puts a larger number of people in supreme control of something, and able to shape it to their personal liking, than do the vast organizations that rule society outside, whether those systems are legal or commercial or even merely social. Even if we were only considering the parents, it is plain that there are more parents than there are policemen or politicians or heads of big businesses or proprietors of hotels. As I shall suggest in a moment, the

THE DRIFT FROM DOMESTICITY

argument actually applies indirectly to the children as well as directly to the parents.

But the main point is that the world *outside* the home is now under a rigid discipline and routine, and it is only inside the home that there is really a place for individuality and liberty. Anyone stepping out of the front-door is obliged to step into a procession, all going the same way and to a great extent even obliged to wear the same uniform. Business, especially big business, is now organized like an army. It is, as some would say, a sort of mild militarism without bloodshed; as I should say, a militarism without the military virtues. But anyhow, it is obvious that a hundred clerks in a bank or a hundred waitresses in a tea-shop are more regimented and under rule than the same individuals when each has gone back to his or her own dwelling or lodging, hung with his or her favorite pictures or fragrant with his or her favorite cheap cigarettes. But this, which is so obvious in the commercial case, is no less true even in the social case.

In practice the pursuit of pleasure is merely the pursuit of fashion. The pursuit of fashion is merely the pursuit of convention; only that it happens to be a new convention. The jazz dances, the joy-rides, the big pleasure parties and hotel entertainments do not make any more provision for a *really* independent taste than did any of the fashions of the past. If a wealthy young lady wants to do what all the other wealthy young ladies are doing, she will find it great fun, simply because youth is fun and society is fun. She will enjoy being modern exactly as her Victorian grandmother enjoyed being Victorian. And quite right, too; but it is the enjoyment of convention, not the enjoyment of liberty. It is perfectly healthy for all young people of all historic periods to herd together, to a reasonable extent, and enthusiastically copy each other. But in that there is nothing particularly fresh and certainly nothing particularly free. The girl who likes shaving her head and powdering her nose and wearing short skirts will find the world organized for her and will march happily with the procession. But a girl who happened to like having her hair down to her heels or loading herself with barbaric gauds and trailing garments or (most awful of all) leaving her nose in its natural state—she will still be well advised to do these things on her own premises. If the Duchess wants to play leapfrog, she must not start suddenly leaping in the manner of a frog across the ballroom of the Babylon Hotel, when it is crowded with the fifty best couples professionally practicing the very latest dance for the instruction of society. The Duchess will find it easier to practice leapfrog to the admiration of her intimate friends in the old oak-paneled hall of Fitzdragon Castle. If the Dean must stand on his head, he will do it with more ease and grace in the calm atmosphere of the Deanery than by attempting to interrupt the program of some social entertainment already organized for philanthropic purposes.

If there is this impersonal routine in commercial and even in social things, it goes without saying that it exists and always must exist in political and legal things. For instance, the punishments of the state must be sweeping generalizations. It is only the punishments of the home that can possibly be adapted to the individual case; because it is only there that the judge can know anything of the individual. If Tommy takes a silver thimble out of a work-basket, his mother may act very differently according as she knows that he did it for fun or for spite or to sell to somebody else or to get somebody into trouble. But if Tomkins takes a silver thimble out of a shop, the law not only can but must punish him according to the rule made for all shoplifters or stealers of silver. It is only the domestic discipline that can show any sympathy or especially any humor. I do not say that the family always does do this; but I say that the state never ought to attempt it. So even if we consider the parents alone as independent princes, and the children merely as subjects, the relative freedom of the family can and often does work to the advantage of those subjects. But so long as the children are children they will always be the subjects of somebody. The question is whether they are to be distributed naturally under their natural princes, as the old phrase went, who normally feel for them what nobody else will feel, a natural affection. It seems to me clear that this normal distribution gives the largest amount of liberty to the largest number of people.

My complaint of the anti-domestic drift is that it is unintelligent. People do not know what they are doing, because they do not know what they are undoing. There are a multitude of modern manifestations, from the largest to the smallest, ranging from a divorce to a picnic party. But each is a separate escape or evasion; and especially an evasion of the point at issue. People ought to decide in a philosophical fashion whether they desire the traditional social order or not; or if there is any particular alternative to be desired. As it is, they treat the public question merely as a mess or medley of private questions. Even in being anti-domestic, they are too much domestic in their test of domesticity. Each family considers only its own case and the result is merely narrow and negative. Each case is an exception to a rule that does not exist. The family, especially in the modern state, stands in need of considerable correction and reconstruction; most things do in the modern state. But the family mansion should be preserved or destroyed or rebuilt; it should not be allowed to fall to pieces brick by brick, because nobody has any historic sense of the object of bricklaying. For instance, the architects of the restoration should rebuild the house with wide and easily opened doors, for the practice of the ancient virtue of hospitality. In other words, private property should be distributed with sufficient decent equality as to allow of a margin for festive intercourse. But the hospitality of the home will always be different from the hospitality of a hotel. And it will be different in being more individual, more independent, more interesting than the hospitality of a hotel. It is perfectly right that the young Browns and the young Robinsons should meet and mix and dance and make asses of themselves, according to the design of their Creator. But there will always be some difference between the Browns entertaining the Robinsons, and the Robinsons entertaining the Browns. And it will be a difference to the advantage of variety, of the potentialities of the mind of man; or, in other words, of life, liberty and the pursuit of happiness.

[From *The Thing: Why I Am a Catholic*]

Woman

A correspondent has written me an able and interesting letter in the matter of some allusions of mine to the subject of communal kitchens. He defends communal kitchens very lucidly from the standpoint of the calculating collectivist; but, like many of his school, he cannot apparently grasp that there is another test of the whole matter, with which such calculation has nothing at all to do. He knows it would be cheaper if a number of us ate at the same time, so as to use the same table. So it would. It would also be cheaper if a number of us slept at different times, so as to use the same pair of trousers. But the question is not how cheap are we buying a thing, but what are we buying? It is cheap to own a slave. And it is cheaper still to be a slave.

My correspondent also says that the habit of dining out in restaurants, etc., is growing. So, I believe, is the habit of committing suicide. I do not desire to connect the two facts together. It seems fairly clear that a man could not dine at a restaurant because he had just committed suicide; and it would be extreme, perhaps, to suggest that he commits suicide because he has just dined at a restaurant. But the two cases, when put side by side, are enough to indicate the falsity and poltroonery of this eternal modern argument from what is in fashion. The question for brave men is not whether a certain thing is increasing; the question is whether we are increasing it. I dine very often in restaurants because the nature of my trade makes it more convenient: but if I thought that by dining in restaurants I was working for the creation of communal meals, I would never enter a restaurant again; I would carry bread and cheese in my pocket or eat chocolate out of automatic machines. For the personal element in some things is sacred. I heard Mr. Will Crooks put it perfectly the other day: "The most sacred thing is to be able to shut your own door."

My correspondent says, "Would not our women be spared the drudgery of cooking and all its attendant worries, leaving them free for higher culture?" The first thing that occurs to me to say about this is very simple, and is, I imagine, a part of all our experience. If my correspondent can find any way of preventing women from worrying, he will indeed be a remarkable man. I think the matter is a much deeper one. First of all, my correspondent overlooks a distinction which is elementary in our human nature. Theoretically, I suppose, every one would like to be freed from worries. But nobody in the world would always like to be freed from worrying occupations. I should very much like (as far as my feelings at the moment go) to be free from the consuming nuisance of writing this article. But it does not follow that I should like to be free from the consuming nuisance of being a journalist. Because we are worried about a thing, it does not follow that we are not interested in it. The truth is the other way. If we are not interested, why on earth should we be worried? Women are worried about housekeeping, but those that are most interested are the most worried. Women are still more worried about their husbands and their children. And I suppose if we strangled the children and poleaxed the husbands it would leave women free for higher culture. That is, it would leave them free to begin to worry about that. For women would worry about higher culture as much as they worry about everything else.

I believe this way of talking about women and their higher culture is almost entirely a growth of the classes which (unlike the journalistic class to which I belong) have always a reasonable amount of money. One odd thing I specially notice. Those who write like this seem entirely to forget the existence of the working and wage-earning classes. They say eternally, like my correspondent, that the ordinary woman is always a drudge. And what, in the name of the Nine Gods, is the ordinary man? These people seem to think that the ordinary man is a Cabinet Minister. They are always talking about man going forth to wield power, to carve his own way, to stamp his individuality on the world, to command and to be obeyed. This may be true of a certain class. Dukes, perhaps, are not drudges; but, then, neither are Duchesses. The Ladies and Gentlemen of the Smart Set are quite free for the higher culture, which consists chiefly of motoring and Bridge. But the ordinary man who typifies and constitutes the millions that make up our civilisation is no more free for the higher culture than his wife is.

Indeed, he is not so free. Of the two sexes the woman is in the more powerful position. For the average woman is at the head of something with which she can do as she likes; the average man has to obey orders and do nothing else. He has to put one dull brick on another dull brick, and do nothing else; he has to add one dull figure to another dull figure, and do nothing else. The woman's world is a small one, perhaps, but she can alter it. The woman can tell the tradesman with whom she deals some realistic things about himself. The clerk who does this to the manager generally gets the sack, or shall we say (to avoid the vulgarism), finds himself free for higher culture. Above all . . . , the woman does work which is in some small degree creative and individual. She can put the flowers or the furniture in fancy arrangements of her own. I fear the bricklayer cannot put the bricks in fancy arrangements of his own, without disaster to himself and others. If the woman is only putting a patch into a carpet, she can choose the thing with regard to colour. I fear it would not do for the office boy dispatching a parcel to choose his stamps with a view to colour; to prefer the tender mauve of the six-penny to the crude scarlet of the penny stamp. A woman cooking may not always cook artistically; still she can cook artistically. She can introduce a personal and imperceptible alteration into the composition of a soup. The clerk is not encouraged to introduce a personal and impercep-tible alteration into the figures in a ledger.

The trouble is that the real question I raised is not discussed. It is argued as a problem in pennies, not as a problem in people. It is not the proposals of these reformers that I feel to be false so much as their temper and their arguments. I am not nearly so certain that communal kitchens are wrong as I am that the defenders of communal kitchens are wrong. Of course, for one thing, there is a vast difference between the communal kitchens of which I spoke and the communal meal (*mon-strum horrendum, informe*) which the darker and wilder mind of my correspondent diabolically calls up. But in both the trouble is that their defenders will not defend them humanly as human institutions. They will not interest themselves in the staring psychological fact that there are some things that a man or a woman, as the case may be, wishes to do for himself or herself. He or she must do it inventively, creatively, artistically, individually—in a word, badly. Choosing your wife (say) is one of these things. Is choosing your husband's dinner one of these things? That is the whole question: it is never asked.

And then the higher culture. I know that culture. I would not set any man free for it if I could help it. The effect of it on the rich men who are free for it is so horrible that it is worse than any of the other amusements of the millionaire—worse than gambling, worse even than philan-thropy. It means thinking the smallest poet in Belgium greater than the greatest poet of England. It means losing every democratic sympathy. It means being unable to talk to a navvy about sport, or about beer, or about the Bible, or about the Derby, or about patriotism, or about anything whatever that he, the navvy, wants to talk about. It means taking literature seriously, a very amateurish thing to do. It means pardoning indecency only when it is gloomy indecency. Its disciples will call a spade a spade: but only when it is a grave-digger's spade. The higher culture is sad, cheap, impudent, unkind, without honesty and without ease. In short, it is "high." That abominable word (also applied to game) admirably describes it.

No; if you were setting women free for something else, I might be more melted. If you can assure me, privately and gravely, that you are setting women free to dance on the mountains like Maenads, or to worship some monstrous goddess, I will make a note of your request. If you are quite sure that the ladies in Brixton, the moment they gave up cooking, will beat great gongs and blow horns to Mumbo-Jumbo, then I will agree that the occupation is at least human and is more or less entertaining. Women have been set free to be Bacchantes; they have been set free to be Virgin Martyrs; they have been set free to be Witches. Do not ask them now to sink so low as the higher culture.

I have my own little notions of the possible emancipation of women; but I suppose I should not be taken very seriously if I propounded them. I should favour anything that would increase the present enormous authority of women and their creative action in their own homes. The average woman, as I have said, is a despot; the average man is a serf. I am for any scheme that any one can suggest that will make the average woman more of a despot. So far from wishing her to get her cooked meals from outside, I should like her to cook more widely and at her own will than she does. So far from getting always the same meals from the same place, let her invent, if she likes, a new dish every day of her life. Let a woman be more of a maker, not less. We are right to talk about "Woman"; only blackguards talk about women. Yet all men talk about men, and that is the whole difference. Men represent the deliberate and democratic element in life. Woman represents the despotic.

[From *All Things Considered*]

The Modern Surrender of Women

Note: In this essay, written over seventy years ago, Chesterton gives his reasons for opposing women's suffrage, an issue being hotly debated at the time.

THERE is a thing which is often called progress, but which only occurs in dull and stale conditions: it is indeed, not progress, but a sort of galloping plagiarism. To carry the same fashion further and further is not a mark of energy, but a mark of fatigue. One can fancy that in the fantastic decline of some Chinese civilization one might find things automatically increasing, simply because everybody had forgotten what the things were meant for. Hats might be bigger than umbrellas, because every one had forgotten to wear them. Walking sticks might be taller than lances, because nobody ever thought of taking them out on a walk. The human mind never goes so fast as that except when it has got into a groove.

The converse is also true. All really honest and courageous thought has a tendency to look like truism. For strong thought about a thing is always thought about its most recent developments. The really bold thinker is never afraid of platitude; because platitudes are the great primeval foundations. The bold thinker is not afraid to say of the hat that it is a covering for the head; when he has said that he knows that he has his hat and his head in the right place. The strong thinker does not shrink from saying that the walking stick is a stick with which one goes walking; then he knows that he has got hold of the right end of the stick. All civilizations show some tendency towards that weak-minded sort of progress which is mere accumulation. Some time ago a well-dressed English gentleman wore two or three waistcoats. It would be easy to be purely progressive about him, to make him wear more and more waistcoats of different colors until he died. Some time ago a Japanese nobleman wore two swords; it would be easy to be progressive and suggest nine swords or twenty-three swords. But the strong thinker does not go forward with the flood, but back to the fountain. If once we think about what a sword is and what it symbolizes, we shall see that a man ought to have one sword because he has one right hand. And if we meditate deeply upon what a waistcoat is, it will become apparent to us, after a brief effort of philology, that a man ought not to have more than one waistcoat unless he has more than one waist. All tame and trivial thought is concerned with following a fashion onward to its logical extremity. All clear and courageous thought is concerned with following it back to its logical root. A man may make hats larger and larger and be only as mad as a hatter. But if he can quite perfectly explain what a hat is he must have the great sanity of Aristotle.

Now, in that quarrel about the function of the two sexes which has lately disturbed a section of our wealthier classes, nothing seems to me more marked than this habit of pursuing a thing to its conclusion when we have not tracked it to its origin. Many of the women who wish for votes urge their case entirely as a development from what exists. They argue from precedent, that most poisonous and senseless of all the products of our Protestant Constitution. Precedent is the opposite of doctrine. These ladies, who believe themselves revolutionary, are really moving along that line of least resistance which is the essence of the evil sort of conservatism. They say, "Men have votes; why shouldn't women have votes?" I have met many able and admirable ladies who were full of reasons why women should have votes. But when I asked them why men should have votes they did not know.

I shall pursue here the opposite course. I shall try to start with a truth, even if it is a truism. I shall try to state the substance of suffrage, instead of pulling it out into long strings like liquorice or treacle till it reaches the end of the world. If the question stands whether a woman should have a vote, I beg leave to begin by asking what a vote is, and even (so far as the subject can be safely approached) what a woman is. But the nature of a vote is the vital and really interesting thing.

I trust that the reader will remember that I am, for the moment, the professor of platitudes. As the man seeking to preserve sanity among hatters would begin by reminding them that hats have to cover heads, so I begin all statements about the vote at the humblest and most evident end. Two things are quite clear about the vote. First that it is entirely concerned with government, that is with coercion. Second, it is entirely concerned with democratic government; that is, with government by chorus, government by public quarrel and public unanimity. First, to desire a vote means to desire the power of coercing others; the power of using a policeman. Second, it means that this power should be given not to princes or officials, but to a human mass, a throng of citizens. If any person does not mean by voting coercion by the will of the masses, then that person does not know what the word means. He (or rather she) is simply stunned with one monosyllable that she does not understand. If a woman wants democracy or mob law, or even riot, I think she should be listened to most seriously and respectfully. But if she only wants the vote, it is a proof that she ought not to have it. She should be refused just as a would-be nun should be refused who has no vocation except a wish to wear the costume.

Now this is exactly where my personal lament begins. I weep for the collapse and complete surrender of women. People tell me that this modern movement is a revolt against man by woman. It seems to me to be the utter submission of woman to man upon every point upon which they ever disagreed. That woman should ask for a vote is not feminism; it is masculism in its last and most insolent triumph. The whole point of view which is peculiar to man is here riding so ruthlessly and contemptuously over the whole point of view that is peculiar to woman that I cannot but regret it, though it is the triumph of my own sex. After all, I am a human being as well as a male, and my pleasure in knowing that masculine prejudices are at last prevailing is poisoned with the thought that after all women do exist, and that their present humiliation cannot be good for the common stock.

The facts themselves, of course, are clear enough. Voting, as has been said, involves two primary principles; it involves the coercive idea, and it involves the collective idea. To push and kick men into their senses, and to push with a throng of arms, to kick with a crowd of legs, that is the quite just and rational meaning of voting; it has no other just or rational meaning. And certainly the privilege should be extended to everybody, certainly the arms and legs might be of any sex, if only this were quite certainly clear and proved—that the coercive and the collective ideas are the whole of human life. But the truth is that the coercive and collective ideas are not only a mere half of human life, but have been from the beginning a mere half of the human species. From the dawn of the world there has been another point of view, the feminine point of view, which was against mere force, but even more against mere argument. This strong feminine position has kept the race healthy for hundreds of centuries. It has never really been weakened until now.

Every good man is half an anarchist. That is, that with half his mind he feels it is a cruel and clumsy business to be always catching his fellows in the man-traps of merely human by-laws, and torturing them with ropes and rods and long terms of living burial. Coercion is necessary, no doubt; but it should be conducted in the presence of some permanent protest on behalf of a humane anarchy. That protest has always been provided by the other half of life called Society; by the enormous success with which women have managed their social empire. They have done it not without cruelty, but quite without coercion. They have made the cold shoulder as unmistakable as the branded shoulder; they have found it quite easy to lock the offenders out, without finding it necessary to lock them in. Not only is one half of the good man an anarchist, but the anarchist is his better half; the anarchist is his wife. It is the woman who stands forever for the futility of mere rules. Women could justly contrast Society's swiftness with the law's delay. It takes such a long time to condemn a man—and such a short time to snub him. Tact is only a name for anarchy when it works well. But this free and persuasive method, for which women have stood from the beginning, has much stronger examples than any mere diplomacies of social life.

The two or three most important things in the world have always been managed without law or government; because they have been managed by women. Can anyone tell me two things more vital to the race than these; what man shall marry what woman, and what shall be the first things taught to their first child? Yet no one has ever been so mad as to suggest that either of these godlike and gigantic tasks should be conducted by law. They are matters of emotional management; of persuasion and disuasion; of discouraging a guest or encouraging a governess. This is the first great argument for the old female point of view, and we could never deny that it had force. The old-fashioned woman really said this: "What can be the use of all your politics and policemen? The moment you come to a really vital question you dare not use them. For a foolish marriage, or a bad education, for a broken heart or a spoilt child, for the things that really matter, your courts of justice can do nothing at all. When one live woman is being neglected by a man, or one live child by a mother, we can do more by our meanest feminine dodges than you can do by the whole apparatus of the British Constitution. A snub from a duchess or a slanging from a fishwife is more likely to put things right than all the votes in the world." That has always been the woman's great case against mere legalist machinery. It is only one half of the truth; but I am sorry to see the women abandon it.

But voting not only stands for the coercive idea of government, but also for the collective idea of democracy. And a surrender to collective democracy is even more of a feminine collapse than a surrender to regimentation and legalism. Woman would be more herself if she refused to touch coercion altogether. That she may be the priestess of society it is necessary that her hands should be as bloodless as a priest's. I think Queen Victoria would have been more powerful still if she had never had to sign a death warrant. But although I disagree with votes for women, I do not necessarily disagree with thrones for women or imperial crowns for women. There is a much stronger case for making Miss Pankhurst a despot than for making her a voter. Among other reasons, there is the fact that she is a despot. Moderns complain of a personal voice in the Papacy; but it is odd to notice that every one of the highly modern and slightly hysterical moral and religious movements of today is run with the most irresponsible despotism: General Booth's despotism in the Salvation Army; Mrs. Eddy's despotism in Christian Science; and the Pankhurst despotism amongst the Suffragettes. But I do not so much complain of this. It was always plain to me that there are two principles in life, the harmony of which is happiness: the horizontal principle called equality and the vertical principle called authority. For we require authority even to impose equality. The first is life considered as a perpetual playground, where the children are under one law and should share and share alike. The second is life considered as the perpetual repetition of the relation of mother and child. I would be much more willing to give women authority than to give them equality. I can imagine that a queen might really be the mother of her people without ceasing to be the mother of her babies. She must be a despotic queen, of course; there must be no nonsense about constitutions. For despotism is, in its nature, a domestic thing; an autocracy is run like a household; that is, it is run without rules.

But voting is government conducted entirely by this other element in man; the sense of fraternity and similarity. Voting is gregarious government. The only reality behind voting is that instinct of men to get together and argue; unless they can fulfill this they are unhappy. In our somewhat morbid age, when representative government has become only an unwieldy oligarchy, and when decent pleasures have stagnated into poison, there is said to be some kind of quarrel between the Parish Council and the Public House. But in a plain and happy society the Public House is the Parish Council. The townsmen argue in the tavern about the politics of the town, invoking abstract principles which cannot be proved, and rules of debate which do not in the least matter; their wives teach the children to say their prayers and wish politics at the bottom of the sea. That is the happiest condition of humanity. But in any case this is the basis of voting: the elders of the tribe talking under the tree: the men of the village shouting at each other at the "Blue Pig"; the great and mysterious mob, singing, fighting and judging in the market place. This is democracy; all voting is only the shadow of this; and if you do not like this you will not like its shadow.

Nothing is more unfair in the current attacks on Christianity than the way in which men specially accuse the Church of things that are far more manifest in the world. Thus people will talk of torture as a disgrace to the Church, whereas it is simply one of the few real disgraces of European civilization, from the Roman Empire to Francis Bacon or Governor Eyre. But of all the instances there is none more unjust than the ordinary charge against religion of being a mere ritual or routine. So, indeed, it sometimes is; but never so much as all other human institutions, especially modern institutions. Talk of clerical government becoming stiff and unmeaning! What, in heaven's name, has become of representative government by this time? Talk of a praying machine; what could one say of the voting machine? I doubt if the dullest peasant or the most reckless brigand ever made the sign of the cross on his body with such a deathlike indifference as many a modern citizen makes the sign of the cross on his ballot papers.

So long as the vote is thus a meaningless and useless thing it is natural that women should want it. I do not say this as a traditional sneer at their unreason; on the contrary, I think their feeling is quite reasonable. If the vote means nothing it must be a mere badge; and if it is a badge it is a badge of superiority. It is exactly because most female suffragettes think that it is a mere formality that they object to the public insult of being kept out of that formality. It is only when we ask ourselves what the vote ultimately means when it means anything, what democracy is when it is direct, that we discover why the folk of all ages, male and female alike, have felt that this function is rather male than female.

Women might like an unreal democracy; and they may possibly be called upon to comply with the forms of one. But they dislike a real democracy; and it is well that they do. For real democracy has its peculiar perils and exaggerations, against which woman has wisely pitted herself from the first. She hates that vagueness in democracy which tends to forget the fact of the family in the theory of the State. She dislikes the democratic tendency to discuss abstractions; or, as she sees it, the tendency to arouse discussions that have no end. To her the Good Citizen of the Revolution is best defined as the man who begins to ask unanswerable questions when it is time to go to bed. Now there is a truth and a corrective value in this attitude; the Good Citizen may really become an uncommonly bad husband. Most men with anything manly about them can remember arguments started some weeks ago which might be going on now but for the interruption of the ladies. It is sufficient here to maintain that woman, as compared at least with man, dislikes this atmosphere of government by deafening and protracted debate; dislikes it and also distrusts it, not by any means without reason. If anyone thinks this too sweeping, it is easy to make an imaginative test. Think of any street in London at a late hour of the evening, and ask yourself in how many of the houses it is likely that the men are yawning and wondering when on earth the women will have done talking.

Thus we see that on both points—the coercive or legal conception, and the collective or democratic conception—a great part of the power and importance of woman from the first has been concerned with balancing, criticising and opposing them. It is the female, as symbol of the family in which there are no laws and no votes, who has been the permanent drag, both on the fantasies of democracy and the pedantries of law. But what shall we do if women cease to make game of us?

The immediate effect of the female suffrage movement will be to make politics much too important; to exaggerate them out of all proportion to the rest of life. For the female suffrage movement is simply the breakdown of the pride of woman; her surrender of that throne of satire, realism and detachment from which she has so long laughed at the solemnities and moderated the manias of the mere politician. Woman tempered the gravity of politics as she tempers the gravity of golf. She reminds us that it is only about things that are slightly unreal that a man can be as solemn as that. The line of life was kept straight and level because the man and the woman were pulling at opposite ends of it in an amicable tug-of-war. But now the woman has suddenly let go. The man is victorious—but on his back. We males permitted ourselves exaggerated fusses and formalities about the art of government, well knowing that there was one at home who could be trusted to dilute such things with plenty of cold water, or occasionally even hot water. We allowed ourselves outrageous pomposities of speech; we talked about the country being ruined if the other party won the election; we talked about the intolerable shame and anger which we felt after Robinson's speech; we talked about Jones or Smith being necessary to England. These things were not exactly lies. They were the emphatic terms of a special art which we knew was not the whole of life. We knew quite well, of course, that the country would not be ruined by politicians half so utterly and sweepingly as it could be ruined by nurse-maids. We knew that our pain at any political speech was not actually as intense as that which a bad dinner or a certain lecture can produce. We knew that Smith is not necessary to England; that nothing is necessary to England except that its males and females should continue to behave as such. But now, to our horror, we find that our fantastic technical language is actually taken seriously. Instead of the old strong, scornful woman, who classed sociology with skittles, and regarded politics as a pretext for the public house, we have now a new converted and submissive sort of woman. Miss Pankhurst owns, with tears in her eyes, that men have been right all along, and that it was only the intellectual weakness of woman that prevented her from seeing the value of a vote until now. This state of things throws out all the balance of my existence. I feel lost without the strong and sensible Mrs. Caudle. I do not know what to do with the prostrate and penitent Miss Pankhurst. I feel that I have deceived her, but not intentionally. The Suffragettes are victims of male exaggeration, but not of male cunning. We did tell women that the vote was of frightful importance; but we never supposed that any woman would believe it. We men exaggerated our side of life as the women exaggerated the dreadfulness of smoking in the drawing room. The war was healthy. It is a lovers' quarrel which should continue through the ages. But an awful and unforeseen thing has happened to us who are masculine: we have won.

[From *The Living Age*, 21 August 1909]

HUMOROUS POEMS

The Song of Right and Wrong

Feast on wine or fast on water
And your honour shall stand sure,
God Almighty's son and daughter
He the valiant, she the pure;
If an angel out of heaven
Brings you other things to drink,
Thank him for his kind attentions,
Go and pour them down the sink.

Tea is like the East he grows in,
A great yellow Mandarin
With urbanity of manner
And unconsciousness of sin;
All the women, like a harem,
At his pig-tail troop along;
And, like all the East he grows in,
He is Poison when he's strong.

Tea, although an Oriental,
Is a gentleman at least;
Cocoa is a cad and coward,
Cocoa is a vulgar beast,
Cocoa is a dull, disloyal,
Lying, crawling cad and clown,
And may very well be grateful
To the fool that takes him down.

As for all the windy waters,
They were rained like tempests down
When good drink had been dishonoured
By the tipplers of the town;

When red wine had brought red ruin
And the death-dance of our times,
Heaven sent us Soda Water
As a torment for our crimes.

[From *Wine, Water and Song*]

Note: In the *New Witness,* Cecil Chesterton rather intemperately accused certain ministers of the Crown of swindling and collusion with regard to private transactions in
shares of a government contract. This was the famous "Marconi affair." Cecil was
prosecuted for libel by one of these ministers. At the trial in the Old Bailey, Cecil was
found guilty and fined one hundred pounds. (He himself had thought that he would
be sentenced to three years in prison.) The *Daily News,* which had supported the
ministers against Cecil, was owned by George Cadbury, a candy manufacturer, and
was known as the Cocoa Press. Thus GKC's denunciation of cocoa in the above poem
and his emphasis on the word "cad" were really an attack on Cadbury and his paper.

Wine and Water

Old Noah he had an ostrich farm and
fowls on the largest scale,
He ate his egg with a ladle in an egg-cup
big as a pail,
And the soup he took was Elephant Soup
and the fish he took was Whale,
But they all were small to the cellar he
took when he set out to sail,
And Noah he often said to his wife when
he sat down to dine,
"I don't care where the water goes if it
doesn't get into the wine."

The cataract of the cliff of heaven fell
blinding off the brink
As if it would wash the stars away as suds
go down a sink,
The seven heavens came roaring down for
the throats of hell to drink,

And Noah he cocked his eye and said,
  "It looks like rain, I think,
The water has drowned the Matterhorn
  as deep as a Mendip mine,
But I don't care where the water goes if
  it doesn't get into the wine."

But Noah he sinned, and we have sinned;
  on tipsy feet we trod,
Till a great big black teetotaller was sent
  to us for a rod,
And you can't get wine at a P.S.A., or
  chapel, or Eisteddfod,
For the Curse of Water has come again
  because of the wrath of God,
And water is on the Bishop's board and
  the Higher Thinker's shrine,
But I don't care where the water goes if
  it doesn't get into the wine.

[From *Wine, Water and Song*]

True Sympathy
or
Prevention of Cruelty to Teachers

I was kind to all my masters
  And I never worked them hard
To goad them to exactitude
  Or speaking by the card.

If one of them should have the air
  Of talking through his hat
And call a curve isosceles
  I let it go at that.

The point was without magnitude;
I knew without regret
Our minds were moving parallel
Because they never met.

Because I could not bear to make
An algebraist cry
I gazed with interest at X
And never thought of Why.

That he should think I thought he thought
That X was ABC
Was far, far happier for him
And possibly for me.

While other teachers raved and died
In reason's wild career,
Men who had driven themselves mad
By making themselves clear,

My teachers laugh and sing and dance,
Aged, but still alive;
Because I often let them say
That two and two are five.

Angles obtuse appeared acute,
Angles acute were quite
Obtuse; but I was more obtuse:
Their angles were all right.

I wore my soul's awakening smile
I felt it was my duty:
Lo! Logic works by Barbara*
And life is ruled by beauty.

And Mathematics merged and met
Its higher unity,
Where Five and Two and Twelve and Four
They were all One to me.

[From *Catholic Herald*, 15 December 1939]

*"Barbara" is the expression for a type of syllogism in formal logic.

On Reading "God"

(Mr. Middleton Murry explains that his book with this title records his farewell to God.)

Murry, on finding *le Bon Dieu*
Chose difficile à croire,
Illogically said "Adieu"
But God said "Au revoir."

[From *G. K.'s: A Miscellany of the First 500 Issues of G. K.'s Weekly*]

Irresponsible Outbreak of One Who, Having Completed a Book of Enormous Length on the Poet Chaucer, Feels Himself Freed from All Bonds of Intellectual Self-Respect and Proposes to Do No Work for an Indefinite Period

"Wot ye not wher ther stout a litel town,
Which that icleped is Bob-up-an-down."

The Canterbury Tales

They babble on of Babylon
They tire me out with Tyre
And Sidon putting side on
I do not much admire.
But the little town Bob-Up-and-Down
That lies beyond the Blee
Along the road our fathers rode,
O that's the town for me.

150

In dome and spire and cupola
It bubbles up and swells
For the company that canter
To the Canterbury Bells.
But when the Land Surveyors come
With maps and books to write,
The little town Bob-Up-and-Down
It bobs down out of sight.

I cannot live in Liverpool,
O lead me not to Leeds,
I'm not a man in Manchester,
Though men be cheap as weeds:
But the little town Bob-Up-and-Down
That bobs towards the sea
And knew its name when Chaucer came,
O that's the town for me.

I'll go and eat my Christmas meat
In that resurgent town
And pledge to fame our Father's name
Till the sky bobs up and down;
And join in sport of every sort
That's played beside the Blee,
Bob-Apple in Bob-Up-and-Down,
O that's the game for me.

Now Huddersfield is Shuddersfield
And Hull is nearly Hell,
Where a Daisy would go crazy
Or a Canterbury Bell,
The little town of Bob-Up-and-Down
Alone is fair and free;
For it can't be found above the ground,
O that's the place for me.

[From *G. K.'s: A Miscellany of the First 500 Issues of G. K.'s Weekly*]

Commercial Candour

(On the outside of a sensational novel is printed the statement: "The back of the cover will tell you the plot")

Our fathers to creed and tradition were tied,
They opened a book to see what was inside,
And of various methods they deemed not the worst
Was to find the first chapter and look at it first.
And so from the first to the second they passed,
Till in servile routine they arrived at the last.
But a literate age, unbenighted by creed,
Can find on two boards all it wishes to read;
For the front of the cover shows somebody shot
And the back of the cover will tell you the plot.

Between, that the book may be handily padded,
Some pages of mere printed matter are added,
Expanding the theme, which in case of great need
The curious reader might very well read
With the zest that is lent to a game worth the winning,
By knowing the end when you start the beginning;
While our barbarous sires, who would read every word
With a morbid desire to find out what occurred,
Went drearily drudging through Dickens and Scott.
But the back of the cover will tell you the plot.

The wild village folk in earth's earliest prime
Could often sit still for an hour at a time
And hear a blind beggar, nor did the tale pall
Because Hector must fight before Hector could fall:
Nor was Scheherazade required, at the worst,
To tell her tales backwards and finish them first;
And the minstrels who sang about battle and banners
Found the rude camp-fire crowd had some notion of manners.
Till Forster (who pelted the people like crooks,
The Irish with buckshot, the English with books),
Established the great educational scheme
Of compulsory schooling, that glorious theme.

Some learnt how to read, and the others forgot,
And the back of the cover will tell you the plot.*

O Genius of Business! O marvellous brain,
Come in place of the priests and the warriors to reign!
O Will to Get On that makes everything go—
O Hustle! O Pep! O Publicity! O!
Shall I spend three-and-sixpence to purchase the book,
Which we all can pick up on the bookstall and look?
Well, it may appear strange, but I think I shall not,
For the back of the cover will tell you the plot.

[From *The Collected Poems of G. K. Chesterton*]

*William E. Forster (1818–1886) was responsible for the Education Act of 1870, which provided for state education in England where voluntary and church-related schools were not sufficient. In 1881 he introduced a coercion act for Ireland, which called for the suspension of *habeas corpus* and for unlimited use of arbitrary arrest and preventive detention.

Lines to a Friend Apprehensive of a Shortage of Food in Beaconsfield*

Lady, you will not, when you come,
Devour us out of house and home,
Nor do I think you come, indeed,
Impelled by undiluted greed,
Or merely seek our poor abodes
To over-eat at Overroads,
Or merely come to make the Rectory
Alter its name to the Refectory,
Out of mere vanity to win
A double or a treble chin,
Or hope to shake this wood and weald,
A larger Mrs. Inglefield.

Dear Freda, no. Food has been seen
Between Hall Barn and Knotty Green.

Men walk our ways, whose pasts reveal
The far-off memory of a meal.
Your fatter friends, through all the dearth,
Fill their appointed space on earth.
Lord Burnham (if by force of will)
Is stouter than Lord Stopford still;
And Becky Child, on closer view,
Is still a shade more thick than you.
And I, a frailer lily, last
—Bent but not broken by the blast.

Shelley, the ethereal bard, who had
A tidy income from his dad,
Sang (as his month's allowance came)
That poets live on love and fame:
The Poet who has penned these lines
On more material matter dines;
And with his fame and love, will take
A casual Ham, a trifling Steak;
And sends, in this disgraceful verse you view,
His fame to blazes and his love to you.

[From Maisie Ward, *Return to Chesterton*]

*GKC wrote this poem to his former secretary Freda Spencer, who was dubious about visiting the Chestertons during a wartime food shortage.

Poem by Oliver Hereford:

G. K. Chesterton

When Plain Folk, such as you or I,
See the Sun sinking in the sky,
We think it is the Setting Sun,
But Mr. Gilbert Chesterton
Is not so easily misled.
He calmly stands upon his head,
And upside-down obtains a new
And Chestertonian point of view.

G. K. CHESTERTON

Observing thus, how from his toes
The sun creeps nearer to his nose,
He cries with wonder and delight,
"How Grand the SUNRISE is to-night!"

[From *The American Magazine*, February 1913]

❦ 10 ❧

RELIGION, MORALITY, THEOLOGY, HERESY

Essay Excerpts

YOU cannot evade the issue of God; whether you talk about pigs or the binomial theory, you are still talking about Him. Now if Christianity be . . . a fragment of metaphysical nonsense invented by a few people, then, of course, defending it will simply mean talking that metaphysical nonsense over and over again. But if Christianity should happen to be true—that is to say, if its God is the real God of the universe—then defending it may mean talking about anything or everything. Things can be irrelevant to the proposition that Christianity is false, but nothing can be irrelevant to the proposition that Christianity is true. Zulus, gardening, butchers' shops, lunatic asylums, housemaids and the French Revolution—all these things not only may have something to do with the Christian God, but must have something to do with Him if He really lives and reigns.

[From the London *Daily News,* 12 December 1903]

YOU are free in our time to say that God does not exist; you are free to say that He exists and is evil; you are free to say (like poor old Renan) that He would like to exist if He could. You may talk of God as a metaphor or mystification; you may water Him down with gallons of long words, or boil Him to the rags of metaphysics; and it is not merely that nobody punishes, but nobody protests. But if you speak of God as a fact, as a thing like a tiger, as a reason for changing one's conduct, then the modern world will stop you somehow if it can. We are long past talking about whether an unbeliever should be punished for being irreverent. It is now thought irreverent to be a believer.

[From *George Bernard Shaw*]

THE elusive, enormous, and nameless thing, with which I have so long wrestled, as with a slippery leviathan, in such places as this, suddenly heaved in sight the other day and took on a sort of formless form. I am always getting these brief glimpses of the monster, though they seldom last long enough for me to make head or tail of it. In this case it appeared in a short letter to the *Daily Express*, which ran, word for word, as follows:

"In reply to your article 'What Youth Wants in Church,' I assert that it does not want sadness, ceremony, or humbug. Youth wants to know only about the present and future, not about what happened 2,000 years ago. If the churches forsake these things, young people will flock to them."

The syntax is a little shaky, and the writer does not mean that the young people will flock to the things that happened 2,000 years ago if only the churches will desert them. He does actually mean (what is much more extraordinary) that the young people will flock to the churches merely because the churches have forsaken all the original objects of their existence. Every feature of every church, from a cross on a spire to an old hymn-book left in a pew, refers more or less to certain things that happened about 2,000 years ago. If we do not want to be reminded of these things, the natural inference is that we do not want any of the buildings built to remind us of them. So far from flocking to them, we shall naturally desire to get away from them; or still more to clear them away. But I cannot understand why something which is unpopular because of what it means should become frightfully popular because it no longer means anything. A War Memorial is a memorial of the war, and I can imagine that those who merely hate the memory might merely hate the memorial. But what would be the sense of saying that, if only all the names of the dead were scraped off the War Memorials, huge pilgrimages would be made from all ends of the earth to visit and venerate the absence of names on a memorial of nothing?

[From *All Is Grist*]

IN all the mess of modern thoughtlessness, that still calls itself modern thought, there is perhaps nothing so stupendously stupid as the common saying, "Religion can never depend on minute disputes about doctrine." It is like saying that life can never depend on minute disputes about medicine. The man who is content to say, "We do not want theologians splitting hairs," will doubtless be content to go on and say, "We do not want surgeons splitting filaments more delicate than hairs." It is a fact that many a man would be dead today, if his doctors had not debated fine shades about doctoring. It is also the fact that European civilization would be dead today, if its doctors of divinity had not debated fine shades about doctrine.

[From *The Resurrection of Rome*]

RIGHT in the middle of all these things [pre-Christian theories about God] stands up an enormous exception. It is quite unlike anything else. It is a thing final like the trump of doom, though it is also a piece of good news; or news that seems too good to be true. It is nothing less than the loud assertion that this mysterious maker of the world has visited his world in person. It declares that really and even recently, or right in the middle of historic times, there did walk into the world this original invisible being; about whom the thinkers make theories and the mythologists hand down myths; the Man Who Made the World. That such a higher personality exists behind all things had indeed always been implied by all the best thinkers, as well as by all the most beautiful legends. But nothing of this sort had ever been implied in any of them. It is simply false to say that the other sages and heroes had claimed to be that mysterious master and maker, of whom the world had dreamed and disputed. Not one of them had ever claimed to be anything of the sort. Not one of their sects or schools had ever claimed that they had claimed to be anything of the sort. The most that any religious prophet had said was that he was the true servant of such a being. The most that any visionary had ever said was that men might catch glimpses of the glory of that spiritual being; or much more often of lesser spiritual beings. The most that any primitive myth had ever suggested was that the Creator was present at the Creation. But that the

Creator was present at scenes a little subsequent to the supper-parties of Horace, and talked with tax-collectors and government officials in the detailed daily life of the Roman Empire, and that this fact continued to be firmly asserted by the whole of that great civilization for more than a thousand years—that is something utterly unlike anything else in nature. It is the one great startling statement that man has made since he spoke his first articulate word, instead of barking like a dog. . . . It makes nothing but dust and nonsense of comparative religion.

[From *The Everlasting Man*]

I F . . . a theological distinction is a thread, all Western history has hung on that thread; if it is a fine point, all our past has been balanced on that point. The subtle distinctions have made the simple Christians: all the men who think drink right and drunkenness wrong; all the men who think marriage normal and polygamy abnormal; all the men who think it wrong to hit first and right to hit back; and . . . all the men who think it right to carve statues and wrong to worship them. These are all, when one comes to think of it, very subtle theological distinctions.

[From *The Resurrection of Rome*]

E ACH one of these Christian or mystical virtues involves a paradox in its own nature, and . . . this is not true of any of the typically pagan or rationalist virtues. Justice insists on finding out a certain thing due to a certain man and giving it to him. Temperance consists in finding out the proper limit of a particular indulgence and adhering to that. But charity means pardoning what is unpardonable, or it is no virtue at all. Hope means hoping when things are hopeless, or it is no virtue at all And faith means believing the incredible, or it is no virtue at all.

[From *Heretics*]

THE Fall is a view of life. It is not only the only enlightening, but the only encouraging view of life. It holds, as against the only real alternative philosophies, those of the Buddhist or the Pessimist or the Promethean, that we have misused a good world, and not merely been entrapped into a bad one. It refers evil back to the wrong use of the will, and thus declares that it can eventually be righted by the right use of the will. Every other creed except that one is some form of surrender to fate. A man who holds this view of life will find it giving light on a thousand things; on which mere evolutionary ethics have not a word to say. For instance, on the colossal contrast between the completeness of man's machines and the continued corruption of his motives; on the fact that no social progress really seems to leave self behind; on the fact that the first and not the last men of any school or revolution are generally the best and purest; as William Penn was better than a Quaker millionaire or Washington better than an American oil magnate; on that proverb that says: "The price of liberty is eternal vigilance," which is only what the theologians say of every other virtue, and is itself only a way of stating the truth of original sin; on those extremes of good and evil by which man exceeds all the animals by the measure of heaven and hell; on that sublime sense of loss that is in the very sound of all great poetry, and nowhere more than in the poetry of pagans and sceptics: "We look before and after, and pine for what is not"; which cries against all prigs and progressives out of the very depths and abysses of the broken heart of man, that happiness is not only a hope, but also in some strange manner a memory; and that we are all kings in exile.

[From *The Thing: Why I Am a Catholic*]

A S for the social justification of murder, that has already begun; and earnest thinkers had better begin at once to think about a nice inoffensive name for it. The case for murder, on modern relative and evolutionary ethics, is quite overwhelming. There is hardly one of us who does not, in looking around his or her social circle, recognize some chatty person or energetic social character whose disappearance, without undue fuss or farewell, would be a bright event for us all. Nor is it true that such a person is dangerous only because he wields unjust legal or social powers. The problem is often purely psychological, and not in the least legal; and no legal emancipations would solve it, but the introduction of that new form of liberty which we may agree to call, perhaps, the practice of Social Subtraction. Or, if we like, we can model the new name on the other names I have mentioned. We may call it Life-Control or Free Death.

[From Come to Think of It]

M OST of our friends and acquaintances continue to entertain a healthy prejudice against Cannibalism. The time when this next step in ethical evolution will be taken seems as yet far distant. But the notion that there is not very much difference between the bodies of men and animals—that is not by any means far distant, but exceedingly near. It is expressed in a hundred ways, as a sort of cosmic communism. We might almost say that it is expressed in every other way except cannibalism.

It is expressed, as in the Voronoff notion, in putting pieces of animals into men. It is expressed, as in the vegetarian notion, in not putting pieces of animals into men. It is expressed in letting a man die as a dog dies, or in thinking it more pathetic that a dog should die than a man. Some are fussy about what happens to the bodies of animals, as if they were quite certain that a rabbit resented being cooked, or that an oyster demanded to be cremated. Some are ostentatiously indifferent to what happens to the bodies of men; and deny all dignity to the dead and all affectionate gesture to the living. But all these have obviously one thing in common; and that is that they regard the human and bestial body as common things. They think of them under a common generalization; or under conditions at best comparative. Among people who have reached this position, the reason for disapproving of cannibalism has already become very vague. It remains as a tradition and an instinct. Fortunately, thank God, though it is now very vague, it is still very strong. But though the number of earnest ethical pioneers who are likely to begin to eat boiled missionary is very small, the number of those among them who would explain their own real reason for not doing so is still smaller.

[From The Thing: Why I Am a Catholic]

NOW, of course, as I say, a Catholic knows the answer [regarding fatalism and suicide]; because he holds the complete philosophy which keeps a man sane; and not some single fragment of it, whether sad or glad, which may easily drive him mad. A Catholic does not kill himself because he does not take it for granted that he will deserve heaven in any case, or that it will not matter at all whether he deserves it at all. He does not profess to know exactly what danger he would run; but he does know what loyalty he would violate and what command or condition he would disregard. He actually thinks that a man might be fitter for heaven because he endured like a man; and that a hero could be a martyr to cancer as St. Lawrence or St. Cecilia were martyrs to cauldrons or gridirons. The faith in a future life, the hope of a future happiness, the belief that God is Love and that loyalty is eternal life, these things do not produce lunacy and anarchy, *if* they are taken along with the other Catholic doctrines about duty and vigilance and watchfulness against the powers of hell. They might produce lunacy and anarchy, if they were taken alone. And the Modernists, that is, the optimists and the sentimentalists, did want us to take them alone. Of course, the same would be true, if somebody took the other doctrines of duty and discipline alone. It would produce another dark age of Puritans rapidly blackening into Pessimists. Indeed, the extremes meet, when they are both ends clipped off what should be a complete thing. Our parable ends poetically with two gibbets side by side; one for the suicidal pessimist and the other for the suicidal optimist.

[From *The Thing: Why I Am a Catholic*]

THE two great movements that have happened since the Reformation can best be defined as the solemn sanctification of two cardinal sins. The aristocratic movement ultimately amounted to the declaration that pride is not a sin. The Manchester or commercial movement which followed it amounted to the assertion that avarice is not a sin. It is in this dogma alone that the industrial movement differed from mankind. A French peasant may grab at gold as much as a Birmingham merchant. But when the French peasant wants to worship a saint he does not worship a man who grabbed at gold, but one who flung it away.

[From *The Living Age*, 17 April 1909]

IF the Church had not renounced the Manicheans it might have become merely Manichean. If it had not renounced the Gnostics it might have become Gnostic. But by the very fact that it did renounce them it proved that it was not either Gnostic or Manichean. At any rate it proved that something was not either Gnostic or Manichean; and what could it be that condemned them, if it was not the original good news of the runners from Bethlehem and the trumpet of the Resurrection? The early Church was ascetic, but she proved that she was not pessimistic, simply by condemning the pessimists. The creed declared that man was sinful, but it did not declare that life was evil, and it proved it by damning those who did. The condemnation of the early heretics is itself condemned as something crabbed and narrow; but it was in truth the very proof that the Church meant to be brotherly and broad. It proved that the primitive Catholics were specially eager to explain that they did *not* think man utterly vile; that they did *not* think life incurably miserable; that they did *not* think marriage a sin or procreation a tragedy. They were ascetic because asceticism was the only possible purge of the sins of the world; but in the very thunder of their anathemas they affirmed forever that their asceticism was not to be anti-human or anti-natural; that they did wish to purge the world and not destroy it. And nothing else except those anathemas could possibly have made it clear, amid a confusion which still confuses them with their mortal enemies. Nothing else but dogma could have resisted the riot of imaginative invention with which the pessimists were waging their war against nature. . . . If the Church had not insisted on theology, it would have melted into a mad mythology of the mystics, yet further removed from reason or even from rationalism; and, above all, yet further removed from life and from the love of life.

[From *The Everlasting Man*]

A man does not come an inch nearer to being a heretic by being a hundred times a critic. Nor does he do so because his criticisms resemble those of critics who are also heretics. He only becomes a heretic at the precise moment when he prefers his criticism to his Catholicism. That is, at the instant of separation in which he thinks the view peculiar to himself more valuable than the creed that unites him to his fellows. At any given moment the Catholic Church is full of people sympathizing with social movements or moral ideas, which may happen to have representatives outside the Church. For the Church is not a movement or a mood or a direction, but the balance of many movements and moods; and membership of it consists of accepting the ultimate arbitrament which strikes the balance between them, not in refusing to admit any of them into the balance at all. A Catholic does not come any nearer to being a Communist by hating the Capitalist corruptions, any more than he comes any nearer to being a Moslem by hating real idolatry or real excess in wine. He accepts the Church's ruling about the use and abuse of wine and images; and after that it is irrelevant how much he happens to hate the abuse of them. A Catholic did not come any nearer to being a Calvinist by dwelling on the omniscience of God and the power of Grace, any more than he came nearer to being an atheist by saying that man possessed reason and freewill.

[From *Chaucer*]

NOT very long after the great Greek Emperor, Leo the Isaurian, had issued a universal proclamation, commanding every single subject in the whole Roman Empire to swear to his hatred of images and his acceptance of Iconoclasm, Pope Gregory III rose up and excommunicated the Iconoclasts. The Emperor called a Council of the Church which supported the imperial view. The Pope condemned the Council. It would be impossible to bring into sharper outline and conflict the claims of the two powers. But in practice, those who knew them to be incompatible felt them to be incommensurate. It is impossible, as I have said, to recreate after all these ages and alterations, the huge disproportion that seemed to exist between the broad daylight of the Empire and the faint shadow in the West. I have compared it to Winchester challenging London; it was more as if the York diocese defied the modern financial position of New York. New Rome seemed as prosperous and promising as New York. It seemed as central and civilized as Paris. It seemed as natural a seat of new experiments as the real New Rome of today. The Emperor had on his side councils and colleges and the bishops of big cities and the whole tone and talk of society and the prestige of the past and the promise of the future. The Pope had on his side deserted streets and barren provinces and frontiers broken by barbarians and the support of rude and uncertain tribes; the Pope had on his side savagery and stupidity and ignorance and desolation; and the Pope was right.

He was right thoroughly; he was right a thousand times; he was right by the creative Christian principle, in which the devil cannot make but only mar; he was right equally by every modern test or taste in beauty and the liberty of the arts; he was right against the Caesarean fad of flat portraits as much as against the Moslem monomania of monotheism; he was right by the whole power and spirit of the wide culture that was already dawning darkly behind; he was as right as the oldest gargoyle of Chartres or the last statuette of Cellini; he was right with the unconscious prophecy of all that has here covered him with the flamboyance and the splendour of Rome; and he was right when every one else was wrong. Realize only that one forgotten fact about that one obscure Pontiff; and then come back to consider afresh, with what detachment and independence you will, the impression that at first puzzled you; the impression that this temple of St. Peter is built to assert rather the firmness and authority and even audacity of its hierarchs than their softness or simplicity or sympathy as holy men. Realize that for many millions of mankind, including those who made this city and this shrine, it is really true; the same thing that happened in the matter of the Iconoclasts has happened again and again; and in the awful silence after some shattering question, one voice has spoken and one signal has saved the world.

[From *The Resurrection of Rome*]

FOR all we know the Reformation may have tried to make a democracy; all that we do know for certain is that it did make an aristocracy, the most powerful aristocracy of modern times. The great English landlords, who are the peers, arose after the destruction of the small English landlords, who were the abbots. The public schools, which were popular in the Middle Ages, became aristocratic after the Reformation. The universities, which were popular in the Middle Ages, became aristocratic after the Reformation. The tramp who went to a monastic inn in the Middle Ages, went to jail and the whipping-post after the Reformation. All this is scarcely denied.

[From *The Living Age*, 26 February 1910]

THE genuine Protestant creed is now hardly held by anybody—least of all by the Protestants. So completely have they lost faith in it, that they have mostly forgotten what is was. If almost any modern man be asked whether we save our souls solely through our theology, or whether doing good (to the poor, for instance) will help us on the road to God, he would answer without hesitation that good works are probably more pleasing to God than theology. It would probably come as quite a surprise to him to learn that, for three hundred years, the faith in faith alone was the badge of a Protestant, the faith in good works the rather shameful badge of a disreputable Papist. The ordinary Englishman . . . would now be in no doubt whatever on the merits of the long quarrel between Catholicism and Calvinism. And that was the most important and intellectual quarrel between Catholicism and Protestantism. If he believes in a God at all, or even if he does not, he would quite certainly prefer a God who has made all men for joy, and desires to save them all, to a God who deliberately made some for involuntary sin and immortal misery. But that was the quarrel; and it was the Catholic who held the first and the Protestant who held the second.

[From *The Thing: Why I Am a Catholic*]

WHEN the reformer says that the principles of the Reformation give freedom to different points of view, he means that they give freedom to the Universalist to curse Rome for having too much predestination and to the Calvinist to curse her for having too little. He means that in that happy family there is a place for the No Popery man who finds Purgatory too tender-hearted and also for the other No Popery man who finds Hell too harsh. He means that the same description can somehow be made to cover the Tolstoyan who blames priests because they permit patriotism and the Diehard who blames priests because they represent Internationalism. After all, the essential aim of true Christianity is that priests should be blamed; and who are we that we should set narrow dogmatic limits to the various ways in which various temperaments may desire to blame them? Why should we allow a cold difficulty of the logician, technically called a contradiction in terms, to stand between us and the warm and broadening human brotherhood of all who are full of sincere and unaffected dislike of their neighbors? Religion is of the heart, not of the head; and as long as all our hearts are full of a hatred for everything that our fathers loved, we can go on flatly contradicting each other for ever about what there is to be hated.

[From *The Catholic Church and Conversion*]

IT sounds harmless to say, as most modern people have said: "Actions are only wrong if they are bad for society." Follow it out, and sooner or later you will have the inhumanity of a hive or a heathen city, establishing slavery as the cheapest and most certain means of production, torturing the slaves for evidence because the individual is nothing to the State, declaring that an innocent man must die for the people, as did the murderers of Christ. Then, perhaps, you will go back to Catholic definitions and find that the Church, while she also says it is our duty to work for society, says other things also which forbid individual injustice. Or again, it sounds quite pious to say, "Our moral conflict should end with a victory of the spiritual over the material." Follow it out and you may end in the madness of the Manicheans, saying that a suicide is good because it is a sacrifice, that a sexual perversion is good because it produces no life, that the devil made the sun and moon because they are material. Then you may begin to guess why Catholicism insists that there are evil spirits as well as good; and that materials also may be sacred, as in the Incarnation or the Mass, in the sacrament of marriage or the resurrection of the body.

[From *Twelve Modern Apostles and Their Creeds*,
an anthology with an Introduction by Dean Inge]

ONE broad characteristic belongs to all the schools of thought that are called broad-minded, and that is that their eloquence ends in a sort of silence not very far removed from sleep. One mark distinguishes all the wild innovations and insurrections of modern intellectualism; one note is apparent in all the new and revolutionary religions that have recently swept the world; and that note is dullness. They are too simple to be true. And meanwhile any one Catholic peasant, while holding one small bead of the rosary in his fingers, can be conscious, not of one eternity, but of a complex and almost a conflict of eternities; as, for example, in the relations of Our Lord and Our Lady, of the fatherhood and childhood of God, of the motherhood and childhood of Mary. Thoughts of that kind have in a supernatural sense something analogous to sex; they breed. They are fruitful and multiply; and there is no end to them. They have innumerable aspects; but the aspect that concerns the argument here is this: that a religion which is rich in this sense always has a number of ideas in reserve. Besides the ideas that are being applied to a particular problem of a particular period, there are a number of rich fields of thought which are in that sense lying fallow. Where a new theory, invented to meet a new problem, rapidly perishes with that problem, the old things are always waiting for other problems when they shall in their turn become new. A new Catholic movement is generally a movement to emphasize some Catholic idea that was only neglected in the sense that it was not till then specially needed; but when it was needed, nothing else can meet the need. In other words, the only way really to meet all the human needs of the future is to pass into the possession of all the Catholic thoughts of the past; and the only way to do that is really to become a Catholic.

[From *Where All Roads Lead*]

N OW of nearly all the dead heresies it may be said that they are not only dead, but damned; that is, they are condemned or would be condemned by common sense, even outside the Church, when once the mood and mania of them is passed. Nobody now wants to revive the Divine Right of Kings which the first Anglicans advanced against the Pope. Nobody now wants to revive the Calvinism which the first Puritans advanced against the King. Nobody now is sorry that the Iconoclasts were prevented from smashing all the statues of Italy. Nobody now is sorry that the Jansenists failed to destroy all the dramas of France. Nobody who knows anything about the Albigensians regrets that they did not convert the world to pessimism and perversion. Nobody who really understands the logic of the Lollards (a much more sympathetic set of people) really wishes that they had succeeded in taking away all political rights and privileges from everybody who was not in a state of grace. "Dominion founded on Grace" was a devout ideal; but considered as a plan for disregarding an Irish policeman controlling the traffic in Piccadilly, until we have discovered whether he has confessed recently to his Irish priest, it is wanting in actuality. In nine cases out of ten the Church simply stood for sanity and social balance against heretics who were sometimes very like lunatics. . . . A study of the true historical cases commonly shows us the spirit of the age going wrong, and the Catholics at least relatively going right. It is a mind surviving a hundred moods.

[From *The Thing: Why I Am a Catholic*]

IT is not true, as the rationalist histories imply, that through the ages orthodoxy has grown old slowly. It is rather heresy that has grown old quickly. The Reformation grew old amazingly quickly. It was the Counter-Reformation that grew young. In England, it is strange to note how soon Puritanism turned into Paganism, or perhaps ultimately into Philistinism. It is strange to note how soon the Puritans degenerated into Whigs. By the end of the seventeenth century English politics had dried up into a wrinkled cynicism that might have been as old as Chinese etiquette. It was the Counter-Reformation that was full of the fire and even of the impatience of youth. It was in the Catholic figures of the sixteenth and seventeenth centuries that we find the spirit of energy, in the only noble sense of novelty. It was people like St. Teresa who reformed; people like Bossuet who challenged; people like Pascal who questioned; people like Suarez who speculated. The counter-attack was like a charge of the old spears of chivalry. And indeed the comparison is very relevant to the generalization. I believe that this renovation, which has certainly happened in our own time, and which has certainly happened in a time so recent as the Reformation, has really happened again and again in the history of Christendom.

Working backwards on the same principle, I will mention at least two examples which I suspect to have been similar; the case of Islam and the case of Arianism. The Church had any number of opportunities of dying, and even of being respectfully interred. But the younger generation always began once again to knock at the door; and never louder than when it was knocking at the lid of the coffin in which it had been prematurely buried. Islam and Arianism were both attempts to broaden the basis to a sane and simple Theism, the former supported by great military success and the latter by great imperial prestige. They ought to have finally established the new system, but for the one perplexing fact, that the old system preserved the only seed and secret of novelty. Any-one reading between the lines of the twelfth-century record can see that the world was permeated by potential Pantheism and Paganism; we can see it in the dread of the Arabian version of Aristotle, in the rumour about great men being Moslems in secret; the old men, seeing the simple faith of the Dark Ages dissolving, might well have thought that the fading of Christendom into Islam would be the next thing to happen. If so, the old men would have been much surprised at what did happen. What did happen was a roar like thunder from thousands and thousands of young men, throwing all their youth into one exultant counter-charge: the Crusades. The actual effect of danger from the younger religion was renewal of our own youth. It was the sons of St. Francis, the Jugglers of God, wandering singing over all the roads of the world; it was the Gothic going up like a flight of arrows; it was a rejuvenation of Europe. And though I know less of the older period, I suspect that the same was true of Athanasian orthodoxy in revolt against Arian offi-cialism. The older men had submitted it to a compromise, and St. Athanasius led the younger like a divine demagogue. The persecuted carried into exile the sacred fire. It was a flaming torch that could be cast out, but could not be trampled out.

[From *Where All Roads Lead*]

A man who finds his way to Catholicism, out of the tangle of modern culture and complexity, must think harder than he has ever thought in his life. He must often deal as grimly with dry abstrac-tions as if he were reading mathematics with the hope of being Senior Wrangler. He must often face the dull and repulsive aspects of duty, as if he were facing the dreariest drudgery in the world. He must realise all the sides upon which the religion may seem sordid or humdrum or humiliating or harsh. He must feel all the counter-attractions of Paganism at least enough to know how attractive are those attractions. But, above all, he must think; above all, he must preserve his intellectual independence; above all, he must use his reason. It would be better to reject the Faith than to accept it as an unreasonable thing. I do not say, and I have never said, that the splendour and wonder of these things can be the same as the final satisfaction in them. I say that all real human religions would recognise the reality of this as a religion; but that is not the same as recognising it as *the* religion. I may say that even the heathen, when they are human, would realise the presence of Christ, their foe and their friend; but it would not always answer the old question: "Your gods and my gods; do you or I know which is the stronger?" I do not say that the man who merely feels these things is by that act accepting this thing. To do that he must reason more closely than any rationalist; yes, and think more freely than any freethinker. He must broaden his mind much more than any of the broadminded; it is the complement of the ancient truth: "Unless your righteousness exceed the righteousness of the Scribes and Pharisees." Unless your inwardness and sincerity exceed that of all the intellectuals who talk about inwardness and sincerity, I do not say that even the miracle of the Phoenix will convince you. But I do say this.

I say that *when* you are convinced, when you are rationally convinced, when you have come to the end of the long road of reason, when you have seen and seen through the tangled arguments of the time, when you have found the answer to them—*then* you will find yourself suddenly in the morning of the world. Then you will find yourself among facts and not arguments, but facts as marvelous as fables; facts like those which the pagans pictured as a land of giants or an age of heroes; you will have returned to the age of the Epic; and the epoch of things achieved.

[From *Christendom in Dublin*]

Note: The "miracle of the Phoenix" refers to the great open-air Mass that Chesterton attended in Phoenix Park, Dublin, during the Eucharistic Congress of 1932.

SUPPOSE that a great commotion arises in the street about something, let us say a lamp-post, which many influential persons desire to pull down. A grey-clad monk, who is the spirit of the Middle Ages, is approached upon the matter, and begins to say, in the arid manner of the Schoolmen, "Let us first of all consider, my brethren, the value of Light. If Light be in itself good—" At this point he is somewhat excusably knocked down. All the people make a rush for the lamp-post, the lamp-post is down in ten minutes, and they go about congratulating each other on their unmedieval practicality. But as things go on they do not work out so easily. Some people have pulled the lamp-post down because they wanted the electric light; some because they wanted old iron; some because they wanted darkness, because their deeds were evil. Some thought it not enough of a lamp-post, some too much; some acted because they wanted to smash municipal machinery; some because they wanted to smash something. And there is war in the night, no man knowing whom he strikes. So, gradually and inevitably, to-day, to-morrow, or the next day, there comes back the conviction that the monk was right after all, and that all depends on what is the philosophy of Light. Only what we might have discussed under the gas-lamp, we must now discuss in the dark.

[From *Heretics*]

A ND, indeed, speaking of Confucianism, I have heard it said that the whole art of fireworks first came from the land of Confucius. There is something not inappropriate in such an origin. The art of coloured glass can truly be called the most typically Christian of all arts or artifices. The art of coloured lights is as essentially Confucian as the art of coloured windows is Christian. Esthetically, they produce somewhat the same impression on the fancy; the impression of something glowing and magical; something at once mysterious and transparent. But the difference between their substance and structure is the whole difference between the great western faith and the great eastern agnosticism. The Christian windows are solid and human, made of heavy lead, of hearty and characteristic colours; but behind them is the light. The colours of the fireworks are as festive and as varied; but behind them is the darkness. They themselves are their only illumination; even as in that stern philosophy, man is his own star. The rockets of ruby and sapphire fade away slowly upon the dome of hollowness and darkness. But the kings and saints in the old Gothic windows, dusky and opaque in this hour of midnight, still contain all their power of full flamboyance, and await the rising of the sun.

[From *Alarms and Discursions*]

A ND those of us who have seen all the normal rules and relations of humanity uprooted by random speculators, as if they were abnormal abuses and almost accidents, will understand why men have sought for something divine if they wished to preserve anything human. They will know why common sense, cast out from some academy of fads and fashions conducted on the lines of a luxurious madhouse, has age after age sought refuge in the high sanity of a sacrament.

[From *The Superstition of Divorce*]

" B UT I think there is more to be said. I think God has given us the love of special places, of a hearth and of a native land, for a good reason."

"I dare say," I said. "What reason?"

"Because otherwise," he said, pointing his pole out at the sky and the abyss, "We might worship that."

"What do you mean?" I demanded.

"Eternity," he said in his harsh voice, "the largest of the idols—the mightiest of the rivals of God."

"You mean pantheism and infinity and all that," I suggested.

"I mean," he said with increasing vehemence, "that if there be a house for me in heaven it will either have a green lamp-post and a hedge, or something quite as positive and personal as a green lamp-post and a hedge. I mean that God bade me love one spot and serve it, and do all things however wild in praise of it, so that this one spot might be a witness against all the infinities and sophistries, that Paradise is some-where and not anywhere, is something and not anything. And I would not be so very much surprised if the house in heaven had a real green lamp-post after all."

[From *Manalive*]

The Outline of Liberty

THERE is a quality needed today for the spread of all truth, and especially religious truth, which is very simple and vivid, but which I find it very difficult to fit with a word. So many words have become catchwords.

I suppose that our critics, in their learned way, would have recourse to the little-known Greek word *paradox,* if I were simply to say that they are not quite broad-minded enough to be Catholics. In their own jargon, being broad-minded so often means being blank-minded.

If I were to say that they suffer from a lack of imagination, they might suppose (heaven help them) that I meant that what we believe in is all imaginary. Nor indeed do either of these two terms define the definite thing I intend. It would be nearer the mark if I said that they cannot see all round a subject; or that they cannot see anything against the background of everything else.

The learned man, of what I may call the Cambridge type, is like a man who should spend years in making a minute ordnance map of the country between Cork and Dublin, and never discover that Ireland is an island. It is not a question of understanding something difficult. It is rather a question of opening the mind wide enough to understand something easy. It is not to be attained by years of labour; it is more likely to be attained in a moment of laziness; when the map-maker who has long been poring over the map with his nose close to Cork, may lean back for a moment and suddenly see Ireland. It is much more difficult to get such men to lean back for a moment and see Christendom.

The Catholic Church is always being defined in terms of the particular quarrel that she happens to have with particular people in a particular place. Because the Protestant sects in Northern Europe, for one or two centuries, disapproved of rosaries and incense and candles and confessional boxes, there was a widespread impression that Roman Catholics were simply people who liked confessional boxes and candles and incense and rosaries. But that is not what a Manichee or a Moslem or a Hindoo or an ancient Greek philosopher would say about Roman Catholics.

Buddhists have incense; Moslems have something very like rosaries; and hardly any healthy human being on earth could conceive why anybody should have any particular hatred of candles. Buddhists would say that Catholics were people who insisted on a personal God and personal immortality. Moslems would say that Catholics were people who believed that God had a Son who assumed human form, and who did not think it idolatrous that He should afterwards assume pictorial or sculptural form. Every group in the world would have its own angle or aspect; and the Protestant would hardly recognise the same object which he had only considered in his own aspect.

Nevertheless, each of these, taken in itself, is in a sense narrow; and to dwell upon it narrows the issue. What we want is to have some general impression of the whole background of humanity, especially of heathen humanity, against which we can see the outline of the object, as, in the map of Ireland, the island is seen against the sea.

Now the real background of all that human heathenry is rather a grey background. There are particular patches, which happen to be close to us in place and time, which have been freshly painted in various ways. So freshly painted that nobody knows yet how long the colours will last. As the Imperialists wanted to paint the map red, so the Internationalists and Idealists now want to paint the map pink. But none of them has painted half so much of the map anything as they, in their optimism, have sometimes supposed. And even in the areas where a sort of official optimism prevails, as in parts of America, there is a great deal more of the old ordinary melancholy of men than anyone could gather from newspaper headlines or political programmes. And I believe that the most general philosophy of men left to themselves, and perhaps the most practical illustration of the Fall of Man, is a vague impression of Fate.

If a man will really talk to the poor, in almost any country, I think he will generally find that they are either Christians or fatalists. This fatalism is more or less varied and complicated, of course, in various places by various mythologies or philosophies. It will generally be found that the mythology is a sort of poetry, embodying a worship of the wild forces of nature; a nature-worship which, when broken up, is called polytheism, and, when united, is called pantheism. But there is sometimes very little left of theism in pantheism.

Then there are whole districts where there is true theism, which is, nevertheless, permeated with a mood of fatalism. That, I suppose, is true at least of large areas of Islam. Then there are what may be called the philosophies of resignation, which probably cover equally large areas of the ancient civilisation of Asia.

We need not insist here on any controversial points against or even about these things. But I take it as certain that all those notes of recurrence and cosmic rhythm, and a cycle beginning and ending with itself, which repeat themselves so frequently in connection with Buddhism and Brahminism and Theosophy, are in a general sense allied to an almost impersonal submission to an ultimately impersonal law. That is the tone of the whole thing; and, as I have said, the tone or tint of it strikes us as rather grey; or at least, neutral and negative.

It is the same with almost all we know of the pagan myths and metaphysics of antiquity. It is a modern slander on pagans to represent paganism as almost identical with pleasure. But anyhow, nobody acquainted with the great Greek and Latin literature, even in the smallest degree, will ever dream of identifying paganism with optimism. It would at least be a great deal nearer the truth to say that there, as everywhere else, the fundamental character of paganism is pessimism. But in any case, it can quite fairly be said that it is fatalism.

Upon this grey background there is one splash or star of silver or gold; a thing like a flame. It is quite exceptional and extraordinary. Of its many extraordinary characters, this is perhaps the chief; that it proclaims Liberty. Or, as the only true meaning of that term, it proclaims Will. In a strange voice, as of a trumpet from heaven, it tells a strange story, of which the very essence is that it is made up of Will, or of a free divergence of Wills.

Will made the world; Will wounded the world; the same Divine Will gave to the world for the second time its chance; the same human Will can for the last time make its choice. That is the real outstanding peculiarity, or eccentricity, of the peculiar sect called Roman Catholics. And if anyone objects to my limiting so large a conception to Roman Catholics, I willingly agree that there are many who value it so much that they obviously ought to be Roman Catholics. But if anyone says that it is not in fact and history bound up with the Faith of Roman Catholicism, it is enough to refer him to the history and the facts.

Nobody especially emphasised this spiritual liberty until the Church was established. People began instantly to question this spiritual liberty, when the Church began to be broken up. The instant a breach, or even a crack, had been made in the dyke of Catholicism, there poured through it the bitter sea of Calvinism, or in other words, of a very cruel form of fatalism. Since that time, it has taken the much duller form of Determinism. This sadness and sense of bondage is so general to mankind that it immediately made its appearance, when the special spiritual message of liberty was silenced or interrupted anywhere. Wherever that message is heard, men think and talk in terms of will and choice; and they see no meaning in any of the philosophies of fate, whether desperate or resigned.

It is idle to talk to a Catholic about optimism or pessimism; for he himself shall decide whether the universe shall be, for him, the best or the worst of all possible worlds. It is useless to tell him that he might be more at one with the universal life as a Buddhist or a pantheist; for he knows that, in that sense, he might be more at one with the universal life as a turnip or a tree. It is his whole hope and glory that he is not at one with the universal life; but stands out from it, an exception and even a miracle.

There is a great passage in the "Paradiso" of Dante, which I wish I knew enough Italian to appreciate or enough English to translate. But I would commend it to those who may fancy that my emphasis on this exceptional quality is a mere modern whitewashing of a medieval superstition; and especially to those who have been taught in laborious detail, by learned and very stupid historians, to regard medievalism as narrow and enchained. For it runs roughly like this:

The mightiest gift that God of his largesse
Made in creation, perfect even as He,
Most of His substance, and to Him most dear,
He gave to the Will and it was Liberty.

[From *The Common Man*]

The New Case for Catholic Schools

ANY amount of nonsense has been talked about the need of novelty, and in that sense there is nothing particularly meritorious about being modern. A man who seriously describes his creed as Modernism might just as well invent a creed called Mondayism, meaning that he puts special faith in the fancies that occurred to him on Monday; or a creed called Morningism, meaning that he believed in the thoughts that occurred to him in the morning but not in the afternoon.

Modernity is only the moment of time in which we happen to find ourselves, and nobody who thinks will suppose that it is bound to be superior, either to the time that comes after it or to the time that went before. But in a relative and rational sense we may congratulate ourselves on knowing the news of the moment, and having realised recent facts or discoveries that some people still ignore.

And it is in that sense that we may truly call the fundamental concept of Catholic Education a scientific fact, and especially a psychological fact. Our demand for a complete culture, based on its own philosophy and religion, is a demand that is really unanswerable, in the light of the most vital and even the most modern psychology. For that matter, for those who care for such things, there could hardly be a *word* more modern than *atmosphere*.

Now, so long as they are engaged in doing anything whatever except arguing with us, our modern and scientific friends are never tired of telling us that education must be treated as a whole; that all parts of the mind affect each other; that nothing is too trivial to be significant and even symbolic; that all thoughts can be coloured by conscious or unconscious emotions; that knowledge can never be in watertight compartments; that what may seem a senseless detail may be the symbol of a deep desire; that nothing is negative, nothing is naked, nothing stands separated and alone.

They use these arguments for all sorts of purposes, some of them sensible enough, some of them almost insanely silly; but this is, broadly speaking, how they argue. And the one thing they do not know is that they are arguing in favour of Catholic education, and especially in favour of Catholic atmosphere in Catholic schools. Perhaps if they did know they would leave off.

As a matter of fact, those who refuse to understand that Catholic children must have an entirely Catholic school are back in the bad old days, as they would express it, when nobody wanted education but only instruction. They are relics of the dead time when it was thought enough to drill pupils in two or three dull and detached lessons that were supposed to be quite mechanical. They descend from the original Philistine who first talked about "The Three R's"; and the joke about him is very symbolic of his type or time. For he was the sort of man who insists very literally on literacy, and, even in doing so, shows himself illiterate.

They were very uneducated rich men who loudly demanded education. And among the marks of their ignorance and stupidity was the particular mark that they regarded letters and figures as dead things, quite separate from each other and from a general view of life. They thought of a boy learning his letters as something quite cut off, for instance, from what is meant by a man of letters. They thought a calculating boy could be made like a calculating machine.

When somebody said to them, therefore, "These things must be taught in a spiritual atmosphere," they thought it was nonsense; they had a vague idea that it meant that a child could only do a simple addition sum when surrounded with the smell of incense. But they thought simple addition much more simple than it is. When the Catholic controversialist said to them, "Even the alphabet can be learnt in a Catholic way," they thought he was a raving bigot, they thought he meant that nobody must ever read anything but a Latin missal.

But he meant what he said, and what he said is thoroughly sound psychology. There is a Catholic view of learning the alphabet; for instance, it prevents you from thinking that the only thing that matters is learning the alphabet; or from despising better people than yourself, if they do not happen to have learnt the alphabet.

The old unpsychological school of instructors used to say: "What possible sense can there be in mixing up arithmetic with religion?" But arithmetic is mixed up with religion, or at the worst with philosophy. It does make a great deal of difference whether the instructor implies that truth is real, or relative, or changeable, or an illusion. The man who said, "Two and two may make five in the fixed stars," was teaching arithmetic in an anti-rational way, and, therefore, in an anti-Catholic way. The Catholic is much more certain about the fixed truths than about the fixed stars.

But I am not now arguing which philosophy is the better; I am only pointing out that every education teaches a philosophy; if not by dogma then by suggestion, by implication, by atmosphere. Every part of that education has a connection with every other part. If it does not all combine to convey some general view of life, it is not education at all.

And the modern educationists, the modern psychologists, the modern men of science, all agree in asserting and reasserting this—until they begin to quarrel with Catholics over Catholic schools.

In short, if there is a psychological truth discoverable by human reason, it is this; that Catholics must either go without Catholic teaching or possess and govern Catholic schools. There is a case for refusing to allow Catholic families to grow up Catholic, by any machinery worth calling education in the existing sense. There is a case for refusing to make any concessions to Catholics at all, and ignoring their idiosyncrasy as if it were an insanity. There is a case for that, because there is and always has been a case for persecution; for the State acting on the principle that certain philosophies are false and dangerous and must be crushed even if they are sincerely held; indeed that they must be crushed, especially if they are sincerely held.

But if Catholics are to teach Catholicism all the time, they cannot merely teach Catholic theology for part of the time. It is our opponents, and not we, who give a really outrageous and superstitious position to dogmatic theology. It is they who suppose that the special "subject" called theology can be put into people by an experiment lasting half an hour; and that this magical inoculation will last them through a week in a world that is soaked through and through with a contrary conception of life.

Theology is only articulate religion; but, strange as it seems to the true Christians who criticise us, it is necessary to have religion as well as theology. And religion, as they are often obliging enough to remind us when this particular problem is not involved, is a thing for every day of the week and not merely for Sunday or Church services.

The truth is that the modern world has committed itself to two totally different and inconsistent conceptions about education. It is always trying to expand the scope of education; and always trying to exclude from it all religion and philosophy. But this is sheer nonsense. You can have an education that teaches atheism because atheism is true, and it can be, from its own point of view, a complete education. But you cannot have an education claiming to teach all truth, and then refusing to discuss whether atheism is true.

Since the coming of the more ambitious psychological education, our schools have claimed to develop all sides of human nature; that is, to produce a complete human being. You cannot do this and totally ignore a great living tradition, which teaches that a complete human being must be a Christian or Catholic human being. You must either persecute it out of existence or allow it to make its own education complete.

When schooling was supposed to consist of spelling, of counting, and making pothooks and hangers, you might make out some kind of case for saying that it could be taught indifferently by a Baptist or Buddhist. But what in the world is the sense of having an education which includes lessons in "citizenship," for instance; and then pretending not to include anything like a moral theory, and ignoring all those who happen to hold that a moral theory depends on a moral theology.

Our schoolmasters profess to bring out every side of the pupil; the aesthetic side; the athletic side; the political side, and so on; and yet they still talk the stale cant of the nineteenth century about public instruction having nothing to do with the religious side. The truth is that, in this matter, it is our enemies who are stick-in-the-mud, and still remain in the stuffy atmosphere of undeveloped and unscientific education; while we are, in this at any rate, on the side of all modern psychologists and serious educationalists in recognising the idea of atmosphere. They sometimes like to call it environment.

[From *The Common Man*]

Babies and Distributism

I hope it is not a secret arrogance to say that I do not think I am exceptionally arrogant; or if I were, my religion would prevent me from being proud of my pride. Nevertheless, for those of such a philosophy, there is a very terrible temptation to intellectual pride, in the welter of wordy and worthless philosophies that surround us to-day. Yet there are not many things that move me to anything like a personal contempt. I do not feel any contempt for an atheist, who is often a man limited and constrained by his own logic to a very sad simplification. I do not feel any contempt for a Bolshevist, who is a man driven to the same negative simplification by a revolt against very positive wrongs. But there is one type of person for whom I feel what I can only call contempt. And that is the popular propagandist of what he or she absurdly describes as Birth-Control.

I despise Birth-Control first because it is a weak and wobbly and cowardly word. It is also an entirely meaningless word; and is used so as to curry favour even with those who would at first recoil from its real meaning. The proceeding these quack doctors recommend does not *control* any birth. It only makes sure that there shall never be any birth to control. It cannot, for instance, determine sex, or even make any selection in the style of the pseudo-science of Eugenics. Normal people can only act so as to produce birth; and these people can only act so as to prevent birth. But these people know perfectly well that they dare not write the plain word Birth-Prevention, in any one of the hundred places where they write the hypocritical word Birth-Control. They know as well as I do that the very word Birth-Prevention would strike a chill into the public, the instant it was blazoned on headlines, or proclaimed on platforms, or scattered in advertisements like any other quack medicine. They dare not call it by its name, because its name is very bad advertising. Therefore they use a conventional and unmeaning word, which may make the quack medicine sound more innocuous.

Second, I despise Birth-Control because it is a weak and wobbly and cowardly thing. It is not even a step along the muddy road they call Eugenics; it is a flat refusal to take the first and most obvious step along the road of Eugenics. Once grant that their philosophy is right, and their course of action is obvious; and they dare not take it; they dare not even declare it. If there is no authority in things which Christendom has called moral, because their origins were mystical, then they are clearly free to ignore all difference between animals and men; and treat men as we treat animals. They need not palter with the stale and timid compromise and convention called Birth-Control. Nobody applies it to the cat. The obvious course for Eugenists is to act towards babies as they act towards kittens. Let all babies be born; and then let us drown those we do not like. I cannot see any objection to it; except the moral or mystical sort of objection that we advance against Birth-Prevention. And that would be real and even reasonable Eugenics; for we could then select the best, or at least the healthiest, and sacrifice what are called the unfit. By the weak compromise of Birth-Prevention, we are very probably sacrificing the fit and only producing the unfit. The births we prevent may be the births of the best and most beautiful children; those we allow, the weakest or worst. Indeed, it is probable; for the habit discourages the early parentage of young and vigorous people; and lets them put off the experience to later years, mostly for mercenary motives. Until I see a real pioneer and progressive leader coming out with a good, bold, scientific programme for drowning babies, I will not join the movement.

But there is a third reason for my contempt, much deeper and therefore much more difficult to express; in which is rooted all my reasons for being anything I am or attempt to be; and above all, for being a Distributist. Perhaps the nearest to a description of it is to say this: that my contempt boils over into bad behaviour when I hear the common suggestion that a birth is avoided because people want to be "free" to go to the cinema or buy a gramophone or a loud-speaker. What makes me want to walk over such people like doormats is that they use the word "free." By every act of that sort they chain themselves to the most servile and mechanical system yet tolerated by men. The cinema is a machine for unrolling certain regular patterns called pictures; expressing the most vulgar millionaire's notion of the taste of the most vulgar millions. The gramophone is a machine for recording such tunes as certain shops and other organisations choose to sell. The wireless is better; but even that is marked by the modern mark of all three; the impotence of the receptive party. The amateur cannot challenge the actor; the householder will find it vain to go and shout into the gramophone; the mob cannot pelt the modern speaker, especially when he is a loud-speaker. It is all a central mechanism giving out to men exactly what their masters think they should have.

Now a child is the very sign and sacrament of personal freedom. He is a fresh free will added to the wills of the world; he is something that his parents have freely chosen to produce and which they freely agree to protect. They can feel that any amusement he gives (which is often considerable) really comes from him and from them, and from nobody else. He has been born without the intervention of any master or lord. He is a creation and a contribution; he is their own creative contribution to creation. He is also a much more beautiful, wonderful, amusing and astonishing thing than any of the stale stories or jingling jazz tunes turned out by the machines. When men no longer feel that he is so, they have lost the appreciation of primary things, and therefore all sense of proportion about the world. People who prefer the mechanical pleasures, to such a miracle, are jaded and enslaved. They are preferring the very dregs of life to the first fountains of life. They are preferring the last, crooked, indirect, borrowed, repeated and exhausted things of our dying Capitalist civilisation, to the reality which is the only rejuvenation of all civilisation. It is they who are hugging the chains of their old slavery; it is the child who is ready for the new world.

[From *The Well and the Shallows*]

On Man: Heir of All the Ages

I F the modern man is indeed the heir of all the ages, he is often the kind of heir who tells the family solicitor to sell the whole damned estate, lock, stock, and barrel, and give him a little ready money to throw away at the races or the nightclubs. He is certainly not the kind of heir who ever visits his estate: and, if he really owns all the historic lands of ancient and modern history, he is a very absentee landlord. He does not really go down the mines on the historic property, whether they are the Caves of the Cave-Men or the Catacombs of the Christians, but is content with a very hasty and often misleading report from a very superficial and sometimes dishonest mining expert. He allows any wild theories, like wild thickets of thorn and brier, to grow all over the garden and even the graveyard. He will always believe modern testimony in a textbook against contemporary testimony on a tombstone. He sells the family portraits with much more than the carelessness of Charles Surface, and seldom knows enough about the family even to save a favourite uncle from the wreck. For the adjective "fast," which was a condemnation when applied to profligates, has become a compliment when applied to progressives. I know there are any number of men in the modern world to whom all this does not in the least apply; but the point is that, even where it is obviously applicable, it is not thought particularly culpable. Nevertheless, there are some of us who do hold that the metaphor of inheritance from human history is a true metaphor, and that any man who is cut off from the past, and content with the future, is a man most unjustly disinherited; and all the more unjustly if he is happy in his lot, and is not permitted even to know what he has lost. And I, for one, believe that the mind of man is at its largest, and especially at its broadest, when it feels the brotherhood of humanity linking it up with remote and primitive and even barbaric things.

Mr. Christopher Dawson has written studies of historic and pre-historic problems which have been admired by men distinguished in every way, and especially distinguished from each other. His work has been most warmly praised by critics as different as Dean Inge and Mr. Aldous Huxley and the Rev. C. C. Martindale. But I, for one, value his researches for one particular reason above the rest: that he has given the first tolerably clear and convincing account of the real stages of what his less lucid predecessors loved to call the Evolution of Religion. Whether myths and mystical cults were really evolved along one consistent line, I do not know. But theories about mythology or cults or mysteries were most certainly not evolved along any consistent line. They cut across each other and almost immediately become a tangle of contradictions. First we had the Sun Myth illuminating everything like the sun, and enabling Bishop Whately to prove that Napoleon was a mythical character. Then we had Herbert Spencer and Grant Allen, who said that everything came from ghosts and graves and the worship of ancestors; and then Professor Frazer, who (with all his genius) could not see the sacred tree for the golden bough. Now whatever else be true of these theories of evolution, they are not evolved. The grave does not grow out of the sun; nor even the oak out of the grave; and on no possible theory is Frazer a development of Spencer. They are contrary guesses; and if there is evidence for all of them (as no doubt there is), the evidence only increases the confusion. Mr. Dawson has ordered the confusion without contradicting the evidence; and his conclusion is that there were, broadly, four stages in the spiritual story of humanity.

The first notion, with which the lowest and most primitive savages seem to have begun, was very like the notion with which many of our High Thinkers hope that all humanity will end. It was a broad belief in what is now called "the spiritual element in life"; in a spirit almost impersonal but still superior to our material minds; of which we may gain encouraging glimpses and visions. This is the stage of the Shaman, or medicine-man, who, as an independent individual mystic, can tap the vast and vague supernatural power that pervades the world. By special magic rites, with special material objects, herbs or stones or what not, he could release the mysterious force. For note that this is not pantheism; the sacred tree is hidden in the wood or the dryad is imprisoned in the tree. Now I could not be content with this magic, whether or no it would suit the Higher Thinkers. But I have no sympathy with a man who has no sympathy with his magic; I count no man large-minded or imaginative who has not sometimes felt like a medicine-man. It is quite natural to me, walking in the woods, to wonder fancifully whether whistling back the note of a certain bird, or tasting the juice of a certain berry, would release a glamour or give back a fairyland. I call that being the heir of all the ages.

The second stage is that of the static archaic culture, in which a whole people live a ritual life, generally founded on the seasons of seed or harvest, in which there is no distinction between sacred and profane, because ploughing or fishing are religious forms; and no distinction between king and priest, because the Sacred Emperor rules the whole round of ritual life like a god. China and Egypt and other cultures were of that sort. Here again, I should be dissatisfied with a religion that was a pageant of nature; for I feel the soul, in Sir Thomas Browne's noble phrase, as something other than the elements, that owes no homage unto the sun. But I am much more dissatisfied with a man, pretending to be a man of culture, who merely despises that ritual. I can never see the pageant of harvest without feeling that it is religious, and it gratifies me to think that I am feeling like the first Emperor of China. I call that being the heir of all the ages.

The third phrase described is the rise of the world religions, the moral and universal religions; for Buddha and Confucius and the Hebrew Prophets and the first Greek philosophers appeared roughly about the same time. And with them appeared the idea expressed in Sir Thomas Browne's phrase: that the soul is greater than the sun. Henceforth the conscience is more than the cosmos. Either it condemns the cosmos, or ignores the cosmos, as in Buddhism; or it gives it a mystical meaning, as in Platonism; or it sees it as an instrument for producing a grander good, as in Judaism and Christianity. Now I do not myself care about the Buddhist extreme, which almost unmakes the world to make the soul. I do not like Nirvana, which seems indistinguishable from death. But I would be seen dead in a field, not in the field of any paradise, negative or positive, with the man who has no admiration for the superb renunciation of Buddha, or for the Western equivalent, the star-defying despair of the Stoics. No man has really been alive who has not some time felt that the skies might fall, so that the justice within his conscience should be done; and in the richer tapestry of the Christian there is also a dark thread of the Stoic. I call that being the heir of all the ages.

I will not complete the four phases here, because the last deals with the more controversial question of the Christian system. I merely use them as a convenient classification to illustrate a neglected truth: that a complete human being ought to have all these things stratified in him, so long as they are in the right order of importance, and that man should be a prince looking from the pinnacle of a tower built by his fathers, and not a contemptuous cad, perpetually kicking down the ladders by which he climbed.

[From *Avowals and Denials*]

11

IF I HAD ONLY ONE SERMON TO PREACH

IF I had only one sermon to preach, it would be a sermon against Pride. The more I see of existence, and especially of modern practical and experimental existence, the more I am convinced of the reality of the old religious thesis; that all evil began with some attempt at superiority; some moment when, as we might say, the very skies were cracked across like a mirror, because there was a sneer in Heaven.

Now the first fact to note about this notion is a rather curious one. Of all such notions, it is the one most generally dismissed in theory and most universally accepted in practice. Modern men imagine that such a theological idea is quite remote from them; and, stated as a theological idea, it probably is remote from them. But, as a matter of fact, it is too close to them to be recognised. It is so completely a part of their minds and morals and instincts, I might almost say of their bodies, that they take it for granted and act on it even before they think of it. It is actually the most popular of all moral ideas; and yet it is almost entirely unknown as a moral idea. No truth is now so unfamiliar as a truth, or so familiar as a fact.

Let us put the fact to a trifling but not unpleasing test. Let us suppose that the reader, or (preferably) the writer, is going into a public-house or some public place of social intercourse; a public tube or tram might do as well, except that it seldom allows of such long and philosophical intercourse as did the old public house. Anyhow, let us suppose any place where men of motley but ordinary types assemble; mostly poor because the majority is poor, some moderately comfortable but rather what is snobbishly called common; an average handful of human beings. Let us suppose that the enquirer, politely approaching this group, opens the conversation in a chatty way by saying, "Theologians are of opinion that it was one of the superior angelic intelligences seeking to become the supreme object of worship, instead of finding his natural joy in worshipping, which dislocated the providential design and frustrated the full joy and completion of the cosmos." After making these remarks the enquirer will gaze round brightly and expectantly at the company for corroboration, at the same time ordering such refreshments as may be ritually fitted to the place or time, or perhaps merely offering cigarettes or cigars to the whole company, to fortify them against the strain. In any case, we may well admit that such a company will find it something of a strain to accept the formula in the above form. Their comments will probably be disjointed and detached; whether they take the form of "Lorlumme" (a beautiful thought slurred somewhat in pronunciation), or even "Gorblimme" (an image more sombre but fortunately more obscure), or merely the unaffected form of "Garn," a statement quite free from doctrinal and denominational teaching, like our State compulsory education. In short, he who shall attempt to state this theory as a theory to the average crowd of the populace will doubtless find that he is talking in an unfamiliar language. Even if he states the matter in the simplified form, that Pride is the worst of the Seven Deadly Sins, he will only produce a vague and rather unfavourable impression that he is preaching. But he is only preaching what everybody else is practising; or at least is wanting everybody else to practise.

Let the scientific enquirer continue to cultivate the patience of science. Let him linger—at any rate let *me* linger—in the place of popular entertainment whatever it may be, and take very careful note (if necessary in a note-book) of the way in which ordinary human beings do really talk about each other. As he is a scientific enquirer with a note-book, it is very likely that he never saw any ordinary human beings before. But if he will listen carefully, he will observe a certain tone taken towards friends, foes and acquaintances; a tone which is, on the whole, creditably genial and considerate, though not without strong likes and dislikes. He will hear abundant if sometimes bewildering allusion to the well-known weaknesses of Old George; but many excuses also, and a certain generous pride in conceding that Old George is quite the gentleman when drunk, or that he told the policeman off proper. Some celebrated idiot, who is always spotting winners that never win, will be treated with almost tender derision; and, especially among the poorest, there will be a true Christian pathos in the reference to those who have been "in trouble" for habits like burglary and petty larceny. And as all these queer types are called up like ghosts by the incantation of gossip, the enquirer will gradually form the impression that there is one kind of man, probably only one kind of man, perhaps, only one man, who is really disliked. The voices take on quite a different tone in speaking of him; there is a hardening and solidification of disapproval and a new coldness in the air. And this will be all the more curious because, by the current modern theories of social or anti-social action, it will not be at all easy to say why he should be such a monster; or what exactly is the matter with him. It will be hinted at only in singular figures of speech, about a gentleman who is mistakenly convinced that he owns the street; or sometimes that he owns the earth. Then one of the social critics will say, "'E comes in 'ere and 'e thinks 'e's Gawd Almighty." Then the scientific enquirer will shut his note-book with a snap and retire from the scene, possibly after paying for any drinks he may have consumed in the cause of social science. He has got what he wanted. He has been intellectually justified. The man in the pub has precisely repeated, word for word, the theological formula about Satan.

Pride is a poison so very poisonous that it not only poisons the virtues; it even poisons the other vices. This is what is felt by the poor men in the public tavern, when they tolerate the tippler or the tipster or even the thief, but feel something fiendishly wrong with the man who bears so close a resemblance to God Almighty. And we all do in fact know that the primary sin of pride has this curiously freezing and hardening effect upon the other sins. A man may be very susceptible and in sex matters rather loose; he may waste himself on passing and unworthy passions, to the hurt of his soul; and yet always retain something which makes friendship with his own sex at least possible, and even faithful and satisfying. But once let that sort of man regard his own weakness as a strength, and you have somebody entirely different. You have the Lady-Killer; the most beastly of all possible bounders; the man whom his own sex almost always has the healthy instinct to hate and despise. A man may be naturally slothful and rather irresponsible; he may neglect many duties through carelessness, and his friends may still understand him, so long as it is really a careless carelessness. But it is the devil and all when it becomes a careful carelessness. It is the devil and all when he becomes a deliberate and self-conscious Bohemian, sponging on principle, preying on society in the name of his own genius (or rather of his own belief in his own genius), taxing the world like a king on the plea that he is a poet, and despising better men than himself who work that he may waste. It is no metaphor to say that it is the devil and all. By the same fine old original religious formula, it is all of the devil. We could go through any number of social types illustrating the same spiritual truth. It would be easy to point out that even the miser, who is half-ashamed of his madness, is a more human and sympathetic type than the millionaire who brags and boasts of his avarice and calls it sanity and simplicity and the strenuous life. It would be easy to point out that even cowardice, as a mere collapse of the nerves, is better than cowardice as an ideal and theory of the intellect; and that a really imaginative person will have more sympathy with men who, like cattle, yield to what they know is panic, than with a certain particular type of prig who preaches something that he calls peace. Men hate priggishness because it is the driest form of pride.

Thus there is a paradox in the whole position. The spiritual idea of the evil of pride, especially spiritual pride, was dismissed as a piece of mysticism not needed by modern morality, which is to be purely social and practical. And, as a fact, it is very specially needed because the morality is social and practical. On the assumption that we need care for nothing except making other human beings happy, this is quite certainly the thing that will make them unhappy. The practical case against pride, as a mere source of social discomfort and discord, is if possible even more self-evident than the more mystical case against it, as a setting up of the self against the soul of the world. And yet though we see this thing on every side in modern life, we really hear very little about it in modern literature and ethical theory. Indeed, a great deal of modern literature and ethics might be meant specially for the encouragement of spiritual pride. Scores of scribes and sages are busy writing about the importance of self-culture and self-realisation; about how every child is to be taught to develop his personality (whatever that may be); about how every man must devote himself to success, and every successful man must devote himself to developing a magnetic and compelling personality; about how every man may become a superman (by taking Our Correspondence Course) or, in the more sophisticated and artistic type of fiction, how one specially superior superman can learn to look down on the mere mob of ordinary supermen, who form the population of that peculiar world. Modern theory, as a whole, is rather encouraging egoism. But we need not be alarmed about that. Modern practice, being exactly like ancient practice, is still heartily discouraging it. The man with the strong magnetic personality is still the man whom those who know him best desire most warmly to kick out of the club. The man in a really acute stage of self-realisation is a no more pleasing object in the club than in the pub. Even the most enlightened and scientific sort of club can see through the superman; and see that he has become a bore. It is in practice that the philosophy of pride breaks down; by the test of the moral instincts of man wherever two or three are gathered together; and it is the mere experience of modern humanity that answers the modern heresy.

There is indeed another practical experience, known to us all, even more pungent and vivid than the actual unpopularity of the bully or the bumptious fool. We all know that there is a thing called egoism that is much deeper than egotism. Of all spiritual diseases it is the most intangible and the most intolerable. It is said to be allied to hysteria; it sometimes looks as if it were allied to diabolic possession. It is that condition in which the victim does a thousand varying things from one unvarying motive of a devouring vanity; and sulks or smiles, slanders or praises, conspires and intrigues or sits still and does nothing, all in one unsleeping vigilance over the social effect of one single person. It is amazing to me that in the modern world, that chatters perpetually about psychology and sociology, about the tyranny with which we are threatened by a few feeble-minded infants, about alcoholic poisoning and the treatment of neurotics, about half a hundred things that are near the subject and never on the spot—it is amazing that these moderns really have so very little to say about the cause and cure of a moral condition that poisons nearly every family and every circle of friends. There is hardly a practical psychologist who has anything to say about it that is half so illuminating as the literal exactitude of the old maxim of the priest; that pride is from hell. For there is something awfully vivid and appallingly fixed, about this madness at its worst, that makes that short and antiquated word seem much more apt than any other. And then, as I say, the learned go wandering away into discourses about drink or tobacco, about the wickedness of wine glasses or the incredible character of public-houses. The wickedest work in this world is symbolised not by a wine glass but by a looking-glass; and it is not done in public-houses, but in the most private of all private houses; which is a house of mirrors.

The phrase would probably be misunderstood; but I should begin my sermon by telling people not to enjoy themselves. I should tell them to enjoy dances and theatres and joy-rides and champagne and oysters; to enjoy jazz and cocktails and night-clubs if they can enjoy nothing better; to enjoy bigamy and burglary and any crime in the calendar, in preference to this other alternative; but never to learn to enjoy themselves. Human beings are happy so long as they retain the receptive power and the power of reaction in surprise and gratitude to something outside. So long as they have this they have, as the greatest minds have always declared, a something that is present in childhood and which can still preserve and invigorate manhood. The moment the self within is consciously felt as something superior to any of the gifts that can be brought to it, or any of the adventures that it may enjoy, there has appeared a sort of self-devouring fastidiousness and a disenchantment in advance, which fulfils all the Tartarean emblems of thirst and despair.

Difficulties can easily be raised, of course, in any such debate by the accident of words being used in different senses; and sometimes in quite contrary senses. For instance, when we speak of somebody being "proud of" something, as of a man being proud of his wife or a people proud of its heroes, we really mean something that is the very opposite of pride. For it implies that the man thinks that something outside himself is needed to give him great glory; and such a glory is really acknowledged as a gift. In the same way, the word will certainly be found misleading, if I say that the worst and most depressing element in the mixed elements of the present and the immediate future, seems to me to be an element of impudence. For there is a kind of impudence that we all find either amusing or bracing; as in the impudence of the guttersnipe. But there again the circumstances disarm the thing of its real evil. The quality commonly called "cheek" is not an assertion of superiority; but rather a bold attempt to balance inferiority. When you walk up to a very wealthy and powerful nobleman and playfully tip his hat over his eyes (as is your custom) you are not suggesting that you yourself are above all human follies, but rather that you are capable of them, and that he also ought to have a wider and richer experience of them. When you dig a Royal Duke in the waistcoat, in your playful manner, you are not taking yourself too seriously, but only, perhaps, not taking him so seriously as is usually thought correct. This sort of impudence may be open to criticism, as it is certainly subject to dangers. But there is a sort of hard intellectual impudence, which really treats itself as intangible to retort or judgment; and there are a certain number among the new generations and social movements, who fall into this fundamental weakness. It is a weakness; for it is simply settling down permanently to believe what even the vain and foolish can only believe by fits and starts, but what all men wish to believe and are often found weak enough to believe; that they themselves constitute the supreme standard of things. Pride consists in a man making his personality the only test, instead of making the truth the test. It is not pride to wish to do well, or even to look well, according to a real test. It is pride to think that a thing looks ill, because it does not look like something characteristic of oneself. Now in the general clouding of clear and abstract standards, there is a real tendency today for a young man (and even possibly a young woman) to fall back on that personal test, simply for lack of any trustworthy impersonal test. No standard being sufficiently secure for the self to be moulded to suit it, all standards may be moulded to suit the self. But the self as a self is a very small thing and something very like an accident. Hence arises a new kind of narrowness; which exists especially in those who boast of breadth. The sceptic feels himself too large to measure life by the largest things; and ends by measuring it by the smallest thing of all. There is produced also a sort of subconscious ossification; which hardens the mind not only against the traditions of the past, but even against the surprises of the future. *Nil admirari* becomes the motto of all nihilists; and it ends, in the most complete and exact sense, in nothing.

If I had only one sermon to preach, I certainly could not end it in honour, without testifying to what is in my knowledge the salt and preservative of all these things. This is but one of a thousand things in which I have found the Catholic Church to be right, when the whole world is perpetually tending to be wrong; and without its witness, I believe that this secret, at once a sanity and a subtlety, would be almost entirely forgotten among men. I know that I for one had hardly heard of positive humility until I came within the range of Catholic influence; and even the things that I love most, such as liberty and the island poetry of England, had in this matter lost the way; and were in a fog of self-deception. Indeed there is no better example of the definition of pride than the definition of patriotism. It is the noblest of all natural affections, exactly so long as it consists of saying, "May I be worthy of England." It is the beginning of one of the blindest forms of Pharisaism when the patriot is content to say, "I am an Englishman." And I cannot count it an accident that the patriot has generally seen the flag as a flame of vision, beyond and better than himself, in countries of the Catholic tradition, like France and Poland and Ireland; and has hardened into this heresy of admiring merely his own breed and bone and inherited type, and himself as a part of it, in the places most remote from that religion, whether in Berlin or Belfast. In short, if I had only one sermon to preach, it would be one that would profoundly annoy the congregation, by bringing to their attention the permanent challenge of the Church. If I had only one sermon to preach, I should feel specially confident that I should not be asked to preach another.

[From *The Common Man*]

❧ 12 ❧

THE FATHER BROWN STORIES

The Origin of Father Brown

The "Father Brown" detective short stories are Chesterton's best-
known works in fiction. These stories, about fifty in all, were originally written for various British periodicals, then collected in five volumes
from 1911 to 1935, and finally incorporated into the *Father Brown
Omnibus*. In the last chapter of his *Autobiography*, GKC describes the
origin of Father Brown:

BUT I mention these [lecture tours throughout England] here only
as leading up to that very accidental meeting in Yorkshire, which
was to have consequences for me rather beyond the appearance of
accident. I had gone to give a lecture at Keighley on the high moors of
the West Riding, and stayed the night with a leading citizen of that little
industrial town; who had assembled a group of local friends such as
could be conceived, I suppose, as likely to be patient with lecturers;
including the curate of the Roman Catholic Church; a small man with a
smooth face and a demure but elfish expression. I was struck by the tact
and humour with which he mingled with his very Yorkshire and very
Protestant company; and I soon found out that they had, in their bluff
way, already learned to appreciate him as something of a character. . . .

I liked him very much, but if you had told me that ten years afterwards I should be a Mormon Missionary in the Cannibal Islands, I
should not have been more surprised than at the suggestion that, fully
fifteen years afterwards, I should be making to him my General Confession and being received into the Church that he served.

Next morning he and I walked over Keighley Gate, the great wall of
the moors that separates Keighley from Wharfedale, for I was visiting
friends in Ilkley; and after a few hours talk on the moors, it was a new

friend whom I introduced to my old friends at my journey's end. He stayed to lunch; he stayed to tea; he stayed to dinner; I am not sure that, under their pressing hospitality, he did not stay the night; and he stayed there many nights and days on later occasions; and it was there that we most often met. It was on one of these visits that the incident occurred, which led me to take the liberty of putting him, or rather part of him, into a string of sensational stories. But I mention it, not because I attach any importance to those stories, but because it has a more vital connection with the other story; the story that I am telling here.

I mentioned to the priest in conversation that I proposed to support in print a certain proposal, it matters not what, in connection with some rather sordid social questions of vice and crime. On this particular point he thought I was in error, or rather in ignorance; and indeed I was. And, merely as a necessary duty and to prevent me from falling into a mare's nest, he told me certain facts he knew about perverted practices which I certainly shall not set down or discuss here. I have confessed on an earlier page that in my own youth I had imagined for myself any amount of iniquity; and it was a curious experience to find that this quiet and pleasant celibate had plumbed those abysses far deeper than I. I had not imagined that the world could hold such horrors. If he had been a professional novelist throwing such filth broadcast on all the bookstalls for boys and babies to pick up, of course he would have been a great creative artist and a herald of the Dawn. As he was only stating them reluctantly, in strict privacy, as a practical necessity, he was, of course, a typical Jesuit whispering poisonous secrets in my ear. When we returned to the house, we found it full of visitors, and fell into special conversation with two hearty and healthy young Cambridge undergraduates who had been walking or cycling across the moors in the spirit of the stern and vigorous English holiday. They were no narrow athletes, however, but interested in various sports and in a breezy way in various arts; and they began to discuss music and landscape with my friend Father O'Connor. I never knew a man who could turn with more ease than he from one topic to another, or who had more unexpected stores of information, often purely technical information, upon all. The talk soon deepened into a discussion on matters more philosophical and moral; and when the priest had left the room, the two young men broke out into generous expressions of admiration, saying truly that he was a remarkable man, and seemed to know a great deal about Palestrina or Baroque architecture, or whatever was the point at the moment. Then there fell a curious reflective silence, at the end of which one of the undergraduates suddenly burst out, "All the same, I don't believe his sort of life is the right one. It's all very well to like religious music and so on, when you're all shut up in a sort of cloister and don't know anything about the real evil in the world. But I don't believe that's the right ideal. I believe in a fellow coming out into the world, and facing the evil that's in it, and knowing something about the dangers and all that. It's a very beautiful thing to be innocent and ignorant; but I think it's a much finer thing not to be afraid of knowledge."

To me, still almost shivering with the appallingly practical facts of which the priest had warned me, this comment came with such a colossal and crushing irony, that I nearly burst into a loud harsh laugh in the drawing-room. For I knew perfectly well that, as regards all the solid Satanism which the priest knew and warred against with all his life, these two Cambridge gentlemen (luckily for them) knew about as much of real evil as two babies in the same perambulator.

And there sprang up in my mind the vague idea of making some artistic use of these comic yet tragic cross-purposes; and constructing a comedy in which a priest should appear to know nothing and in fact know more about crime than the criminals. I afterwards summed up the special idea in the story called "The Blue Cross," otherwise very slight and improbable, and continued it through the interminable series of tales with which I have afflicted the world. In short, I permitted myself the grave liberty of taking my friend and knocking him about; beating his hat and umbrella shapeless, untidying his clothes, punching his intelligent countenance into a condition of pudding-faced fatuity, and generally disguising Father O'Connor as Father Brown.

[From *Autobiography*]

Father Brown, Flambeau, and
Grandison Chace

Flambeau was an arch-criminal, a swindler and thief wanted by "the police of two hemispheres." In the story "The Blue Cross," Father Brown ingeniously outwits Flambeau, who nevertheless continues— for a while—in his life of crime. Flambeau's personality and previous exploits are described thus in "The Blue Cross":

IT is many years now since this colossus of crime suddenly ceased keeping the world in a turmoil; and when he ceased, as they said after the death of Roland, there was a great quiet upon the earth. But in his best days (I mean, of course, his worst) Flambeau was a figure as statuesque and international as the Kaiser. Almost every morning the daily paper announced that he had escaped the consequences of one extraordinary crime by committing another. He was a Gascon of gigantic stature and bodily daring; and the wildest tales were told of his outbursts of athletic humour; how he turned the *juge d'instruction* upside down and stood him on his head, "to clear his mind"; how he ran down the Rue de Rivoli with a policeman under each arm. It is due to him to say that his fantastic physical strength was generally employed in such bloodless though undignified scenes; his real crimes were chiefly those of ingenious and wholesale robbery. But each of his thefts was almost a new sin, and would make a story by itself. It was he who ran the great Tyrolean Dairy Company in London, with no dairies, no cows, no carts, no milk, but with some thousand subscribers. These he served by the simple operation of moving the little milk-cans outside people's doors to the doors of his own customers. . . . A sweeping simplicity, however, marked many of his experiments. It is said he once repainted all the numbers in a street in the dead of night merely to divert one traveller into a trap. It is quite certain that he invented a portable pillar-box, which he put up at corners in quiet suburbs on the chance of strangers dropping postal orders into it. Lastly he was known to be a startling acrobat; despite his huge figure, he could leap like a grasshopper and melt into the tree-tops like a monkey. . . .

[From *The Innocence of Father Brown*]

In the story "The Flying Stars," Flambeau commits his last crime, after which he becomes a friend and sometimes assistant to Father Brown. The story involves a masquerade at a wealthy man's home. Flambeau appears disguised as a distant relative of the host. He arranges the masquerade, disguises himself as a harlequin, and manages to steal the three enormous diamonds known as the "flying stars" from a visiting financier, Sir Leopold Fischer. The host's daughter is engaged to a young man who proclaims to be a socialist and who is suspected of the theft. Flambeau is escaping—he has just climbed a tree in the garden and is about to jump over the wall when Father Brown accosts him from below.

THE silvery figure among the green leaves seems to linger as if hypnotised, though his escape is easy behind him; he is staring at the man below.

"Oh, yes," says the man below, "I know all about it. I know you not only forced the pantomime, but put it to a double use. You were going to steal the stones quietly; and news came by an accomplice that you were already suspected, and a capable police officer was coming to rout you up that very night. A common thief would have been thankful for the warning and fled; but you are a poet. You already had the clever notion of hiding the jewels in a blaze of false stage jewellery. Now, you saw that if the dress were a harlequin's the appearance of a policeman would be quite in keeping. The worthy officer started from Putney police station to find you, and walked into the queerest trap ever set in this world. When the front door opened he walked straight on to the stage of a Christmas pantomime, where he could be kicked, clubbed, stunned and drugged by the dancing harlequin, amid roars of laughter from all the most respectable people in Putney. Oh, you will never do anything better. And now, by the way, you might give me back those diamonds."

The green branch on which the glittering figure swung, rustled as if in astonishment; but the voice went on:

"I want you to give them back, Flambeau, and I want you to give up this life. There is still youth and honour and humour in you; don't fancy they will last in that trade. Men may keep a sort of level of good, but no man has ever been able to keep on one level of evil. That road goes down and down. The kind man drinks and turns cruel; the frank man kills and lies about it. Many a man I've known started like you to be an honest outlaw, a merry robber of the rich, and ended stamped into slime. Maurice Blum started out as an anarchist of principle, a father of the poor; he ended a greasy spy and tale-bearer that both sides used and despised. Harry Burke started his free money movement sincerely enough; now he's sponging on a half-starved sister for endless brandies and sodas. Lord Amber went into wild society in a sort of chivalry; now he's paying blackmail to the lowest vultures in London. Captain Barillon was the great gentleman-apache before your time; he died in a madhouse, screaming with fear of the "narks" and receivers that had betrayed him and hunted him down. I know the woods look very free behind you, Flambeau; I know that in a flash you could melt into them like a monkey. But some day you will be an old grey monkey, Flambeau. You will sit up in your free forest cold at heart and close to death, and the tree-tops will be very bare."

Everything continued still, as if the small man below held the other in the tree in some long invisible leash; and he went on:

"Your downward steps have begun. You used to boast of doing nothing mean, but you are doing something mean tonight. You are leaving suspicion on an honest boy with a good deal against him already; you are separating him from the woman he loves and who loves him. But you will do meaner things than that before you die."

Three flashing diamonds fell from the tree to the turf. The small man stooped to pick them up, and when he looked up again the green cage of the tree was emptied of its silver bird.

The restoration of the gems (accidentally picked up by Father Brown, of all people) ended the evening in uproarious triumph; and Sir Leopold, in his height of good humour, even told the priest that though he himself had broader views, he could respect those whose creed required them to be cloistered and ignorant of this world.

[From *The Innocence of Father Brown*]

The first story in *The Secret of Father Brown* is not a detective adventure as such, but a story in which Father Brown explains his "method" to a friend of his, the American Grandison Chace. Chace has mentioned that certain groups in America, including the Second Sight Sisterhood of Indianapolis, apparently believe that Father Brown has some preternatural ability related to "thought-forms" by which he solves the crimes.

FATHER Brown was still staring at the stove; then he said quite loud, yet as if hardly aware that anyone heard him:

"Oh, I say. This will never do."

"I don't exactly know how it's to be helped," said Mr. Chace humorously. "The Second Sight Sisterhood want a lot of holding down. The only way I can think of stopping it is for you to tell us the secret after all."

Father Brown groaned. He put his head on his hands and remained a moment, as if full of a silent convulsion of thought. Then he lifted his head and said in a dull voice:

"Very well. I must tell the secret."

His eye rolled darkly over the whole darkling scene, from the red eyes of the little stove to the stark expanse of the ancient wall, over which were standing out, more and more brightly, the strong stars of the south.

"The secret is," he said; and then stopped as if unable to go on. Then he began again and said:

"You see, it was I who killed all those people."

"What?" repeated the other in a small voice out of a vast silence.

"You see, I had murdered them all myself," explained Father Brown patiently. "So, of course, I knew how it was done."

Grandison Chace had risen to his great height like a man lifted to the ceiling by a sort of slow explosion. Staring down at the other he repeated his incredulous question.

"I had planned out each of the crimes very carefully," went on Father Brown. "I had thought out exactly how a thing like that could be done, and in what style or state of mind a man could really do it. And when I was quite sure that I felt exactly like the murderer myself, of course I knew who he was."

Chace gradually released a sort of broken sigh.

"You frightened me all right," he said. "For the minute I really did think you meant you were the murderer. Just for the minute I kind of saw it splashed over all the papers in the States: 'Saintly Sleuth Exposed as Killer: Hundred Crimes of Father Brown.' Why, of course, if it's just a figure of speech and means you tried to reconstruct the psychology—"

Father Brown rapped sharply on the stove with the short pipe he was about to fill; one of his very rare spasms of annoyance contracted his face.

"No, no, no," he said, almost angrily. "I don't mean just a figure of speech. This is what comes of trying to talk about deep things. . . . What's the good of words? . . . If you try to talk about a truth that's merely moral, people will always think it's merely metaphorical. A real live man with two legs once said to me: 'I only believe in the Holy Ghost in a spiritual sense.' Naturally, I said: 'In what other sense could you believe it?' And *then* he thought I meant he needn't believe in anything except evolution, or ethical fellowship, or some bilge. . . . I mean that I really did see myself, and my real self, committing the murder. I didn't actually kill the men by material means; but that's not the point. Any brick or bit of machinery might have killed them by material means. I mean that I thought and thought about how a man might come to be like that, until I realised that I really *was* like that, in everything except actual final consent to the action. It was once suggested to me by a friend of mine, as a sort of religious exercise. I believe he got it from Pope Leo XIII, who was always rather a hero of mine."

"I'm afraid," said the American, in tones that were still doubtful, and keeping his eye on the priest rather as if he were a wild animal, "that you'd have to explain a lot to me, before I knew what you were talking about. The science of detection—"

Father Brown snapped his fingers with the same animated annoyance. "That's it," he cried, "that's just where we part company. Science is a grand thing when you can get it; in its real sense one of the grandest words in the world. But what do these men mean, nine times out of ten, when they use it nowadays? When they say detection is a science? When they say criminology is a science? They mean getting *outside* a man and studying him as if he were a gigantic insect; in what they would call a dry impartial light; in what I should call a dead and dehumanised light. They mean getting a long way off him, as if he were a distant prehistoric monster; staring at the shape of his 'criminal skull' as if it were a sort of eerie growth like the horn of a rhinoceros's nose. When the scientist talks about a type, he never means himself, but always his neighbour; probably his poorer neighbor. I don't deny the dry light may sometimes do good; though in one sense it's the very reverse of science. So far from being knowledge, it's actually suppression of what we know. It's treating a friend as a stranger, and pretending that something familiar is really remote and mysterious. It's like saying that a man has a proboscis between the eyes, or that he falls down in a fit of insensibility once every twenty-four hours. Well, what you call 'the secret' is exactly the opposite. I don't try to get outside the man. I try to get inside the murderer. . . . Indeed it's much more than that, don't you see? I *am* inside a man. I am always inside a man, moving his arms and legs; but I wait till I know I am inside a murderer, thinking his thoughts, wrestling with his passions; till I have bent myself into the posture of his hunched and peering hatred; till I see the world with his bloodshot and squinting eyes, looking between the blinkers of his half-witted concentration; looking up the short and sharp perspective of a straight road to a pool of blood. Till I am really a murderer."

"Oh," said Mr. Chace, regarding him with a long grim face, and added: "And that is what you call a religious exercise."

"Yes," said Father Brown. "That is what I call a religious exercise."
After an instant's silence he resumed, "It's so real a religious exercise that I'd rather not have said anything about it. But I simply couldn't have you going off and telling all your countrymen that I had a secret magic connected with Thought-Forms, could I? I've put it badly, but it's true. No man's really any good till he knows how bad he is, or might be; till he's realised exactly how much right he has to all this snobbery, and sneering, and talking about 'criminals,' as if they were apes in a forest ten thousand miles away; till he's got rid of all the dirty self-deception of talking about low types and deficient skulls; till he's squeezed out of his soul the last drop of the oil of the Pharisees; till his only hope is somehow or other to have captured one criminal, and kept him safe and sane under his own hat."

[From *The Secret of Father Brown*]

In the last story in *The Secret of Father Brown*, Father Brown and Grandison Chace are together again, this time at the home of one of Father Brown's friends known as Monsieur Duroc. Father Brown and Chace are speaking of the remoteness of crime and criminals.

"THERE are two ways of renouncing the devil," he [Father Brown] said; "and the difference is perhaps the deepest chasm in modern religion. One is to have a horror of him because he is so far off; and the other is to have it because he is so near. And no virtue and vice are so much divided as those two virtues."

They did not answer and he went on in the same heavy tone, as if he were dropping words like molten lead.

"You may think a crime horrible because you could never commit it. I think it horrible because I could commit it. You think of it as something like an eruption of Vesuvius; but that would not really be so terrible as this house catching fire. If a criminal suddenly appeared in this room—"

"If a criminal appeared in this room," said Chace, smiling, "I think you would be a good deal too favourable to him. Apparently you would start by telling him that you were a criminal yourself and explaining how perfectly natural it was that he should have picked his father's pocket or cut his mother's throat. Frankly, I don't think it's practical. I think that the practical effect would be that no criminal would ever reform. It's easy enough to theorize and take hypothetical cases; but we all know we're only talking in the air. Sitting here in M. Duroc's nice comfortable house, conscious of our respectability and all the rest of it, it just gives us a theatrical thrill to talk about thieves and murderers and the mysteries of their souls. But the people who really have to deal with thieves and murderers have to deal with them differently. We are safe by the fireside; and we know the house is not on fire. We know there is not a criminal in the room."

The M. Duroc to whom allusion had been made rose slowly from what had been called his fireside, and his huge shadow flung from the fire seemed to cover everything and darken even the very night above him.

"There *is* a criminal in this room," he said. "I am one. I am Flambeau, and the police of two hemispheres are still hunting for me."

The American remained gazing at him with eyes of stony brightness; he seemed unable to speak or move.

"There is nothing mystical or metaphorical or vicarious about my confession," said Flambeau. "I stole for twenty years with these two hands; I fled from the police on these two feet. I hope you will admit that my judges and pursuers really had to deal with crime. Do you think I do not know all about their way of reprehending it? Have I not heard the sermons of the righteous and seen the cold stare of the respectable; have I not been lectured in the lofty and distant style, asked how it was possible for anyone to fall so low, told that no decent person could ever have dreamed of such depravity? Do you think all that ever did anything but make me laugh? Only my friend told me that he knew exactly why I stole; and I have never stolen since."

Father Brown made a gesture as of deprecation; and Grandison Chace at last let out a long breath like a whistle.

"I have told you the exact truth," said Flambeau; "and it is open to you to hand me over to the police."

There was an instant of profound stillness in which could be faintly heard the belated laughter of Flambeau's children in the high dark house above them, and the crunching and snorting of the great grey pigs in the twilight. And then it was cloven by a high voice, vibrant and with a touch of offence, almost surprising for those who do not understand the sensitive American spirit and how near, in spite of commonplace contrasts, it can sometimes come to the chivalry of Spain.

"Monsieur Duroc," he said rather stiffly. "We have been friends, I hope, for some considerable period; and I should be pretty much pained to suppose you thought me capable of playing you such a trick while I was enjoying your hospitality, and the society of your family, merely because you chose to tell me a little of your own autobiography of your own free will. And when you spoke merely in defence of your friend—

no, sir, I can't imagine any gentleman double-crossing another under such circumstances; it would be a damned sight better to be a dirty informer and sell men's blood for money. But in a case like this—! Could you conceive any man being such a Judas?"

"I could try," said Father Brown.

[From *The Secret of Father Brown*]

The Conclusion of
"The Hammer of God"

This story involves two brothers, one of whom is found murdered. The Reverend Wilfrid Bohun is the curator of the village church. His brother, Colonel Bohun, was a dissolute philanderer who had been making a play for the blacksmith's wife. The Reverend Wilfrid is a sort of "loner," fond of exploring and praying in the galleries and high places of the church. The colonel was found killed by a tremendous blow from a hammer—the blow shattered the green steel helmet that he had been wearing. The blacksmith, who might have had the strength to commit the crime, has an unshakeable alibi. The village idiot is then suspected, and this suspicion is encouraged by the Reverend Wilfrid. In this climactic scene Father Brown and Wilfrid enter the church, and Father Brown climbs up onto one of the high galleries.

"COME up here, Mr. Bohun," he called. "The air will do you good."

Bohun followed him, and came out on a kind of stone gallery or balcony outside the building, from which one could see the illimitable plain in which their small hill stood, wooded away to the purple horizon and dotted with villages and farms. Clear and square, but quite small beneath them, was the blacksmith's yard, where the inspector still stood taking notes and the corpse still lay like a smashed fly.

"Might be the map of the world, mightn't it?" said Father Brown.

"Yes," said Bohun very gravely, and nodded his head. . . .

"I think there is something rather dangerous about standing on these high places even to pray," said Father Brown. "Heights were made to be looked at, not to be looked from."

"Do you mean that one may fall over," asked Wilfrid.

"I mean that one's soul may fall if one's body doesn't," said the other priest.

"I scarcely understand you," remarked Bohun indistinctly.

"Look at that blacksmith, for instance," went on Father Brown calmly; "a good man, but not a Christian—hard, imperious, unforgiving. Well, his Scotch religion was made up by men who prayed on hills and high crags, and learnt to look down on the world more than to look up at heaven. Humility is the mother of giants. One sees great things from the valley; only small things from the peak."

"But he—he didn't do it," said Bohun tremulously.

"No," said the other in an odd voice; "we know he didn't do it."

After a moment he resumed, looking tranquilly out over the plain with his pale grey eyes. "I knew a man," he said, "who began by worshipping with others before the altar, but who grew fond of high and lonely places to pray from, corners or niches in the belfry or the spire. And once in one of those dizzy places, where the whole world seemed to turn under him like a wheel, his brain turned also, and he fancied he was God. So that, though he was a good man, he committed a great crime."

Wilfrid's face was turned away, but his bony hands turned blue and white as they tightened on the parapet of stone.

"He thought it was given to *him* to judge the world and strike down the sinner. He would never have had such a thought if he had been kneeling with other men upon a floor. But he saw all men walking about like insects. He saw one especially strutting just below him, insolent and evident by a bright green hat—a poisonous insect."

Rooks cawed round the corners of the belfry; but there was no other sound till Father Brown went on.

"This also tempted him, that he had in his hand one of the most awful engines of nature; I mean gravitation, that mad and quickening rush by which all earth's creatures fly back to her heart when released. See, the inspector is strutting just below us in the smithy. If I were to toss a pebble over this parapet it would be something like a bullet by the time it struck him. If I were to drop a hammer—even a small hammer—"

Wilfrid Bohun threw one leg over the parapet, and Father Brown had him in a minute by the collar.

"Not by that door," he said quite gently; "that door leads to hell."

Bohun staggered back against the wall, and stared at him with frightful eyes.

"How do you know all this?" he cried. "Are you a devil?"

"I am a man," answered Father Brown gravely; "and therefore have all devils in my heart. Listen to me," he said after a short pause. "I know what you did—at least, I can guess the great part of it. When you left your brother you were racked with no unrighteous rage, to the extent even that you snatched up a small hammer, half inclined to kill him with his foulness on his mouth. Recoiling, you thrust it under your buttoned coat instead, and rushed into the church. You pray wildly in many places, under the angel window, upon the platform above, and a higher platform still, from which you could see the colonel's Eastern hat like the back of a green beetle crawling about. Then something snapped in your soul, and you let God's thunderbolt fall."

Wilfrid put a weak hand to his head, and asked in a low voice: "How did you know that his hat looked like a green beetle?"

"Oh, that," said the other with the shadow of a smile, "that was common sense. But hear me further. I say I know all this; but no one else shall know it. The next step is for you; I shall take no more steps; I will seal this with the seal of confession. If you ask me why, there are many reasons, and only one that concerns you. I leave things to you because you have not yet gone very far wrong, as assassins go. You did not help to fix the crime on the smith when it was easy; or on his wife, when that was easy. You tried to fix it on the imbecile because you knew that he could not suffer. That was one of the gleams that it is my business to find in assassins. And now come down into the village, and go your own way as free as the wind; for I have said my last word."

They went down the winding stairs in utter silence, and came out into the sunlight by the smithy. Wilfrid Bohun carefully unlatched the wooden gate of the yard, and going up to the inspector, said: "I wish to give myself up; I have killed my brother."

[From *The Innocence of Father Brown*]

The Conclusion of
"The Chief Mourner of Marne"

This story involves a strange duel. Because of a rivalry, James Mair and his cousin, Maurice Mair, fight a duel. Maurice, who is a poor shot, falls, and James, immediately overcome by remorse, rushes to help him. Later, "James" travels abroad for several years and then secludes himself, as the Marquis of Marne, in his castle. His rather superficial and remote friends, who think that he has been unduly influenced by priestly teachings, want him to end his self-penance. Father Brown reasons to the correct story, which is this: Maurice faked his fall in the duel and shot James at point-blank range after James rushed over to help him. It was *Maurice*, and not James, who travelled and hid himself, not as an act of penance but to keep his identity secret. Maurice has finally repented of his crime. Because of the circumstances, there is a dramatic encounter between the Marquis and a woman who used to be James' friend, and it is necessary for Father Brown to reveal the secrets of the murder, the changed identity, and Maurice's repentance.

THE rest of the company had risen and stood staring down at the narrator with pale faces. "Are you sure of this?" asked Sir John at last, in a thick voice.

"I am sure of it," said Father Brown, "and now I leave Maurice Mair, the present Marquis of Marne, to your Christian charity. You seemed to me to give it almost too large a place; but how fortunate it is for poor sinners like this man that you err so much on the side of mercy, and are ready to be reconciled to all mankind."

"Hang it all," exploded the general, "if you think I'm going to be reconciled to a filthy viper like that, I tell you I wouldn't say a word to save him from hell. I said I could pardon a regular decent duel, but of all the treacherous assassins—"

"He ought to be lynched," cried Cockspur excitedly. "He ought to burn alive like a nigger in the States. And if there is such a thing as burning forever, he jolly well—"

"I wouldn't touch him with a barge pole myself," said Mallow.

"There is a limit to human charity," said Lady Outram, trembling all over.

"There is," said Father Brown drily," and that is the real difference between human charity and Christian charity. You must forgive me if I was not altogether crushed by your contempt for my uncharitableness today; or by the lectures you read me about pardon for every sinner. For it seems to me that you only pardon the sins that you don't really think sinful. You only forgive criminals when they commit what you don't regard as crimes, but rather as conventions. So you tolerate a conventional duel, just as you tolerate a conventional divorce. You forgive because there isn't anything to be forgiven."

"But hang it all," cried Mallow, "you don't expect us to be able to pardon a vile thing like this?"

"No," said the priest, "but *we* have to be able to pardon it."

He stood up abruptly and looked round at them.

"We have to touch such men, not with a barge pole, but with a benediction," he said. "We have to say the word that will save them from hell. We alone are left to deliver them from despair when your human charity deserts them. Go on your own primrose path pardoning all your favourite vices and being generous to your fashionable crimes; and leave us in the darkness, vampires of the night, to console those who really need consolation; who do things really indefensible, things that neither the world nor they themselves can defend; and none but a priest will pardon. Leave us with the men who commit the mean and revolting and real crimes; mean as St. Peter when the cock crew, and yet the dawn came."

"The dawn," repeated Mallow doubtfully. "You mean hope—for *him?*"

"Yes," replied the other. "Let me ask you one question. You are great ladies and men of honour and secure of yourselves; you would never, you can tell yourselves, stoop to such squalid treason as that. But tell me this. If any of you had so stooped, which of you, years afterwards, when you were old and rich and safe, would have been driven by conscience or confessor to tell such a story of yourself? You say you could not commit so base a crime. Could you confess so base a crime?"

The others gathered their possessions together and drifted by twos and threes out of the room in silence. And Father Brown, also in silence, went back to the melancholy castle of Marne.

[From *The Secret of Father Brown*]

The Last Paragraph

This is the last paragraph of the last Father Brown story, which is entitled "The Insoluble Problem."

H E raised his eyes and saw through the veil of incense smoke and of twinkling lights that Benediction was drawing to its end while the procession waited. The sense of accumulated riches of time and tradition pressed past him like a crowd moving in rank after rank, through unending centuries; and high above them all, like a garland of unfading flames, like the sun of our mortal midnight, the great monstrance blazed against the darkness of the vaulted shadows, as it blazes against the black enigma of the universe. For some are convinced that this enigma also is an Insoluble Problem. And others have equal certitude that it has but one solution.

[From *The Scandal of Father Brown*]

❧ 13 ❧

EXCERPTS FROM
ST. THOMAS AQUINAS

Remarks by Étienne Gilson, noted philosopher and exponent of Thomism:
Chesterton makes one despair. I have been studying St. Thomas all
my life and I could never have written such a book.

[From Maisie Ward, *Gilbert Keith Chesterton*]

I consider it as being without possible comparison the best book ever
written on St. Thomas. Nothing short of genius can account for such
an achievement. Everybody will no doubt admit that it is a "clever"
book, but the few readers who have spent twenty or thirty years in
studying St. Thomas Aquinas, and who, perhaps, have themselves
published two or three volumes on the subject, cannot fail to perceive
that the so-called "wit" of Chesterton has put their scholarship to
shame. He has guessed all that which they had tried to demonstrate,
and he has said all that which they were more or less clumsily attempting to express in academic formulas. Chesterton was one of the deepest thinkers who ever existed; he was deep because he was right; and
he could not help being right; but he could not either help being
modest and charitable, so he left it to those who could understand him
to know that he was right, and deep; to the others, he apologized for
being right, and he made up for being deep by being witty. That is all
they can see of him.

[From Cyril Clemens, *Chesterton as Seen by His Contemporaries*]

IT will not be possible to conceal much longer from anybody the fact
that St. Thomas Aquinas was one of the great liberators of the human
intellect. The sectarians of the seventeenth and eighteenth centuries
were essentially obscurantists, and they guarded an obscurantist legend

that the Schoolman was an obscurantist. This was wearing thin even in the nineteenth century; it will be impossible in the twentieth. It has nothing to do with the truth of their theology or his; but only with the truth of historical proportion, which begins to reappear as quarrels begin to die down. Simply as one of the facts that bulk big in history, it is true to say that Thomas was a very great man who reconciled religion with reason, who expanded it towards experimental science, who insisted that the senses were the windows of the soul and that the reason had a divine right to feed upon facts, and that it was the business of the Faith to digest the strong meat of the toughest and most practical of pagan philosophies. It is a fact, like the military strategy of Napoleon, that Aquinas was thus fighting for all that is liberal and enlightened, as compared with his rivals, or for that matter his successors and supplanters. Those who, for other reasons, honestly accept the final effect of the Reformation will none the less face the fact, that it was the Schoolman who was the Reformer; and that the later Reformers were by comparison reactionaries. I use the word not as a reproach from my own standpoint, but as a fact from the ordinary modern progressive standpoint. For instance, they riveted the mind back to the literal sufficiency of the Hebrew Scriptures; when St. Thomas had already spoken of the Spirit giving grace to the Greek philosophies. He insisted on the social duty of works; they only on the spiritual duty of faith. It was the very life of the Thomist teaching that Reason can be trusted: it was the very life of the Lutheran teaching that Reason is utterly untrustworthy.

[From Chapter 1]

NOBODY can understand the greatness of the thirteenth century, who does not realise that it was a great growth of new things produced by a living thing. In that sense it was really bolder and freer than what we call the Renaissance, which was a resurrection of old things discovered in a dead thing. In that sense medievalism was not a Renascence, but rather a Nascence. It did not model its temples upon the tombs, or call up dead gods from Hades. It made an architecture as new as modern engineering: indeed it still remains the most modern architecture. Only it was followed at the Renaissance by a more antiquated architecture. In that sense the Renaissance might be called the Relapse. Whatever may be said of the Gothic and the Gospel according to St. Thomas, they were not a Relapse. It was a new thrust like the titanic thrust of Gothic engineering; and its strength was in a God who makes all things new.

[From Chapter 1]

WHEN we praise the practical value of the Aristotelian Revolution, and the originality of Aquinas in leading it, we do not mean that the Scholastic philosophers before him had not been philosophers, or had not been highly philosophical, or had not been in touch with ancient philosophy. In so far as there was ever a bad break in philosophical history, it was not before St. Thomas, or at the beginning of medieval history; it was after St. Thomas and at the beginning of modern history. The great intellectual tradition that comes down to us from Pythagoras and Plato was never interrupted or lost through such trifles as the sack of Rome, the triumph of Attila or all the barbarian invasions of the Dark Ages. It was only lost after the introduction of printing, the discovery of America, the founding of the Royal Society and all the enlightenment of the Renaissance and the modern world. It was there, if anywhere, that there was lost or impatiently snapped the long thin delicate thread that had descended from distant antiquity; the thread of that unusual human hobby; the habit of thinking. This is proved by the fact that the printed books of this later period largely had to wait for the eighteenth century, or the end of the seventeenth century, to find even the names of the new philosophers; who were at the best a new kind of philosophers. But the decline of the Empire, the Dark Ages and the early Middle Ages, though too much tempted to neglect what was opposed to Platonic philosophy, had never neglected philosophy. In that sense St. Thomas, like most other very original men, has a long and clear pedigree. He himself is constantly referring back to the authorities from St. Augustine to St. Anselm, and from St. Anselm to St. Albert, and even when he differs, he also defers.

[From Chapter 3]

H IS main business was to defend the Faith against the abuse of Aristotle; and he boldly did it by supporting the use of Aristotle. He knew perfectly well that armies of atheists and anarchists were roaring applause in the background at his Aristotelian victory over all he held most dear. Nevertheless, it was never the existence of atheists, any more than Arabs or Aristotelian pagans, that disturbed the extraordinary controversial composure of Thomas Aquinas. The real peril that followed on the victory he had won for Aristotle was vividly presented in the curious case of Siger of Brabant; and it is well worth study, for anyone who would begin to comprehend the strange history of Christendom. It is marked by one rather queer quality; which has always been the unique note of the Faith, though it is not noticed by its modern enemies, and rarely by its modern friends. It is the fact symbolised in the legend of Antichrist, who was the double of Christ; in the profound proverb that the Devil is the ape of God. It is the fact that falsehood is never so false as when it is very nearly true. It is when the stab comes near the nerve of truth, that the Christian conscience cries out in pain. And Siger of Brabant, following on some of the Arabian Aristotelians, advanced a theory which most modern newspaper readers would instantly have declared to be the same as the theory of St. Thomas. That was what finally roused St. Thomas to his last and most emphatic protest. He had won his battle for a wider scope of philosophy and science; he had cleared the ground for a general understanding about faith and enquiry; an understanding that has generally been observed among Catholics, and certainly never deserted without disaster. It was the idea that the scientist should go on exploring and experimenting freely, so long as he did not claim an infallibility and finality which it was against his own principles to claim. Meanwhile the Church should go on developing and defining, about supernatural things, so long as she did not claim a right to alter the deposit of faith, which it was against her own principles to claim. And when he had said this, Siger of Brabant got up and said something so horribly like it, and so horribly unlike, that (like Antichrist) he might have deceived the very elect.

Siger of Brabant said this: the Church must be right theologically, but she can be wrong scientifically. There are two truths; the truth of the supernatural world, and the truth of the natural world, which contradicts the supernatural world. While we are being naturalists, we can suppose that Christianity is all nonsense; but then, when we remember that we are Christians, we must admit that Christianity is true even if it is nonsense. In other words, Siger of Brabant split the human head in two, like the blow in an old legend of battle; and declared that a man has two minds, with one of which he must entirely believe and with the other may utterly disbelieve. To many this would at least seem like a parody of Thomism. As a fact, it was the assassination of Thomism. It was not two ways of finding the same truth; it was an untruthful way of pretending that there are two truths. And it is extraordinarily interesting to note that this is the one occasion when the Dumb Ox really came out like a wild bull. When he stood up to answer Siger of Brabant, he was altogether transfigured, and the very style of his sentences, which is a thing like the tone of a man's voice, is suddenly altered. He had never been angry with any of the enemies who disagreed with him. But these enemies had attempted the worst treachery: they had made him agree with him.

Those who complain that theologians draw fine distinctions could hardly find a better example of their own folly. In fact, a fine distinction can be a flat contradiction. It was notably so in this case. St. Thomas was willing to allow the one truth to be approached by two paths, precisely *because* he was sure there was only one truth. Because the Faith was the one truth, nothing discovered in nature could ultimately contradict the Faith. Because the Faith was the one truth, nothing really deduced from the Faith could ultimately contradict the facts. It was in truth a curiously daring confidence in the reality of his religion; and though some may linger to dispute it, it has been justified. The scientific facts, which were supposed to contradict the Faith in the nineteenth century, are nearly all of them regarded as unscientific fictions in the twentieth century. Even the materialists have fled from materialism; and those who lectured us about determinism in psychology are already talking about indeterminism in matter. But whether his confidence was right or wrong, it was specially and supremely a confidence that there is one truth which cannot contradict itself.

[From Chapter 3]

THIS great intellectual creation was a Christian and Catholic creation and cannot be understood as anything else. It was Aquinas who baptised Aristotle, when Aristotle could not have baptised Aquinas; it was a purely Christian miracle which raised the great Pagan from the dead. And this is proved in three ways (as St. Thomas himself might say), which it will be well to summarise as a sort of summary of this book.

First, in the life of St. Thomas, it is proved in the fact that only his huge and solid orthodoxy could have supported so many things which then seemed to be unorthodox. Charity covers a multitude of sins; and in that sense orthodoxy covers a multitude of heresies; or things which are hastily mistaken for heresies. It was precisely because his personal Catholicism was so convincing, that his impersonal Aristotelianism was given the benefit of the doubt. He did not smell of the faggot because he did smell of the firebrand; of the firebrand he had so instantly and instinctively snatched up, under a real assault on essential Catholic ethics. A typically cynical modern phrase refers to the man who is so good that he is good for nothing. St. Thomas was so good that he was good for everything; that his warrant held good for what others considered the most wild and daring speculations, ending in the worship of nothing. Whether or no he baptised Aristotle, he was truly the godfather of Aristotle; he was his sponsor; he swore that the old Greek would do no harm; and the whole world trusted his word.

Second, in the philosophy of St. Thomas, it is proved by the fact that everything depended on the new Christian *motive* for the study of facts, as distinct from truths. The Thomist philosophy began with the lowest roots of thought, the senses and the truisms of the reason; and a Pagan sage might have scorned such things, as he scorned the servile arts. But the materialism, which is merely cynicism in a Pagan, can be Christian humility in a Christian. St. Thomas was willing to begin by recording the facts and sensations of the material world, just as he would have been willing to begin by washing up the plates and dishes in the monastery. The point of his Aristotelianism was that even if common sense about concrete things really was a sort of servile labour, he must not be ashamed to be *servus servorum Dei*. Among heathens the mere sceptic might become the mere cynic; Diogenes in his tub had always a touch of the tub-thumper; but even the dirt of the cynics was dignified into dust and ashes among the saints. If we miss that, we miss the whole meaning of the greatest revolution in history. There was a new *motive* for beginning with the most material, and even with the meanest things.

Third, in the theology of St. Thomas, it is proved by the tremendous truth that supports all that theology; or any other Christian theology. There really was a new reason for regarding the senses, and the sensations of the body, and the experiences of the common man, with a reverence at which great Aristotle would have stared, and no man in the ancient world could have begun to understand. The Body was no longer what it was when Plato and Porphyry and the old mystics had left it for dead. It had hung upon a gibbet. It had risen from a tomb. It was no longer possible for the soul to despise the senses, which had been the organs of something that was more than man. Plato might despise the flesh; but God had not despised it. The senses had truly become sanctified; as they are blessed one by one at a Catholic baptism. "Seeing is believing" was no longer the platitude of a mere idiot, or common individual, as in Plato's world; it was mixed up with real conditions of real belief. Those revolving mirrors that send messages to the brain of man, that light that breaks upon the brain, these had truly revealed to God himself the path to Bethany or the light on the high rock of Jerusalem. These ears that resound with common noises had reported also to the secret knowledge of God the noise of the crowd that strewed palms and the crowd that cried for Crucifixion. After the Incarnation had become the idea that is central in our civilisation, it was inevitable that there should be a return to materialism, in the sense of the serious value of matter and the making of the body. When once Christ had risen, it was inevitable that Aristotle should rise again.

Those are three real reasons, and very sufficient reasons, for the general support given by the saint to a solid and objective philosophy. And yet there was something else, very vast and vague, to which I have tried to give a faint expression by the interposition of this chapter. It is difficult to express it fully, without the awful peril of being popular, or what the Modernists quite wrongly imagine to be popular; in short, passing from religion to religiosity. But there is a general tone and temper of Aquinas, which it is as difficult to avoid as daylight in a great house of windows. It is that *positive* position of his mind, which is filled and soaked as with sunshine with the warmth of the wonder of created things. There is a certain private audacity, in his communion, by which men add to their private names the tremendous titles of the Trinity and the Redemption; so that some nun may be called "of the Holy Ghost"; or a man bear such a burden as the title of St. John of the Cross. In this sense, the man we study may specially be called St. Thomas of the Creator. The Arabs have a phrase about the hundred names of God; but they also inherit the tradition of a tremendous name unspeakable because it expresses Being itself, dumb and yet dreadful as an instant inaudible shout; the proclamation of the Absolute. And perhaps no other man ever came so near to calling the Creator by His own name, which can only be written I Am.

[From Chapter 4]

THE philosophy of St. Thomas stands founded on the universal common conviction that eggs are eggs. The Hegelian may say that an egg is really a hen, because it is a part of an endless process of Becoming; the Berkeleian may hold that poached eggs only exist as a dream exists; since it is quite as easy to call the dream the cause of the eggs as the eggs the cause of the dream; the Pragmatist may believe that we get the best out of scrambled eggs by forgetting that they ever were eggs, and only remembering the scramble. But no pupil of St. Thomas needs to addle his brains in order adequately to addle his eggs; to put his head at any peculiar angle in looking at eggs, or squinting at eggs, or winking the other eye in order to see a new simplification of eggs. The Thomist stands in the broad daylight of the brotherhood of men, in their common consciousness that eggs are not hens or dreams or mere practical assumptions; but things attested by the Authority of the Senses, which is from God.

Thus, even those who appreciate the metaphysical depth of Thomism in other matters have expressed surprise that he does not deal at all with what many now think the main metaphysical question; whether we can prove that the primary act of recognition of any reality is real. The answer is that St. Thomas recognised instantly, what so many modern sceptics have begun to suspect rather laboriously; that a man must either answer that question in the affirmative, or else never answer any question, never ask any question, never even exist intellectually, to answer or to ask. I suppose it is true in a sense that a man can be a fundamental sceptic, but he cannot be anything else; certainly not even a defender of fundamental scepticism. If a man feels that all the movements of his own mind are meaningless, then his mind is meaningless, and he is meaningless; and it does not mean anything to attempt to discover his meaning. Most fundamental sceptics appear to survive, because they are not consistently sceptical and not at all fundamental. They will first deny everything and then admit something, if for the sake of argument—or often rather of attack without argument. I saw an almost startling example of this essential frivolity in the professor of final scepticism, in a paper the other day. A man wrote to say that he accepted nothing but Solipsism, and added that he had often wondered it was not a more common philosophy. Now Solipsism simply means that a man believes in his own existence, but not in anybody or anything else. And it never struck this simple sophist, that if his philosophy was true, there obviously were no other philosophers to profess it.

[From Chapter 6]

S T. Thomas Aquinas closely resembles the great Professor Huxley, the Agnostic who invented the word Agnosticism. He is like him in his way of starting the argument, and he is unlike everybody else, before and after, until the Huxleyan age. He adopts almost literally the Huxleyan definition of the Agnostic method; "To follow reason as far as it will go"; the only question is—where does it go? He lays down the almost startlingly modern or materialist statement; "Everything that is in the intellect has been in the senses." This is where he began, as much as any modern man of science, nay, as much as any modern materialist who can now hardly be called a man of science; at the very opposite end of enquiry from that of the mere mystic. The Platonists, or at least the Neo-Platonists, all tended to the view that the mind was lit entirely from within; St. Thomas insisted that it was lit by five windows, that we call the windows of the senses. But he wanted the light from without to shine on what was within. He wanted to study the nature of Man, and not merely of such moss and mushrooms as he might see through the window, and which he valued as the first enlightening experience of man. And starting from this point, he proceeds to climb the House of Man, step by step and story by story, until he has come out on the highest tower and beheld the largest vision.

In other words, he is an anthropologist, with a complete theory of Man, right or wrong. Now the modern Anthropologists, who call themselves Agnostics, completely failed to be Anthropologists at all. Under their limitations, they could not get a complete theory of Man, let alone a complete theory of nature. They began by ruling out something which they called the Unknowable. The incomprehensibility was almost comprehensible, if we could really understand the Unknowable in the sense of the Ultimate. But it rapidly became apparent that all sorts of things were Unknowable, which were exactly the things that a man has got to know. It is necessary to know whether he is responsible or irresponsible, perfect or imperfect, perfectible or unperfectible, mortal or immortal, doomed or free, not in order to understand God, but in order to understand Man. Nothing that leaves these things under a cloud of religious doubt can possibly pretend to be a Science of Man; it shrinks from anthropology as completely as from theology. Has a man free will; or is his sense of choice an illusion? Has he a conscience, or has his conscience any authority; or is it only the prejudice of the tribal past? Is there any real hope of settling these things by human reason; and has *that* any authority? Is he to regard death as final; and is he to regard miraculous help as possible? Now it is all nonsense to say that these are unknowable in any remote sense, like the distinction between the Cherubim and the Seraphim, or the Procession of the Holy Ghost. The Schoolmen may have shot too far beyond our limits in pursuing the Cherubim and Seraphim. But in asking whether a man can choose or whether a man will die, they were asking ordinary questions in n..tural history; like whether a cat can scratch or whether a dog can smell. Nothing calling itself a complete Science of Man can shirk them. And the great Agnostics did shirk them.

[From Chapter 7]

AQUINAS has affirmed that our first sense of fact is a fact; and he cannot go back on it without falsehood. But when we come to look at the fact or facts, as we know them, we observe that they have a rather queer character; which has made many moderns grow strangely and restlessly sceptical about them. For instance, they are largely in a state of change, from being one thing to being another; or their qualities are relative to other things; or they appear to move incessantly; or they appear to vanish entirely. At this point, as I say, many sages lose hold of the first principle of reality, which they would concede at first; and fall back on saying that there is nothing except change; or nothing except comparison; or nothing except flux; or in effect that there is nothing at all. Aquinas turns the whole argument the other way, keeping in line with his first realisation of reality. There is no doubt about the being of being, even if it does sometimes look like becoming; that is because what we see is not the fullness of being; or (to continue a sort of colloquial slang) we never see being being as much as it can. Ice is melted into cold water and cold water is heated into hot water; it cannot be all three at once. But this does not make water unreal or even relative; it only means that its being is limited to being one thing at a time. But the fullness of being is everything that it can be; and without it the lesser or approximate forms of being cannot be explained as anything; unless they are explained away as nothing.

This crude outline can only at the best be historical rather than philosophical. It is impossible to compress into it the metaphysical proofs of such an idea; especially in the medieval metaphysical language. But this distinction in philosophy is tremendous as a turning point in history. Most thinkers, on realising the apparent mutability of being, have really forgotten their own realisation of the being, and believed only in the mutability. They cannot even say that a thing changes into another thing; for them there is no instant in the process at which it is a thing at all. It is only a change. It would be more logical to call it nothing changing into nothing, than to say (on these principles) that there ever was or will be a moment when the thing is itself. St. Thomas maintains that the ordinary thing at any moment is something; but it is not everything that it could be. There is a fullness of being, in which it could be everything that it can be. Thus, while most sages come at last to nothing but naked change, he comes to the ultimate thing that is unchangeable, because it is all the other things at once. While they describe a change which is really a change in nothing, he describes a changelessness which includes the changes of everything. Things change because they are not complete; but their reality can only be explained as part of something that is complete. It is God.

[From Chapter 7]

S T. Thomas could as truly say, of having seen merely a stick or a stone, what St. Paul said of having seen the rending of the secret heavens, "I was not disobedient to the heavenly vision." For though the stick or the stone is an earthly vision, it is through them that St. Thomas finds his way to heaven; and the point is that he is obedient to the vision; he does not go back on it. Nearly all the other sages who have led or misled mankind do, on one excuse or another, go back on it. They dissolve the stick or the stone in chemical solutions of scepticism; either in the medium of mere time and change; or in the difficulties of classification of unique units; or in the difficulty of recognising variety while admitting unity. The first of these three is called debate about flux or formless transition; the second is the debate about Nominalism and Realism, or the existence of general ideas; the third is called the ancient metaphysical riddle of the One and the Many. But they can all be reduced under a rough image to this same statement about St. Thomas. He is still true to the first truth and refusing the first treason. He will not deny what he has seen, though it be a secondary and diverse reality. He will not take away the numbers he first thought of, though there may be quite a number of them.

He has seen grass; and will not say he has not seen grass, because it today is and tomorrow is cast into the oven. That is the substance of all scepticism about change, transition, transformism and the rest. He will not say that there is no grass but only growth. If grass grows and withers, it can only mean that it is part of a greater thing, which is even more real; not that the grass is less real than it looks. St. Thomas has a really logical right to say, in the words of the modern mystic, A.E.: "I begin by the grass to be bound again to the Lord."

He has seen grass and grain; and he will not say that they do not differ, because there is something common to grass and grain. Nor will he say that there is nothing common to grass and grain, because they do really differ. He will not say, with the extreme Nominalists, that because grain can be differentiated into all sorts of fruitage, or grass trodden into mire with any kind of weed, therefore there can be no *classification* to distinguish weeds from slime or to draw a fine distinction between cattle-food and cattle. He will not say with the extreme Platonists, on the other hand, that he saw the perfect fruit in his own head by shutting his eyes, *before* he saw any difference between grain and grass. He saw one thing and then another thing, and then a common quality; but he does not pretend that he saw the quality before the thing.

He has seen grass and gravel; that is to say, he has seen things really different; things not classified together like grass and grain. The first flash of fact shows us a world of really strange things; not merely strange to us, but strange to each other. The separate things need have nothing in common except Being. Everything is Being; but it is not true that everything is Unity. It is here, as I have said, that St. Thomas does definitely, one might say defiantly, part company with the Pantheist and the Monist. All things are; but among the things that are is the thing called difference, quite as much as the thing called similarity. And here again we begin to be bound again to the Lord, not only by the universality of grass, but by the incompatibility of grass and gravel. For this world of different and varied beings is especially the world of the Christian Creator; the world of created things, like things made by an artist; as compared with the world that is only one thing, with a sort of shimmering and shifting veil of misleading change; which is the conception of so many of the ancient religions of Asia and the modern sophistries of Germany. In the face of these, St. Thomas still stands stubborn in the same obstinate objective fidelity. He has seen grass and gravel; and he is not disobedient to the heavenly vision.

To sum up; the reality of things, the mutability of things, the diversity of things, and all other such things that can be attributed to things, is followed carefully by the medieval philosopher, without losing touch with the original point of the reality. There is no space in this book to specify the thousand steps of thought by which he shows that he is right.

But the point is that, even apart from being right, he is real. He is a realist in a rather curious sense of his own, which is a third thing, distinct from the almost contrary medieval and modern meanings of the word. Even the doubts and difficulties about reality have driven him to believe in more reality rather than less. The *deceitfulness* of things which has had so sad an effect on so many sages, has almost a contrary effect on this sage. If things deceive us, it is by being more real than they seem. As ends in themselves they always deceive us; but as things tending to a greater end, they are even more real than we think them. If they seem to have a relative unreality (so to speak) it is because they are potential and not actual; they are unfulfilled, like packets of seeds or boxes of fireworks. They have it in them to be more real than they are. And there is an upper world of what the Schoolmen called Fruition, or Fulfillment, in which all this relative relativity becomes actuality; in which the trees burst into flower or the rockets into flame.

Here I leave the reader, on the very lowest rung of those ladders of logic, by which St. Thomas besieged and mounted the House of Man. It is enough to say that by arguments as honest and laborious, he climbed up to the turrets and talked with angels on the roofs of gold. This is, in a very rude outline, his philosophy; it is impossible in such an outline to describe his theology. Anyone writing so small a book about so big a man, must leave out something. Those who know him best will best understand why, after some considerable consideration, I have left out the only important thing.

[From Chapter 7]

M. Maritain has used an admirable metaphor, in his book *Theonas,* when he says that the external fact *fertilises* the internal intelligence, as the bee fertilises the flower. Anyhow, upon that marriage, or whatever it may be called, the whole system of St. Thomas is founded; God made Man so that he was capable of coming in contact with reality; and those whom God hath joined, let no man put asunder.

Now, it is worthy of remark that it is the only working philosophy. Of nearly all other philosophies it is strictly true that their followers work in spite of them, or do not work at all. No sceptics work sceptically; no fatalists work fatalistically; all without exception work on the principle that it is possible to assume what it is not possible to believe. No materialist who thinks his mind was made up for him, by mud and blood and heredity, has any hesitation in making up his mind. No sceptic who believes that truth is subjective has any hesitation about treating it as objective.

Thus St. Thomas' work has a constructive quality absent from almost all cosmic systems after him. For he is already building a house, while the newer speculators are still at the stage of testing the rungs of a ladder, demonstrating the hopeless softness of the unbaked bricks, chemically analysing the spirit in the spirit-level, and generally quarrelling about whether they can even make the tools that will make the house. Aquinas is whole intellectual aeons ahead of them, over and above the common chronological sense of saying a man is in advance of his age; he is ages in advance of our age. For he has thrown out a bridge across the abyss of the first doubt, and found reality beyond and begun to build on it. Most modern philosophies are not philosophy but philosophic doubt; that is, doubt about whether there can be any philosophy. If we accept St. Thomas' fundamental act or argument in the acceptance of reality, the further deductions from it will be equally real; they will be things and not words. Unlike Kant and most of the Hegelians, he has a faith that is not merely a doubt about doubt. It is not merely what is commonly called a faith about faith; it is a faith about fact. From this point he can go forward, and deduce and develop and decide, like a man planning a city and sitting in a judgment-seat. But never since that time has any thinking man of that eminence thought that there is any real evidence for anything, not even the evidence of his senses, that was strong enough to bear the weight of a definite deduction.

[From Chapter 8]

Remarks by Maisie Ward:
When we were told that Gilbert was writing a book on St. Thomas and that we might have the American rights, my husband felt a quiver of apprehension. Was Chesterton for once undertaking a task beyond his knowledge? Such masses of research had recently been done on St. Thomas by experts of such high standing and he could not possibly have read it all. Nor should we have been entirely reassured had we heard what Dorothy Collins told us later concerning the writing of it.

He began by rapidly dictating to Dorothy about half the book. So far he had consulted no authorities but at this stage he said to her: "I want you to go to London and get me some books."

"What books?" asked Dorothy.

"I don't know," said G. K.

She wrote therefore to Father O'Connor and from him got a list of classic and more recent books on St. Thomas. G. K. "flipped them rapidly through," which is, says Dorothy, the only way she ever saw him read, and then dictated to her the rest of his own book without referring to them again.

[From Maisie Ward, *Gilbert Keith Chesterton*]

Remark by Hugh Kenner:
When late in life he came to grips with systematic philosophy, he was able to produce without apparent effort a profound study of St. Thomas Aquinas, because St. Thomas expounded in an orderly and systematic fashion what Gilbert Chesterton had been seeing and saying all his life.

[From Hugh Kenner, *Paradox in Chesterton*]

❧ 14 ❧

THE ARCHITECT
OF SPEARS

THE other day, in the town of Lincoln, I suffered an optical illusion which accidentally revealed to me the strange greatness of the Gothic architecture. Its secret is not, I think, satisfactorily explained in most of the discussions on the subject. It is said that the Gothic eclipses the classical by a certain richness and complexity, at once lively and mysterious. This is true; but Oriental decoration is equally rich and complex, yet it awakens a widely different sentiment. No man ever got out of a Turkey carpet the emotions that he got from a cathedral tower. Over all the exquisite ornament of Arabia and India there is the presence of something stiff and heartless, of something tortured and silent. Dwarfed trees and crooked serpents, heavy flowers and hunchbacked birds accentuate by the very splendour and contrast of their colour the servility and monotony of their shapes. It is like the vision of a sneering sage, who sees the whole universe as a pattern. Certainly no one ever felt like this about Gothic, even if he happens to dislike it. Or, again, some will say that it is the liberty of the Middle Ages in the use of the comic or even the coarse that makes the Gothic more interesting than the Greek. There is more truth in this; indeed, there is real truth in it. Few of the old Christian cathedrals would have passed the Censor of Plays. We talk of the inimitable grandeur of the old cathedrals; but indeed it is rather their gaiety that we do not dare to imitate. We should be rather surprised if a chorister suddenly began singing "Bill Bailey" in church. Yet that would only be doing in music what the medievals did in sculpture. They put into a Miserere seat the very scenes that we put into a music-hall song: comic domestic scenes similar to the spilling of the beer and the hanging out of the washing. But though the gaiety of Gothic is one of its features, it also is not the secret of its unique effect. We see a domestic topsy-turvydom in many Japanese sketches. But delightful as these are, with their fairy tree-tops, paper houses, and toddling, infantile inhabitants, the pleasure they give is of a kind quite different from the joy and

227

energy of the gargoyles. Some have even been so shallow and illiterate as to maintain that our pleasure in medieval building is a mere pleasure in what is barbaric, in what is rough, shapeless, or crumbling like the rocks. This can be dismissed after the same fashion; South Sea idols, with painted eyes and radiating bristles, are a delight to the eye; but they do not affect it in at all the same way as Westminster Abbey. Some again (going to another and almost equally foolish extreme) ignore the coarse and comic in medievalism; and praise the pointed arch only for its utter purity and simplicity, as of a saint with his hands joined in prayer. Here, again, the uniqueness is missed. There are Renaissance things (such as the ethereal silvery drawings of Raphael), there are even pagan things (such as the Praying Boy) which express as fresh and austere a piety. None of these explanations explain. And I never saw what was the real point about Gothic till I came into the town of Lincoln, and saw it behind a row of furniture-vans.

I did not know they were furniture-vans; at the first glance and in the smoky distance I thought they were a row of cottages. A low stone wall cut off the wheels, and the vans were somewhat of the same colour as the yellowish clay or stone of the buildings around them. I had come across that interminable Eastern plain which is like the open sea, and all the more so because the one small hill and tower of Lincoln stands up in it like a lighthouse. I had climbed the sharp, crooked streets up to this ecclesiastical citadel; just in front of me was a flourishing and richly coloured kitchen garden; beyond that was the low stone wall; beyond that the row of vans that looked like houses; and beyond and above that, straight and swift and dark, light as a flight of birds, and terrible as the Tower of Babel, Lincoln Cathedral seemed to rise out of human sight.

As I looked at it I asked myself the questions that I have asked here; what was the soul in all those stones? They were varied, but it was not variety; they were solemn, but it was not solemnity; they were farcical, but it was not farce. What is it in them that thrills and soothes a man of our blood and history, that is not there in an Egyptian pyramid or an Indian temple or a Chinese pagoda? All of a sudden the vans I had mistaken for cottages began to move away to the left. In the start this gave to my eye and mind I really fancied that the Cathedral was moving towards the right. The two huge towers seemed to start striding across the plain like the two legs of some giant whose body was covered with the clouds. Then I saw what it was.

The truth about Gothic is, first, that it is alive, and second, that it is on the march. It is the Church Militant; it is the only fighting architecture. All its spires are spears at rest; and all its stones are stones asleep in a catapult. In that instant of illusion, I could hear the arches clash like swords as they crossed each other. The mighty and numberless columns seemed to go swinging by like the huge feet of imperial elephants. The graven foliage wreathed and blew like banners going into battle; the silence was deafening with all the mingled noises of a military march; the great bell shook down, as the organ shook up its thunder. The thirsty-throated gargoyles shouted like trumpets from all the roofs and pinnacles as they passed; and from the lectern in the core of the cathedral the eagle of the awful evangelist clashed his wings of brass.

And amid all the noises I seemed to hear the voice of a man shouting in the midst like one ordering regiments hither and thither in the fight; the voice of the great half-military master-builder; the architect of spears. I could almost fancy he wore armour while he made that church; and I knew indeed that, under a scriptural figure, he had borne in either hand the trowel and the sword.

I could imagine for the moment that the whole of that house of life had marched out of the sacred East, alive and interlocked, like an army. Some Eastern nomad had found it solid and silent in the red circle of the desert. He had slept by it as by a world-forgotten pyramid; and had been woke at midnight by the wings of stone and brass, the tramping of the tall pillars, the trumpets of the waterspouts. On such a night every snake or sea-beast must have turned and twisted in every crypt or corner of the architecture. And the fiercely coloured saints marching eternally in the flamboyant windows would have carried their glorioles like torches across dark lands and distant seas; till the whole mountain of music and darkness and lights descended roaring on the lonely Lincoln hill. So for some hundred and sixty seconds I saw the battle-beauty of the Gothic; then the last furniture-van shifted itself away; and I saw only a church tower in a quiet English town, round which the English birds were floating.

[From *A Miscellany of Men*]

15

SOCIAL AND POLITICAL POEMS

Elegy in a Country Churchyard

The men that worked for England
They have their graves at home:
And bees and birds of England
About the cross can roam.

But they that fought for England,
Following a falling star,
Alas, alas for England
They have their graves afar.

And they that rule in England,
In stately conclave met,
Alas, alas for England
They have no graves as yet.

[From *The Ballad of St. Barbara*]

By a Reactionary

Smoke rolls in stinking, suffocating wrack
On Shakespeare's land, turning the green one black;
The crowds that once to harvest home would come
Hope for no harvest and possess no home,
While poor old tramps that liked a little ale,
In natural procession pass to gaol;
Because the world must, like the tramp, move on,
There does not seem much else that can be done.

As Lord Vangelt said in the House of Peers:
"None of us want Reaction." (Tory cheers.)

So doubtful doctors punch and prod and prick
A man thought dead; and when there's not a kick
Left in the corpse, no twitch or faint contraction;
The doctors say: "See . . . there is no Reaction."

[From *The Collected Poems of G. K. Chesterton*]

The Secret People

Smile at us, pay us, pass us; but do not quite forget;
For we are the people of England, that never have spoken yet.
There is many a fat farmer that drinks less cheerfully,
There is many a free French peasant who is richer and sadder than
we.
There are no folk in the whole world so helpless or so wise.
There is hunger in our bellies, there is laughter in our eyes;
You laugh at us and love us, both mugs and eyes are wet;
Only you do not know us. For we have not spoken yet.

The fine French kings came over in a flutter of flags and dames.
We liked their smiles and battles, but we never could say their
names.
The blood ran red to Bosworth and the high French lords went
down;
There was naught but a naked people under a naked crown.
And the eyes of the King's Servants turned terribly every way,
And the gold of the King's Servants rose higher every day.
They burnt the homes of the shaven men, that had been quaint
and kind,
Till there was no bed in a monk's house, nor food that man could
find.
The inns of God where no man paid, that were the wall of the
weak,
The King's Servants ate them all. And still we did not speak.

And the face of the King's Servants grew greater than the King:
He tricked them, and they trapped him, and stood round him in a
ring.

231

The new grave lords closed round him, that had eaten the abbey's
    fruits,
And the men of the new religion, with their bibles in their boots,
We saw their shoulders moving, to menace or discuss,
And some were pure and some were vile; but none took heed of
    us.
We saw the King as they killed him, and his face was proud and
    pale;
And a few men talked of freedom, while England talked of ale.

A war that we understood not came over the world and woke
Americans, Frenchmen, Irish; but we knew not the things they
    spoke.
They talked about rights and nature and peace and the people's
    reign:
And the squires, our masters, bade us fight; and scorned us never
    again.
Weak if we be for ever, none could condemn us then;
Men called us serfs and drudges; men knew that we were men.
In foam and flame at Trafalgar, on Albuera plains,
We did and died like lions, to keep ourselves in chains.
We lay in living ruins; firing and fearing not
The strange fierce face of the Frenchmen who knew for what they
    fought,
And the man who seemed to be more than man we strained
    against and broke;
And we broke our own rights with him. And still we never spoke.

Our patch of glory ended; we never heard guns again.
But the squire seemed struck in the saddle; he was foolish, as if in
    pain.
He leaned on a staggering lawyer, he clutched a cringing Jew,
He was stricken; it may be, after all, he was stricken at Waterloo.
Or perhaps the shades of the shaven men, whose spoil is in his
    house,
Come back in shining shapes at last to spoil his last carouse:
We only know the last sad squires ride slowly towards the sea,
And a new people takes the land: and still it is not we.

They have given us into the hand of new unhappy lords,
Lords without anger and honour, who dare not carry their
    swords.

They fight by shuffling papers; they have bright dead alien eyes;
They look at our labour and laughter as a tired man looks at flies.
And the load of their loveless pity is worse than the ancient
    wrongs,
Their doors are shut in the evening; and they know no songs.

We hear men speaking for us of new laws strong and sweet,
Yet is there no man speaketh as we speak in the street.
It may be we shall rise the last as Frenchmen rose the first,
Our wrath come after Russia's wrath and our wrath be the worst.
It may be we are meant to mark with our riot and our rest
God's scorn for all men governing. It may be beer is best.
But we are the people of England; and we have not spoken yet.
Smile at us, pay us, pass us. But do not quite forget.

[From *Poems*]

Note: The "King's Servants" in the second stanza were the high-placed civil servants of
Henry VIII who carried out the confiscation of the monasteries. The "King's Servants" in the third stanza were the group of noblemen who killed King Charles I in
1649.

The Old Song
(On the Embankment
in Stormy Weather)

A livid sky on London
And like the iron steeds that rear
A shock of engines halted,
And I knew the end was near:
And something said that far away, over the hills and far away,
There came a crawling thunder and the end of all things here.
For London Bridge is broken down, broken down, broken down,
As digging lets the daylight on the sunken streets of yore,
The lightning looked on London town, the broken bridge of
    London town,
The ending of a broken road where men shall go no more.

I saw the kings of London town,
The kings that buy and sell,
They built it up with penny loaves
And penny lies as well:

And where the streets were paved with gold the shrivelled paper
    shone for gold,
The scorching light of promises that pave the streets of hell.
For penny loaves will melt away, melt away, melt away,
Mock the mean that haggled in the grain they did not grow;
With hungry faces in the gate, a hundred thousand in the gate,
A thunder-flash on London and the finding of the foe.

I heard the hundred pin-makers
Slow down their racking din,
Till in the stillness men could hear
The dropping of the pin:
And somewhere men without the wall, beneath the wood, without
    the wall,
Had found the place where London ends and England can begin.
For pins and needles bend and break, bend and break, bend and
    break,
Faster than the breaking spears or the bending of the bow,
Of pageants pale in thunder-light, 'twixt thunder-load and
    thunder-light,
The Hundreds marching on the hills in the wars of long ago.

I saw great Cobbett riding,
The horseman of the shires;
And his face was red with judgment
And a light of Luddite fires:
And south to Sussex and the sea the lights leapt up for liberty,
The trumpet of the yeomanry, the hammer of the squires;
For bars of iron rust away, rust away, rust away,
Rend before the hammer and the horseman riding in,
Crying that all men at the last, and at the worst and at the last,
Have found the place where England ends and England can begin.

His horse-hoofs go before you,
Far beyond your bursting tyres;
And time is bridged behind him
And our sons are with our sires.
A trailing meteor on the Downs he rides above the rotting towns,
The Horseman of Apocalypse, the Rider of the Shires.

For London Bridge is broken down, broken down, broken down;
Blow the horn of Huntingdon from Scotland to the sea—
. . . Only a flash of thunder-light, a flying dream of thunder-light,
Had shown under the shattered sky a people that were free.

[From *The Ballad of St. Barbara*]

Notes: William Cobbett (1762–1835) was a pugnacious idealist and propagandist, a
farmer who wrote a hundred books. He was devoted to a rural, self-sufficient England, and he was strongly opposed to the banking system, stockjobbers, public
corruption, sinecures, and "tax-eaters." Chesterton's biography of Cobbett was published in 1925.

The Luddites were broadloom weavers and framework knitters who lost their
jobs because of mechanization. In 1811 they began rioting and destroying textile-mill machinery.

The Appeal of the Peers

(On their rejection of Mr. Lloyd George's land budget of 1909)

Would you call upon the people; in what ear shall it be told?
Call on God, whose name is pity, though our sins be very old.
Will you call on street and township? Who but you have made the
    smoke
Something heavier than a vapour? Something sharper than a joke?
Who but you have taxed the townsmen of their tired and ugly
    tilth?
Who but you have made men forfeit for their right to live in filth?

Will you call on croft and village? On what village will you call
That four centuries of your lordship have not left a tithe too
    small?
Hamlets breaking, homesteads drifting, peasants tramping, towns
    erased:
Lo, my lords, we gave you England, and you gave us back a
    waste.
Yea, a desert labelled England, where you know (and well you
    know)
That the village Hampdens wither and the village idiots grow;
That the pride of grass grows mighty and the hope of men grows
    small.
Will you call on croft and village? Let the rabbits hear your call.

Will you call on crest and scutcheon? We might heed you, if we
knew
Even one gutter-thief whose millions could not cut his way to
you.
If there lived on earth one upstart from whose filthy face you
shrank,
We would hear, my lords, more gravely of the grace and scorn of
rank.
Now, if in your mob of merchants, usurers, idlers, cads, you keep
One that did have Norman fathers, let your Norman fathers sleep.
Let God's good grass grow above them, where their pointed
pennons blew;
They were thieves and thugs and smiters; they were better men
than you!

Will you call on cross and altar? And in God's name where were
you
When the crashing walls of convents let the Tudor axes through?
Tell us of your deeds, Crusaders. Waken Ariosto's muse;
How you stood the church's champion, when the church had land
to lose—
You, the Russells, with the ashes of a hundred altars shod,
You, the Howards, with your wallets bursting with the gold of
God.
Will you call on cross and altar? Will you name the holy name?
No, by Heaven, you shall not name it. Smite your very mouths
for shame!
Would you call upon the people? Would you waken these things
then?
Call on God, whose name is Pity—Do not ask too much of men!

[From *Forever Freedom*]

☙ 16 ❧

SOCIETY, HISTORY, POLITICS

Essay Excerpts

IT is the fashion to talk of institutions as cold and cramping things. The truth is that when people are in exceptionally high spirits, really wild with freedom and invention, they always must, and they always do, create institutions. When men are weary they fall into anarchy; but while they are gay and vigorous they invariably make rules. This, which is true of all the churches and republics of history, is also true of the most trivial parlour game or the most unsophisticated meadow romp. We are never free until some institution frees us, and liberty cannot exist till it is declared by authority.

[From *Manalive*]

OUR civilization has decided, and very justly decided, that determining the guilt or innocence of men is a thing too important to be trusted to trained men. If it wishes for light upon that awful matter, it asks men who know no more law than I know, but who can feel the things that I felt in the jury box. When it wants a library catalogued, or the solar system discovered, or any trifle of that kind, it uses up its specialists. But when it wishes anything done which is really serious, it collects twelve of the ordinary men standing round. The same thing was done, if I remember right, by the Founder of Christianity.

[From *Tremendous Trifles*]

237

I know not where that man hides and cowers, probably among the millions who had fled to the criminal dens and lairs of the United States, who actually originated the phrase about "making good." If I knew who he was, I would write a life of him; having first killed him, of course, to make the biography complete. He must have been rather a great man in his own perverted and repulsive fashion, for he managed to sum up the supreme essential falsehood of a whole century and a whole civilization in one exactly appropriate phrase, a phrase that is all the more appropriate because it is idiotic. He must be rather like one of the great poisoners, for indeed he has poisoned the whole modern mind. He must be much more than one of the great conspirators, for, as Mr. Wells would say, it is an entirely open conspiracy. He has managed to put all the current contemporary philosophies into one phrase that means nothing. Everybody whose instincts are on the side of such sophistry instantly seizes on it, because of its ambiguity. With one single twist of bad grammar or bad logic, it tangles up together the two things that have been in sharp contrast and contradiction in every decent religion or moral system in history—the idea of moral greatness and the idea of mere material success. And yet making good is not even making sense. It will not really serve to make a sentence, let alone a good sentence or a true sentence.

Thus we can say of one of these abject beings who happen to live in Hoxton or the Harrow Road that he makes good beer-barrels; that he makes good drain-pipes; that he makes good penny-whistles or good pork-pies; but not that he makes good. It does not make sense; it does not make a sentence. And this ambiguous phrase about making good was invented because it was ambiguous; it was invented by the man who did not make pies or pipes or barrels or anything in the East End, but only scooped the profit on other men's work and went off with it to live in the West End. That is all that is meant by making good. It did not matter so much so long as people refrained from describing it as making good; so long as they were content to describe it as making money. Considered merely as one of the mild forms of rascality very common among human beings, it might really be described as mild or even as human. But by the fatal and blasting hypocrisy of this one American catchword, it was transformed from a matter of unmoral adventure to a matter of thoroughly immoral morality. The phrase "making good," merely because it contains the word "good," always carries some shadowy suggestion that the man who has merely done well for himself must also have really done well; done well as in the old creeds and codes of morals; done well in the sight of God and humanity. And that is not merely immorality, it is blasphemy; for it is practically saying that the selfish man is the saint, and that Judas with the bag is greater than Jesus with the cross.

[From *All I Survey*]

I believe that if by some method the local public-house could be as definite and isolated a place as the local post office or the local railway station, if all types of people passed through it for all types of refreshment, you would have the same safeguard against a man behaving in a disgusting way in a tavern that you have at present against his behaving in a disgusting way in a post office: simply the presence of his ordinary sensible neighbors. In such a place the kind of lunatic who wants to drink an unlimited number of whiskies would be treated with the same severity with which the post-office authorities would treat an amiable lunatic who had an appetite for licking an unlimited number of stamps. It is a small matter whether in either case a technical refusal would be officially employed. It is an essential matter that in both cases the authorities could rapidly communicate with the friends and family of the mentally afflicted person. At least, the postmistress would not dangle a strip of tempting sixpenny stamps before the enthusiast's eyes as he was being dragged away with his tongue out. If we made drinking open and official we might be taking one step towards making it careless. In such things to be careless is to be sane: for neither drunkards nor Moslems can be careless about drink.

[From *All Things Considered*]

THE disadvantage of men not knowing the past is that they do not know the present. History is a hill or high point of vantage, from which alone men see the town in which they live or the age in which they are living. Without some such contrast or comparison, without some such shifting of the point of view, we should see nothing whatever of our own social surroundings. We should take them for granted, as the only possible social surroundings. We should be as unconscious of them as we are, for the most part, of the hair growing on our heads or the air passing through our lungs. It is the variety of the human story that brings out sharply the last turn that the road has taken, and it is the view under the arch of the gateway which tells us that we are entering a town.

[From *All I Survey*]

THE vital mistake that is made about the French Revolution is merely this—that every one talks about it as the introduction of a new idea. It was not the introduction of a new idea; there are no new ideas. Or if there are new ideas, they would not cause the least irritation if they were introduced into political society; because the world having never got used to them there would be no mass of men ready to fight for them at a moment's notice. That which was irritating about the French Revolution was this—that it was not the introduction of a new ideal, but the practical fulfillment of an old one. From the time of the first fairy tales men had always believed ideally in equality; they had always thought that something ought to be done, if anything could be done, to redress the balance between Cinderella and the ugly sisters. The irritating thing about the French was not that they said this ought to be done; everybody said that. The irritating thing about the French was that they did it. They proposed to carry out into a positive scheme what had been the vision of humanity; and humanity was naturally annoyed. The kings of Europe did not make war upon the Revolution because it was a blasphemy, but because it was a copy-book maxim which had been just too accurately copied. It was a platitude which they had always held in theory unexpectedly put into practice. The tyrants did not hate democracy because it was a paradox; they hated it because it was a truism which seemed in some danger of coming true.

[From *Appreciations and Criticisms of the Works of Charles Dickens*]

IF you wish for a sharp test to divide the true romantic from the false (a valuable thing when considering the claims of a poet, a son-in-law, or a professor of modern history), about the best I can think of is this: that the false romantic likes castles as much as cathedrals. If the poet or the lover admires the ruins of a feudal fortress as much as the ruins of a religious house, then what he admires is ruins; and he is a ruin himself. He likes medievalism because it is now dead, not because it was once alive; and his pleasure in the poetic past is as frivolous as a fancy-dress ball. For the castles only bear witness to ambitions, to ambitions that are dead; dead by being frustrated or dead by being fulfilled. But the cathedrals bear witness not to ambitions but to ideals; and to ideals that are still alive. They are more than alive, indeed they are immortal because they are ideals that no man has ever been able either to frustrate or to fulfill.

[From *Lunacy and Letters*]

Note: Both Chesterton and Hilaire Belloc elaborated the socio-economic concepts of Distributism, GKC in *The Outline of Sanity* and Belloc in *The Servile State*. These ideas were the basis of the Distributist League, of which Chesterton was the first president. Distributism advocated a greater and more equitable distribution of property; GKC and Belloc believed that a man should be able to own his own home and a farmer his own farm, in contrast to the prevalent notorious concentration of property in the hands of the few. Like all of the recent Popes from Leo XIII on, Chesterton was opposed alike to state socialism and to laissez-faire big business, both of which he saw as being socially despotic and resulting in a dull, inferior standardization of products. In this growing "business government" he detected disturbing trends:

P RIVATE things are already public in the worst sense of the word; that is, they are impersonal and dehumanized. Public things are already private in the worst sense of the word; that is, they are mysterious and secretive and largely corrupt. The new sort of Business Government will combine everything that is bad in all the plans for a better world. There will be no eccentricity; no humour; no noble disdain of the world. There will be nothing but a loathsome thing called Social Service; which means slavery without loyalty.

[From *The Outline of Sanity*]

I have long been acquainted, and not a little amused, with the sort of practical man who will certainly say that I generalize because there is no practical plan. The truth is that I generalize because there are so many practical plans. I know myself four or five schemes that have been drawn up, more or less drastically, for the diffusion of capital. The most cautious, from a capitalist standpoint, is the gradual extension of profit-sharing. A more stringently democratic form of the same thing is the management of every business (if it *cannot* be a small business) by a guild or group clubbing their contributions and dividing their results. Some Distributists dislike the idea of the workman having shares only where he has work; they think he would be more independent if his little capital were invested elsewhere; but they all agree that he ought to have the capital to invest. Others continue to call themselves Distributists because they would give every citizen a dividend out of much larger national systems of production. I deliberately draw out my general principles so as to cover as many as possible of these alternative business schemes. But I object to being told that I am covering so many because I know there are none. If I tell a man he is too luxurious and extravagant, and that he ought to economize in something, I am not bound to give him a list of his luxuries. The point is that he will be all the better for cutting down any of his luxuries. And my point is that modern society would be all the better for cutting up property by any of these processes. This does not mean that I have not my own favourite form; personally I prefer the second type of division given in the above list of examples. But my main business is to point out that *any* reversal of the rush to concentrate property will be an improvement on the present state of things.

[From *The Outline of Sanity*]

PERHAPS it may startle you, but I am a Bolshevist. By that I mean a democratic Bolshevist, and not a Socialistic Bolshevist. I do not believe in any one class, either the capitalistic or official, ruling the masses. I believe that the best interests of freedom will be obtained by a general distribution of property among as many of the people as possible. This would, of course, entail the breaking up of the large landed estates of England, but it is the only means to an end.

[From the *New York American*, 11 January 1921]

Note: Chesterton praised local, autonomous developments in culture and the arts, of which he pointed out numerous examples— from the building of cathedrals in the Middle Ages to the making of subtly different kinds of cheeses in many small English villages. And he opposed the tendency towards widespread standardization of products, a development often related to economic imperialism:

> Our principal exports, all labelled and packed,
> At the ends of the earth are delivered intact:
> Our soap or our salmon can travel in tins
> Between the two poles and as like as two pins;
> So that Lancashire merchants whenever they like
> Can water the beer of a man in Klondike
> Or poison the meat of a man in Bombay;
> And that is the meaning of Empire Day.

[From *The Ballad of St. Barbara;*
excerpt from the poem "Songs of Education: II. Geography"]

YOU will hear everlastingly, in all discussions about newspapers, companies, aristocracies, or party politics, this argument that the rich man cannot be bribed. The fact is, of course, that the rich man is bribed; he has been bribed already. That is why he is a rich man. The whole case for Christianity is that a man who is dependent upon the luxuries of this life is a corrupt man, spiritually corrupt, politically corrupt, financially corrupt. There is one thing that Christ and all the Christian saints have said with a sort of savage monotony. They have said simply that to be rich is to be in peculiar danger of moral wreck. It is not demonstrably un-Christian to kill the rich as violaters of definable justice. It is not demonstrably un-Christian to crown the rich as convenient rulers of society. It is not certainly un-Christian to rebel against the rich or to submit to the rich. But it is quite certainly un-Christian to trust the rich, to regard the rich as more morally safe than the poor.

[From *Orthodoxy*]

IT is really not so repulsive to see the poor asking for money as to see the rich asking for more money. And advertisement is the rich asking for more money. A man would be annoyed if he found himself in a mob of millionaires, all holding out their silk hats for a penny; or all shouting with one voice, "Give me money." Yet advertisement does really assault the eye very much as such a shout would assault the ear. "Budge's Boots are the Best" simply means "Give me money"; "Use Seraphic Soap" simply means "Give me money." It is a complete mistake to suppose that common people make our towns commonplace, with unsightly things like advertisements. Most of those whose wares are thus placarded everywhere are very wealthy gentlemen with coronets and country seats, men who are probably very particular about the artistic adornment of their own homes. They disfigure their towns in order to decorate their houses.

[From *The New Jerusalem*]

WE are incessantly told, indeed, that the modern scientific appliances, even those like the telephone, which are now universally applied, are the miracles of man, and the marvels of science, and the wonders of the new world. But though the inventions are talked of in this way, they are not treated in this way. Or, rather, if they are so talked of in theory, they are not so talked of in practice. There has certainly been a rush of discovery, a rapid series of inventions; and, in one sense, the activity is marvellous and the rapidity might well look like magic. But it has been a rapidity in things going stale; a rush downhill to the flat and dreary world of the prosaic; a haste of marvellous things to lose their marvellous character; a deluge of wonders to destroy wonder. This may be the improvement of machinery, but it cannot possibly be the improvement of man. And since it is not the improvement of man, it cannot possibly be progress. Man is the creature that progress professes to improve; it is not a race of wheels against wheels, or a wrestling match of engines against engines.

[From *As I Was Saying*]

I am certain that nothing solid can be built . . . upon the utterly unphilosophical philosophy of blind buying and selling; of bullying people into purchasing what they do not want; of making it badly so that they may break it and imagine that they want it again; of keeping rubbish in rapid circulation like a dust-storm in a desert.

[From *The Well and the Shallows*]

FEUDAL manorial life was not a democracy; but it could have been much more easily turned into a democracy. Later peasant life, as in France or Switzerland, actually has been quite easily turned into a democracy. But it is horribly hard to turn what is called modern industrial democracy into a democracy.

That is why many men are now beginning to say that the democratic ideal is no longer in touch with the modern spirit. I strongly agree; and I naturally prefer the democratic ideal, which is at least an ideal, and therefore, an idea, to the modern spirit, which is simply modern and, therefore, already becoming ancient. I notice that the cranks, whom it would be more polite to call the idealists, are already hastening to shed this ideal. A well-known Pacifist, with whom I argued in Radical papers in my Radical days, and who then passed as a pattern Republican of the New Republic, went out of his way the other day to say, "The voice of the people is commonly the voice of Satan." The truth is that these Liberals never did really believe in popular government, any more than in anything else that was popular, such as public-houses or the Dublin Sweepstake. They did not believe in the democracy they invoked against kings and priests. But I did believe in it; and I do believe in it, though I much preferred to invoke it against prigs and faddists. I still believe it would be the most human sort of government, if it could be once more attempted in a more human time.

Unfortunately, humanitarianism has been the mark of an unhuman time. And by inhumanity, I do not mean merely cruelty; I mean the condition in which even cruelty ceases to be human. I mean the condition in which the rich man, instead of hanging six or seven of his enemies because he hates them, merely beggars and starves to death six or seven thousand people whom he does not hate, and has never seen, because they live at the other side of the world. I mean the condition in which the courtier or pander of the rich man, instead of excitedly mixing a rare, original poison for the Borgias, or carving an exquisite ornamental poignard for the political purposes of the Medici, works monotonously in a factory turning out a small type of screw, which will fit into a plate he will never see; to form part of a gun he will never see; to be used in a battle he will never see, and about the merits of which he knows far less than the Renaissance rascal knew about the purposes of the poison and the dagger. In short, what is the matter with industrialism is indirection; the fact that nothing is straightforward; that all its ways are crooked even when they are meant to be straight. Into this most indirect of all systems we tried to fit the most direct of all ideas. Democracy, an ideal which is simple to excess, was vainly applied to a society which was complex to the point of craziness. It is not so very surprising that such a vision has faded in such an environment. Personally, I like the vision; but it takes all sorts to make a world, and there are actually human beings, walking about quite calmly in the daylight, who appear to like the environment.

[From *All I Survey*]

I read in any number of *New Leaders* and Labour weeklies, and all sorts of papers supposed to be both progressive and popular, that the working-classes will now take over the government of the country; that the majority of manual workers will have their proper proportional right to rule in all matters of education and humanitarian reform; that the poor will at last inherit the earth. But if I say that one workman is capable of deciding about the education of one child, that he has the right to select a certain school or resist a certain system, I shall have all those progressive papers roaring at me as a rotten reactionary. Why the workman should be clever enough to vote a curriculum for everybody else's children, but not clever enough to choose one for his own children, I cannot for the life of me imagine. If I say that a decent coster-monger is to be trusted with a donkey, or a decent rat-catcher with a dog, I shall be denounced as an obstacle to humanitarian legislation. But there is no objection to trusting a crowd of costermongers and rat-catchers to decide about the humanitarian legislation. And what is true of these particular cases of proprietorship is true of the whole case of property. When the meek inherit the earth, it must only mean that the mob inherits the earth. It must not mean that the man inherits even the smallest portion of the earth. The mob is meek enough, certainly, when it is thus herded to its pastures by its sociological and educational pastors. It does not really mean that the many sheep, but that the few shepherds, will rule over all the meadows. And when the nomadic shepherd finds himself confronted with the static or domestic peasant, with the man who is actually ruling his own small meadow like a realm, there is always a collision and a sort of civil war in the country-side. In any case, the original paradox remains: that it was regarded as a simple thing that all the meadows should belong to all the men, but a frantic and fantastic thing that any man should own any meadow.

[From *All Is Grist*]

BUT the thing which is really required for the proper working of democracy is not merely the democratic system, or even the democratic philosophy, but the democratic emotion. The democratic emotion, like most elementary and indispensable things, is a thing difficult to describe at any time. But it is peculiarly difficult to describe it in our enlightened age, for the simple reason that it is peculiarly difficult to find it. It is a certain instinctive attitude which feels the things in which all men agree to be unspeakably important, and all the things in which they differ (such as mere brains) to be almost unspeakably unimportant. The nearest approach to it in our ordinary life would be the promptitude with which we should consider mere humanity in any circumstance of shock or death. We should say, after a somewhat disturbing discovery, "There is a dead man under the sofa." We should not be likely to say, "There is a dead man of considerable personal refinement under the sofa." We should say, "A woman has fallen into the water." We should not say, "A highly educated woman has fallen into the water." Nobody would say, "There are the remains of a clear thinker in your back garden." Nobody would say, "Unless you hurry up and stop him, a man with a very fine ear for music will have jumped off that cliff." But this emotion, which all of us have in connection with such things as birth and death, is to some people native and constant at all ordinary times and in all ordinary places. It was native to St. Francis of Assisi. It was native to Walt Whitman. In this strange and splendid degree it cannot be expected, perhaps, to pervade a whole commonwealth or a whole civilization; but one commonwealth may have it much more than another commonwealth, one civilization much more than another civilization. No community, perhaps, ever had it so much as the early Franciscans. No community, perhaps, ever had it so little as ours.

[From *Heretics*]

SUPPOSE a Bedouin tribe wanders about the desert and adores the moon (nobody in the desert would be likely to adore the sun) and suppose all its habits, meals, marriages, lustrations and legends revolve around the lunar symbol. If such a tribe picked up out of pity a wandering Jew or Fire-worshipper, I think it would be quite justified in giving him food and shelter but refusing office and power. For these moon-worshippers might almost be men in the moon: their religion is as separate, rounded and remote as the moon itself. But if they conquered and ruled sixteen cities of Jews and Fire-worshippers, then the situation would be very different: certainly at least they would not have the same right to enforce politically the tests of their belief. The distinction is clear: moon worship was the root and meaning of their simple tribe: but clearly it is not the root and meaning of their composite empire. That must rest on some other principle of unity, because the differences are there. These people may have come together by force or affinity or political fate, but they have not come together to worship the moon.

[From *The Living Age*, 12 November 1910]

Note: Chesterton's *The Crimes of England* is a devastating attack on Prussian military aggression. The first chapter is in the form of a letter to a hypothetical Prussian professor, Professor Whirlwind. It ends as follows:

I have therefore thought it advisable to provide you with a catalogue of the real crimes of England; and I have selected them on a principle which cannot fail to interest and please you. On many occasions we have been very wrong indeed. We were very wrong indeed when we took part in preventing Europe from putting a term to the impious piracies of Frederick the Great. We were very wrong indeed when we allowed the triumph over Napoleon to be soiled with the mire and blood of Blucher's sullen savages. We were very wrong indeed when we allowed the peaceful King of Denmark to be robbed in broad daylight by a brigand named Bismarck; and when we allowed the Prussian swashbucklers to enslave and silence the French provinces which they could neither govern nor persuade. We were very wrong indeed when we flung to such hungry adventurers a position so important as Heligoland. We were very wrong indeed when we praised the soulless Prussian education and copied the soulless Prussian laws. Knowing that you will mingle your tears with mine over this record of English wrong-doing, I dedicate it to you, and I remain,

Yours reverently,
G. K. Chesterton

Note: In this allegory against Prussianism, the horse is Prussia, the haddock is England, the nightingale is Italy, and the oyster is Greece. Chesterton does not identify the nationality of the cat.

THE horse asserts that all other creatures are morally bound to sacrifice their interests to his, on the specific ground that he possesses all noble and necessary qualities, and is an end in himself. It is pointed out in answer that when climbing a tree the horse is less graceful than the cat; that lovers and poets seldom urge the horse to make a noise all night like the nightingale; that when submerged for some long time under water, he is less happy than the haddock; and that when he is cut open pearls are less often found in him than in an oyster. He is not content to answer (though, being a muddle-headed horse, he does use this answer also) that having an undivided hoof is more than pearls or oceans or all ascension or song. He reflects for a few years on the subject of cats; and at last discovers in the cat "the characteristic equine quality of caudality, or a tail"; so that cats *are* horses, and wave on every treetop the tail which is the equine banner. Nightingales are found to have legs, which explains their power of song. Haddocks are vertebrates; and therefore are sea-horses. And though the oyster outwardly presents dissimilarities which seem to divide him from the horse, he is by the all-filling nature-might of the same horse-moving energy sustained.

Now this horse is intellectually the wrong horse. It is not perhaps going too far to say that this horse is a donkey. For it is obviously within even the intellectual resources of a haddock to answer, "But if a haddock is a horse, why should I yield to you any more than you to me? Why should that singing horse commonly called the nightingale, or that climbing horse hitherto known as the cat, fall down and worship you because of your horsehood? If all our native faculties are the accomplishments of a horse—why then you are only another horse without any accomplishments." When thus gently reasoned with, the horse flings up his heels, kicks the cat, crushes the oyster, eats the haddock and pursues the nightingale, and that is how the war began.

[From *The Crimes of England*]

THOSE who now think too little of the Allied Cause are those who once thought too much of it. Those who are disappointed with the great defence of civilization are those who expected too much of it. A rather unstable genius like Mr. H. G. Wells is typical of the whole contradiction. He began by calling the Allied effort, The War That Will End War. He has ended by saying, through his rather equivocal mask of Mr. Clissold, that it was no better than a forest fire and that it settled nothing. It is hard to say which of the two statements is the more absurd. It settled exactly what it set out to settle. But that was something rather more rational and modest than what Mr. Wells had settled that it was to settle. To tell a soldier defending his country that it is The War That Will End War is exactly like telling a workman, naturally rather reluctant to do his day's work, that it is The Work That Will End Work. We never promised to put a final end to all war or all work or all worry. We only said that we were bound to endure something very bad because the alternative was something worse. In short, we said what every man on the defensive has to say. Mr. Brown is attacked by a burglar and manages to save his life and property. It is absurd to turn round on him and say, "After all, what has come out of the battle in the back-garden? It is the same old Septimus Brown, with the same face, the same trousers, the same temper a little uncertain at breakfast, the same taste for telling the anecdote about the bookmaker at Brighton." It is absurd to complain that Mr. Brown has not been turned into a Greek god merely by being bashed on the head by a burglar. He had a right to defend himself; he had a right to save himself; and what he saved was himself, so far no better and no worse. If he had gone out to purify the world by shooting all possible burglars, it would not have been a defensive war. And it would not have been a defensible one.

[From *Autobiography*]

IT is all nonsense to say that we Europeans could not have an agreement about disarmament. We could have it right enough if we were Europeans. We could have it well enough if we loved our civilization as much as we hate each other. People cannot love Europe, because Europe is either a map or else a mystical lady who was carried off by a bull. But men could love Christendom, because it was an idea.

Therefore, with all the heartiness proper to one who is wholly ignorant of the subject, I throw down my two private doubts, which are almost strong enough to be called suggestions. First, I gravely doubt whether our hurried emulation in arms is not a great deal too much a mere breathless and crazy copying. If the other schoolboy throws big snowballs, it is the mere instinct to throw bigger ones; but it might be much better strategy to keep one's head, to throw a smaller snowball and to throw it straight. In short, I disbelieve in this modern war exactly because it is always talked of as a war of guns and ships, and never as a war of men. And secondly, I doubt whether this competition of longer spears or larger ships need go on at all, if once the nations could find something positive upon which to combine.

Of course they cannot combine on mere peace; peace is a negation, like darkness. Is there any affectation or institution or creed on which we can combine?—that is increasingly the question. It is our dreadful condition that we agree too much on all the things in which we ought to vary—arms, methods, and the arts of war. And we differ hopelessly on all the things on which we ought to agree—motives, reasons, and beliefs. In the things of life and love we are separated; in the things of death and blood we imitate each other. In a healthy existence the inmost thing should be secure, but the outer gestures energetic and varied. But with modern Europe it is the limbs that are heavy and the heart that has unrest.

[From *The New York Times*, 11 April 1909]

THERE is a wild hypothesis now hardening in the minds of many which has nothing to do with any philosophical case of pacifism, let alone peace. It is the notion that not fighting, as such, would prevent somebody else from fighting, or from taking all he wanted without fighting. It assumes that every pacifist is some strange sort of blend of a lion-tamer and a mesmerist, who would hold up invading armies with his glittering eye, like the Ancient Mariner. The pacifist would paralyse the militarist in all his actions, both militant and post-militant. Now, there is no sort of sense or even meaning in this notion at all. . . . There have been many great and good men in the past who have said that they would never need to resist spoliation or invasion, or would not care if it were irresistible. But they were almost always one of two types, and were thinking only of one or two truths. In some of them it meant: "My mind to me a kingdom is. The inner life is so deep and precious that I do not care if I am beggared or made an outlaw or even a slave." In the others it meant: "I know that my avenger liveth. The judgment of this world may beggar or enslave me, but I shall have justice when I appeal to a higher court." Both these moral attitudes mean something and something very worthy of all possible respect. But neither of these two types was ever such a fool as to say that he *could* not be beggared or enslaved, merely because he stood stock still like a post and did not resist beggary or enslavement. Neither of them was so silly as to suppose that there were not men in the world, wicked or resolute or fanatical or mechanically servile enough, to do unpleasant things to them, while they were content to do nothing. The Stoic claimed to endure pain with patience; but he never claimed that his patience would prevent anybody from causing him pain. The martyr endured tortures to assert his belief in truth; but he never asserted his disbelief in torture. The hazy notion, that has been gathering more and more substance in the modern mind, is quite different and is really unreasonable. Men who have no intention of abandoning their country's wealth, not to mention their own, men who rightly insist on comfort for their countrymen and not infrequently for themselves, still seem to have formed a strange idea that they can keep all these things in all conceivable circumstances, solely and entirely by refusing to defend them. They seem to fancy they could bring the whole reign of violence and pride to an end, instantly and entirely, merely by doing nothing. Now it is not easy to do anything by doing nothing. . . .

Does anybody believe that Hitler or Stalin or Mussolini would ruin all his plans because a Quaker did not propose to interfere with them?

[From *As I Was Saying*]

About Education

I have dared to suggest that it would be rather a good thing if educated Englishmen knew a little history. I am not worrying about uneducated Englishmen. They do know a little history; a very little history, perhaps, but genuine so far as it goes; they do remember what their father and grandfather said; in what town or village they were born; what was the tone of the society round them; and their testimony, so far as it goes, is true. Any lawyer will tell you that uneducated witnesses are much better than educated witnesses, because they have not been elaborately educated to see what is not there. But it is a bad thing that an educated men, trained to have a taste for many good things, such as music or landscape, should know nothing of the songs of his fathers, and should appreciate the landscape without appreciating the land. Now, the nuisance of it is this: that if I say that people should be taught history, I shall have the horrible appearance of presenting myself as a historian. But that is almost the contrary of my contention. I only know a very little history; and even that very little is enough to tell me that much more important and powerful and successful persons than myself know no history at all.

It is not a question of somebody being a scholar; it is a question of something not being taught in the school. If I found that educated people were not aware that there is any difference between addition and subtraction, I should think myself justified in saying that something had happened to arithmetic in the schools; but it would not imply that I am a mathematician, which is absurd; still less that I could discuss the higher mathematics with Professor Einstein. If I found my most cultivated acquaintances alluding to Vienna as the capital of Spain, or the Volga as the chief river of America I should feel the geographical studies had become a little vague; in spite of the fact that my own knowledge of geography is very vague indeed. In short, an ordinary man is only justified in complaining of the neglect of a subject when he realizes that the schools neglect even the very little that he knows. He may himself have had heavy and laborious difficulties even in mastering the alphabet; but he still has the right to consider it rather odd that people do know the alphabet of arithmetic and do not know the alphabet of history. For the question concerns, in the most emphatic sense, the alphabet of history; the elements of history; or what has been called, in a famous title, the outline of history. I know nothing whatever about electricity, except that it lights bulbs and rings bells, and does all sorts of fantastic things round me, to which I do not happen to attach much importance, as compared with candles or gongs. I know the name comes from the ancient Greek word for amber; but I also know that its modern use has been mainly modern. I mean that, until it was analysed and utilized in the last few centuries by scientific men like Volta or Galvani, few people appreciated the importance of electricity; except those who had the brief but brilliant experience of being struck by lightning. In other words, I mean that, though I know next to nothing about electricity, I know something about the history of electricity, since I know that, before Volta and the rest, it had no history at all.

Now compare that sort of rudimentary information possessed by one ignorant Englishman about a branch of physics with the complete ignorance of almost all Englishmen about a parallel point of history. Millions of men who know much more about electricity than I do (and nobody could know less) are at this moment convinced that internationalism is a new ideal; and that this kind of ethics is as recent as electricity—or, rather, as recent as electricians. Talk to almost anybody in a train or a tram, and you will find he believes that we all emerged out of savage separate tribes, and that the idea of friendship with foreigners is part of a modern ideal of fraternity. Perhaps he will vaguely suppose that the Communists were the first Cosmopolitans; that nothing can link up nations but the Third or Fourth or Fifth or Sixth International, and the alliance of the Proletarians Of All Lands. But that is only a possibility; for the Communists are still a small minority. But even if he is quite a mild and moderate citizen, of the older parties, you will find he believes that national bigotry is merely a thing of the past; or perhaps that international brotherhood can only be a thing of the future. He will say it is due to the growth of liberal ideas, which have widened the narrow sympathies of the nation and the tribe. He may even hold that Mr. Wells invented the World State; even if he has not exactly founded the World State. But, anyhow, he will almost certainly believe, in one way or another, that going back into the past means going back into more and more partisan patches of patriotism; that the world began by being jingo and has gradually grown more sympathetic with justice to the foreigner.

Now, that is a black-and-white blunder about the outline of history; just as it would be a blunder to say that any prehistoric man was an electrician if he was struck by a thunderbolt. It is completely and colossally the contrary of the fact. Europe is now very national, and some may say very narrow. But certainly it was once much less national and much less narrow. Personally, I rather like nationalism; and I know there are much worse things than narrowness. But I am talking about a historical fact, a plain and primary historical fact; a fact that stands in history exactly as addition and subtraction stand in arithmetic. Nobody who does not know it knows the alphabet of our human history. The fact is, of course, that a narrow nationality has grown steadily and strongly for the last six hundred years; and European nations are much more divided now than they were in the time of the Holy Roman Empire, to say nothing of the Pagan Roman Empire. The French and English who fought each other at Crecy were more like each other than the French and English who supported each other at Mons. Our nationalities, whether good or bad (and they are good enough for me) did in historical fact emerge into separate existence out of a common cosmopolitan civilization, dating from the days of the Caesars, and still recognized in the days of the medieval Popes. Now, I am not arguing here about what importance is to be attached to this historical fact; still less about what deductions are to be drawn from it. I only say that the fact is not properly recognized as a fact like the fact of electricity. I only say that I should be universally regarded as an idiot if I were quite so ignorant of electricity as most of my countrymen are of history.

I think it rather important to press the point; because it is at this moment a point of peril. Everybody is asking in a distracted fashion whether the great nations can understand each other; and nearly everybody is insisting that it must be an entirely new sort of understanding. Now, it is surely not unimportant to point out that all these great nations formed part of one common and completely united civilization for about sixteen hundred years. I do not want them to fade back into the pagan unity of the first century or the feudal unity of the fourteenth. But if anybody says that they cannot find a unity, it is not irrelevant to say that they did find it, for much more than a thousand years. It is more hopeful to say that international brotherhood was the whole historic background from which we came than to say that it may or may not appear as an untried Utopia.

[From *As I Was Saying*]

On Turnpikes and Medievalism

OPENING my newspaper the other day, I saw a short but emphatic leaderette entitled "A Relic of Medievalism." It expressed a profound indignation upon the fact that somewhere or other, in some fairly remote corner of this country, there is a turnpike-gate, with a toll. It insisted that this antiquated tyranny is unsupportable, because it is supremely important that our road traffic should go very fast; presumably a little faster than it does. So it described the momentary delay in this place as a relic of medievalism. I fear the future will look at that sentence, somewhat sadly and a little contemptuously, as a very typical relic of modernism. I mean it will be a melancholy relic of the only period in all human history when people were proud of being modern. For though today is always today and the moment is always modern, we are the only men in all history who fell back upon bragging about the mere fact that today is not yesterday. I fear that some in the future will explain it by saying that we had previous little else to brag about. For, whatever the medieval faults, they went with one merit. Medieval people never worried about being medieval, and modern people do worry horribly about being modern.

To begin with, note the queer, automatic assumption that it must always mean throwing mud at a thing to call it a relic of medievalism. The modern world contains a good many relics of medievalism, and most of us would be surprised if the argument were logically enforced even against the things that are commonly called medieval. We should express regret if somebody blew up Westminster Abbey, because it is a relic of medievalism. Doubts would trouble us if the Government burned all existing copies of Dante's *Divine Comedy* and Chaucer's *Canterbury Tales*, because they are quite certainly relics of medievalism. We could not throw ourselves into unreserved and enthusiastic rejoicing even if the Tower of Giotto were destroyed as a relic of medievalism. And only just lately, in Oxford and Paris (themselves, alas! relics of medievalism), there has been a perverse and pedantic revival of the Thomist Philosophy and the logical method of the medieval Schoolmen. Similarly, curious and restless minds, among the very youngest artists and art critics, have unaccountably gone back even further into the barbaric period than the limit of the Tower of Giotto, and are even now telling us to look back to the austerity of Cimabue and the Byzantine diagrams of the Dark Ages. These relics must be more medieval even than medievalism.

But, in fact, this queer phase would not cover only what is commonly called medievalism. If a relic of medievalism only means something that has come down to us from medieval times, such writers would probably be surprised at the size and solidity of the relics. If I told these honest pressmen that the Press is a relic of medievalism, they would probably prove their love of a cliché by accusing me of a paradox. But it is at least cértain that the Printing Press is a relic of medievalism. It was discovered and established by entirely medieval men, steeped in medieval ideas, stuffed with the religion and social spirit of the Middle Ages. There are no more typically medieval words than those noble words of the eulogy that was pronounced by the great English printer on the great English poet; the words of Caxton upon Chaucer. If I were to say that Parliament is a relic of medievalism, I should be on even stronger ground; for, while the Press did at least come at the end of the Middle Ages, the Parliaments came much more nearly at the beginning of the Middle Ages. They began, I think, in Spain and the provinces of the Pyrenees; but our own traditional date, connecting them with the revolt of Simon de Montfort, if not strictly accurate, does roughly represent the time. I need not say that half the great educational foundations, not only Oxford and Cambridge, but Glasgow and Paris, are relics of medievalism. It would seem rather hard on the poor journalistic reformer if he is not allowed to pull down a little turnpike-gate till he has proved his right to pull down all these relics of medievalism.

Next we have, of course, the very considerable historic doubt about whether the turnpike-gate is a relic of medievalism. I do not know what was the date of this particular turnpike; but turnpikes and tolls of that description were perhaps most widely present, most practically enforced, or, at least, most generally noted, in the eighteenth century. When Pitt and Dundas, both of them roaring drunk, jumped over a turnpike-gate and were fired at with a blunderbuss, I hope nobody will suggest that those two great politicians were relics of medievalism. Nobody surely could be more modern than Pitt and Dundas, for one of them was a great financial statesman, depending entirely on the bankers, and the other was a swindler. It is possible, of course, that some such local toll was really medieval, but I rather doubt whether the journalist even inquired whether it was medieval. He probably regards everything that happened before the time of Jazz and the Yellow Press as medieval. For him medieval only means old, and old only means bad; so that we come to the last question, which ought to have been the first question, of whether a turnpike is necessarily bad.

If we were really relics of medievalism—that is, if we had really been taught to think—we should have put that question first, and discussed whether a thing is bad or good before discussing whether it is modern or medieval. There is no space to discuss it here at length, but a very simple test in the matter may be made. The aim and effect of tolls is simply this: that those who use the roads shall pay for the roads. As it is, the poor people of a district, including those who never stir from their villages, and hardly from their firesides, pay to maintain roads which are ploughed up and torn to pieces by the cars and lorries of rich men and big businesses, coming from London and the distant cities. It is not self-evident that this is a more just arrangement than that by which wayfarers pay to keep up the way, even if that arrangement were a relic of medievalism.

Lastly, we might well ask, is it indeed so certain that our roads suffer from the slowness of petrol traffic; and that, if we can only make every sort of motor go faster and faster, we shall all be saved at last? That motors are more important than men is doubtless an admitted principle of a truly modern philosophy; nevertheless, it might be well to keep some sort of reasonable ratio between them, and decide exactly how many human beings should be killed by each car in the course of each year. And I fear that a mere policy of the acceleration of traffic may take us beyond the normal modern recognition of murder into something resembling a recognition of massacre. And about this, I for one still have a scruple; which is probably a relic of medievalism.

[From *All I Survey*]

The Fool

FOR many years I had sought him, and at last I found him in a club. I had been told that he was everywhere; but I had almost begun to think that he was nowhere. I had been assured that there were millions of him; but before my late discovery I inclined to think that there were none of him. After my late discovery I am sure that there is one; and I incline to think that there are several, say, a few hundreds, but unfortunately most of them occupying important positions. When I say "him," I mean the entire idiot.

I have never been able to discover that "stupid public" of which so many literary men complain. The people one actually meets in trains or at tea-parties seem to me quite bright and interesting; certainly quite enough so to call for the full exertion of one's own wits. And even when I have heard brilliant "conversationalists" conversing with other people, the conversation had much more equality and give and take than this age of intellectual snobs will admit. I have sometimes felt tired, like other people; but rather tired with men's talk and variety than with their stolidity or sameness; therefore it was that I sometimes longed to find the refreshment of a single fool.

But it was denied me. Turn where I would I found this monotonous brilliancy of the general intelligence, this ruthless, ceaseless sparkle of humour and good sense. The "mostly fools" theory has been used in an anti-democratic sense; but when I found at last my priceless ass, I did not find him in what is commonly called the democracy; nor in the aristocracy either. The man of democracy generally talks quite rationally, sometimes on the anti-democratic side, but always with an idea of giving reasons for what he says and referring to the realities of his experience. Nor is it the aristocracy that is stupid; at least, not that section of the aristocracy which represents it in politics. They are often cynical, especially about money, but even their boredom tends to make them a little eager for any real information or originality. If a man like Mr. Winston Churchill or Mr. Wyndham made up his mind for any reason to attack Syndicalism he would find out what it was first. Not so the man I found in the club.

He was very well dressed; he had a heavy but handsome face; his black clothes suggested the City and his grey moustaches the Army; but the whole suggested that he did not really belong to either, but was one of those who dabble in shares and who play at soldiers. There was some third element about him that was neither mercantile nor military. His manners were a shade too gentlemanly to be quite those of a gentleman. They involved an unction and over-emphasis of the club-man: and I suddenly remembered feeling the same thing in some old actors or old playgoers who had modelled themselves on actors. As I came in he said, "If I was the Government," and then put a cigar in his mouth which he lit carefully with long intakes of breath. Then he took the cigar out of his mouth again and said, "I'd give it 'em," as if it were quite a separate sentence. But even while his mouth was stopped with the cigar his companion or interlocutor leaped to his feet and said with great heartiness, snatching up a hat, "Well, I must be off. Tuesday!" I dislike these dark suspicions, but I certainly fancied I recognized the sudden geniality with which one takes leave of a bore.

When, therefore, he removed the narcotic stopper from his mouth it was to me that he addressed the belated epigram, "I'd give it 'em."

"What would you give them," I asked, "the minimum wage?"

"I'd give them beans," he said. "I'd shoot 'em down—shoot 'em down, every man Jack of them. I lost my best train yesterday, and here's the whole country paralysed, and here's a handful of obstinate fellows standing between the country and coal. I'd shoot 'em down!"

"That would surely be a little harsh," I pleaded. "After all, they are not under martial law, though I suppose two or three of them have commissions in the Yeomanry."

"Commissions in the Yeomanry!" he repeated, and his eyes and face, which became startling and separate, like those of a boiled lobster, made me feel that he had something of the kind himself.

"Besides," I continued, "wouldn't it be quite enough to confiscate their money?"

"Well, I'd send them all to penal servitude, anyhow," he said, "and I'd confiscate their funds as well."

"The policy is daring and full of difficulty," I replied, "but I do not say that it is wholly outside the extreme rights of the republic. But you must remember that though the facts of property have become quite fantastic, yet the sentiment of property still exists. These coal-owners, though they have not earned the mines, though they could not work the mines, do quite honestly feel that they own the mines. Hence your suggestion of shooting them down, or even of confiscating their property, raises very—"

"What do you mean?" asked the man with the cigar, with a bullying eye. "Who yer talking about?"

"I'm talking about what you were talking about," I replied; "as you put it so perfectly, about the handful of obstinate fellows who are standing between the country and the coal. I mean the men who are selling their own coal for fancy prices, and who, as long as they can get those prices, care as little for national starvation as most merchant princes and pirates have cared for the provinces that were wasted or the peoples that were enslaved just before their ships came home. But though I am a bit of a revolutionist myself, I cannot quite go with you in the extreme violence you suggest. You say—"

"I say," he cried, bursting through my speech with a really splendid energy like that of some noble beast, "I say I'd take all those blasted miners and—"

I had risen slowly to my feet, for I was profoundly moved; and I stood staring at that mental monster.

"Oh," I said, "so it is the *miners* who are all to be sent to penal servitude, so that we may get more coal. It is the *miners* who are to be shot dead, every man Jack of them; for if once they are all shot dead they will start mining again. . . . You must forgive me, sir; I know I seem somewhat moved. . . . The fact is, I have just found something . . . something I have been looking for for years."

"Well," he asked, with no unfriendly stare, "and what have you found?"

"No," I answered, shaking my head sadly, "I do not think it would be quite kind to tell you what I have found."

He had a hundred virtues, including the capital virtue of good humour, and we had no difficulty in changing the subject and forgetting the disagreement. He talked about society, his town friends and his country sports, and I discovered in the course of it that he was a county magistrate, a Member of Parliament, and a director of several important companies. He was also that other thing, which I did not tell him.

The moral is that a certain sort of person does exist, to whose glory this article is dedicated. He is not the ordinary man. He is not the miner, who is sharp enough to ask for the necessities of existence. He is not the mine-owner, who is sharp enough to get a great deal more, by selling his coal at the best possible moment. He is not the aristocratic politician, who has a cynical but a fair sympathy with both economic opportunities. But he is the man who appears in scores of public places open to the upper middle class or (that less known but more powerful section) the lower upper class. Men like this all over the country are really saying whatever comes into their heads in their capacities of justice of the peace, candidate for Parliament, Colonel of the Yeomanry, old family doctor, Poor Law guardian, coroner, or, above all, arbiter in trade disputes. He suffers, in the literal sense, from softening of the brain; he has softened it by always taking the view of everything most comfortable for his country, his class, and his private personality. He is a deadly public danger. But as I have given him his name at the beginning of this article there is no need for me to repeat it at the end.

[From *A Miscellany of Men*]

❧ 17 ❧

SHORT QUOTATIONS

These epigrams or "miniquotes" are, of course, necessarily taken out of context. In fact, because of Chesterton's unique style, they are more out of context than one would expect. In many cases, they would seem to be only tenuously related—if at all—to the subjects of the essays and books from which they are taken. The quotation about socialist and capitalist systems, for example, is from the essay "On Boys." The saying about the morality of a great writer being the morality he takes for granted is from *The Superstition of Divorce*. And the statement about doing (or not doing) clever things in education is from an essay on Queen Victoria. It is characteristic of Chesterton's thinking that he drew from an extremely wide source of ideas and experiences in order to nail down an argument. Thus, in order to appreciate the amazing way his mind integrates diverse elements, one is driven to read his books. (The sources of these quotations are provided at the end of this section.)

THERE is less difference than many suppose between the ideal Socialist system, in which the big businesses are run by the State, and the present Capitalist system, in which the State is run by the big businesses. (1)

THE morality of a great writer is not the morality he teaches, but the morality he takes for granted. (2)

IN psychology, in sociology, above all in education, we are learning to do a great many clever things. Unless we are much mistaken the next great task will be to learn not to do them. (3)

THERE is no such thing as being a gentleman at important moments; it is at unimportant moments that a man is a gentleman. (4)

WE must find some common ground in a general philosophy of life, and that is exactly what the fashions of our age seldom give us. Without this it is equally irrational to be old-fashioned and to be newfangled, for each is merely a fashion, or possibly a fangle; whatever that may be. (5)

THE most sentimental thing in the world is to hide your feelings; it is making too much of them. (6)

LOST somewhere in the enormous plains of time, there wanders a dwarf who is the image of God, who has produced on a yet more dwarfish scale an image of creation. The pigmy picture of God we call Man; the pigmy picture of creation we call Art. (7)

MONARCHY in its healthiest days had the same bias as democracy: the belief in human nature when entrusted with power. A king was only the first citizen who received the franchise. (8)

THE critic instinctively avoids the admission that Hamlet's was a struggle between duty and inclination; and tries to substitute a struggle between consciousness and sub-consciousness. He gives Hamlet a complex to avoid giving him a conscience. (9)

FOR religion all men are equal, as all pennies are equal, because the only value in any of them is that they bear the image of the king. (10)

I have heard that in some debating clubs there is a rule that the members may discuss anything except religion and politics. I cannot imagine what they do discuss; but it is quite evident that they have ruled out the only two subjects which are either important or amusing. (11)

FOR he was a sincere man, and in spite of his superficial airs and graces, at root a humble one. And it is always the humble man who talks too much; the proud man watches himself too closely. (12)

IN truth there are only two kinds of people; those who accept dogmas and know it, and those who accept dogmas and don't know it. (13)

A self-conscious simplicity may well be far more intrinsically ornate than luxury itself. (14)

BUT all conservatism is based upon the idea that if you leave things alone you leave them as they are. But you do not. If you leave a thing alone you leave it to a torrent of change. If you leave a white post alone it will soon be a black post. If you particularly want it to be white you must always be painting it again; that is, you must always be having a revolution. (15)

WE make our friends; we make our enemies; but God makes our next-door neighbor. (16)

THERE is a great deal of difference between the eager man who wants to read a book, and the tired man who wants a book to read. (17)

IT is quaint that people talk of separating dogma from education. Dogma is actually the only thing that cannot be separated from education. It *is* education. A teacher who is not dogmatic is simply a teacher who is not teaching. (18)

NOW there are very deep reasons for talking about the weather, reasons that are delicate as well as deep. . . . Jones and Brown talk about the weather: but so do Milton and Shelley. (19)

IF a ballad speaks of St. George or Robin Hood going to the court of King Arthur, it means, not so much that they were all alive then, but rather that they are all alive still. (20)

HE [H. G. Wells] thought that the object of opening the mind is simply opening the mind. Whereas I am incurably convinced that the object of opening the mind, as of opening the mouth, is to shut it again on something solid. (21)

THE first thing to note, as typical of the modern tone, is a certain effect of toleration which actually results in timidity. Religious liberty might be supposed to mean that everybody is free to discuss religion. In practice it means that hardly anybody is allowed to mention it. (22)

IN a quite serious sense it is more important to read the newspaper than to read Shakespeare. It is more important because citizenship must be more important than art. (23)

DESPAIR does not lie in being weary of suffering, but in being weary of joy. (24)

TO complain that I could only be married once was like complaining that I had only been born once. (25)

WE lose our bearings entirely by speaking of the "lower classes" when we mean humanity minus ourselves. (26)

BEING a nation means standing up to your equals, whereas being an empire only means kicking your inferiors. (27)

I prefer the gossip of the many to the scandal of the few. I distrust the narrow individualism of the artist, trusting rather the national communism of the craftsman. I think there is one thing more important than the man of genius—and that is the genius of man. (28)

IN most modern people there is a battle between the new opinions, which they do not follow out to their end, and the old traditions, which they do not trace back to their beginning. If they followed the new notions forward, it would lead them to Bedlam. If they followed the better instincts backward it would lead them to Rome. (29)

ONE must not think primarily of a French Peasant, any more than of a German Measle. The plural of the word is its proper form; you cannot have a Peasant until you have a peasantry. The essence of the Peasant ideal is equality; and you cannot be equal all by yourself. (30)

THE real argument against aristocracy is that it always means the rule of the ignorant. For the most dangerous of all forms of ignorance is ignorance of work. (31)

TRUTH, of course, must of necessity be stranger than fiction, for we have made fiction to suit ourselves. (32)

THE worst argument in the world is a date. For it is actually taking as fixed the one thing that we really know is fugitive and staking all upon to-day at the moment when it is turning into yesterday. (33)

STATE education is simply Conscription applied to culture, or to the destruction of culture. (34)

IF a man cannot make a fool of himself, we may be quite certain that the effort is superfluous. (35)

DO not be proud of the fact that your grandmother was shocked at something which you are accustomed to seeing or hearing without being shocked. . . . It may be that your grandmother was an extremely lively and vital animal, and that you are a paralytic. (36)

HE [Herbert Spencer] popularized this contemptible notion that the size of the solar system ought to over-awe the spiritual dogma of man. Why should a man surrender his dignity to the solar system any more than to a whale? (37)

CHILDREN (and grown-up people too) have in their ownership an obscure idea even of loyalty to the thing. A little boy who has gone to bed without his toy gun does not only feel that he is sad without the gun. He also feels that in some transcendental way the gun will be sad without him. (38)

THE ordinary modern progressive position is that this is a bad universe, but will certainly get better. I say it is certainly a good universe, even if it gets worse. (39)

WHEN we talk of wild poetry, we sometimes forget the parallel of wild flowers. They exist to show that a thing may be more modest and delicate for being wild. (40)

NO traditions in this world are so ancient as the traditions that lead to modern upheaval and innovation. Nothing nowadays is so conservative as a revolution. (41)

RIGHT is right, even if nobody does it. Wrong is wrong, even if everybody is wrong about it. (42)

THEY have invented a new phrase, a phrase that is a black-and-white contradiction in two words—"free love"—as if a lover ever had been, or ever could be, free. It is the nature of love to bind itself, and the institution of marriage merely paid the average man the compliment of taking him at his word. (43)

SORROW and pessimism are indeed, in a sense, opposite things, since sorrow is founded on the value of something, and pessimism upon the value of nothing. (44)

THE whole aim of marriage is to fight through and survive the instant when incompatibility becomes unquestionable. For a man and a woman, as such, are incompatible. (45)

REAL mystics don't hide mysteries, they reveal them. They set a thing up in broad daylight, and when you've seen it it's still a mystery. But the mystagogues hide a thing in darkness and secrecy, and when you find it, it's a platitude. (46)

FOR under the smooth legal surface of our society there are already moving very lawless things. We are always near the breaking-point when we care only for what is legal and nothing for what is lawful. Unless we have a moral principle about such delicate matters as marriage and murder, the whole world will become a welter of exceptions with no rules. There will be so many hard cases that everything will go soft. (47)

IF a thing is worth doing, it is worth doing badly. (48)

I have no particular objection to people going about in cars; though I may regret the curious evolution of the human form in America, where wheels have completely taken the place of legs. (49)

REAL development is not leaving things behind, as on a road, but drawing life from them, as from a root. (50)

POWERFUL men who have powerful passions use much of their strength in forging chains for themselves; they alone know how strong the chains need to be. (51)

THE error of Diogenes lay in the fact that he omitted to notice that every man is both an honest man and a dishonest man. Diogenes looked for his honest man inside every crypt and cavern; but he never thought of looking inside the thief. And there is where the Founder of Christianity found the honest man; He found him on a gibbet and promised him paradise. (52)

CHRISTIANITY has died many times and risen again; for it had a god who knew the way out of the grave. (53)

THE pagan determined with admirable sense to enjoy himself. But by the end of his civilization he had discovered that a man cannot enjoy himself and continue to enjoy anything else. (54)

IT appears to us that of all the fairy-tales none contains so vital a moral truth as the old story, existing in many forms, of Beauty and the Beast. There is written, with all the authority of a human scripture, the eternal and essential truth that until we love a thing in all its ugliness we cannot make it beautiful. (55)

THE world rebelled against the Golden Rule of Christianity; and found itself helpless under the Brazen Rule of commerce and the Iron Rule of war. (56)

PROGRESS should mean that we are always changing the world to suit the vision. Progress does mean (just now) that we are always changing the vision. . . . We are not altering the real to suit the ideal. We are altering the ideal: it is easier. (57)

A sort of Theosophist said to me, "Good and evil, truth and falsehood, folly and wisdom are only aspects of the same upward movement of the universe." Even at that stage it occurred to me to ask, "Supposing there is no difference between good and bad, or between false and true, what is the difference between up and down?" (58)

MOST men now are not so much rushing to extremes as merely sliding to extremes; and even reaching the most violent extremes by being almost entirely passive. (59)

OBVIOUSLY a suicide is the opposite of a martyr. A martyr is a man who cares so much for something outside him, that he forgets his own personal life. A suicide is a man who cares so little for anything outside him, that he wants to see the last of everything. (60)

IT is a sufficient proof that we are not an essentially democratic state that we are always wondering what we shall do with the poor. If we were democrats, we should be wondering what the poor will do with us. (61)

A piece of peculiarly bad advice is constantly given to modern writers, especially to modern theologians; that they should adapt themselves to the spirit of the age. If there is one thing that has made shipwreck of mankind from the beginning it has been the spirit of the age, which always means exaggerating still further something that is grossly exaggerated already. (62)

CHRIST said "Seek first the kingdom, and all these things shall be added unto you." Buddha said "Seek first the kingdom, and then you will need none of these things." (63)

IT is quite possible to be a pagan and hate the Church; it is equally possible to be a pessimist and hate the universe. But there is one Church exactly as there is one universe; and no wise man will wander about looking for another. (64)

BOOKS without morality in them are books that send one to sleep standing up. (65)

FOR the whole point of a home is that it is a hotch-potch. And mine, at any rate, rises to that austere domestic ideal. The whole point of one's own house is that it is not only a number of totally different things, which are nevertheless one thing, but it is one in which we still value even the things that we forget. (66)

THERE is no better test of the truth of serious fiction than the simple truths to be found in a fairy tale or an old ballad. Now, in the whole of folk-lore there is no such thing as free love. (67)

THE greatest poets of the world have a certain serenity, because they have not bothered to invent a small philosophy, but have rather inherited a large philosophy. It is, nine times out of ten, a philosophy which very great men share with very ordinary men. (68)

WE do not want, as the newspapers say, a Church that will move with the world. We want a Church that will move the world. (69)

[WE should] call a halt to the centralization of capital. The Socialist says we have too many capitalists. I say we have too few. The scattering of capital among a great many will solve the problem. (70)

THE practical tendency of all trade and business today is towards big commercial combinations, often more imperial, more impersonal, more international than many a communist commonwealth. (71)

I was not overwhelmed in childhood by being told of remote stars which the sun never reached, any more than in manhood by being told of the empire on which the sun never set. I had no use for an empire that had no sunsets. (72)

THERE is more simplicity in the man who eats caviar on impulse than in the man who eats grape-nuts on principle. (73)

NOW men in their aspect of equality and debate adore the idea of rules; they develop and complicate them greatly to excess. A man finds far more regulations and definitions in his club, where there are rules, than in his home, where there is a ruler. (74)

FOR when once people have begun to believe that prosperity is the reward of virtue their next calamity is obvious. If prosperity is regarded as the reward of virtue, it will be regarded as the symptom of virtue. (75)

TRADITION may be explained as an extension of the franchise. Tradition means giving the vote to the most obscure of all classes, our ancestors. It is the democracy of the dead. Tradition refuses to submit to the small and arrogant oligarchy of those who merely happen to be walking about. (76)

SPIRITUAL doctrines do not actually limit the mind as do materialistic denials. Even if I believe in immortality I need not think about it. But if I disbelieve in immortality I must not think about it. In the first case the road is open and I can go as far as I like; in the second the road is shut. (77)

THERE is something to be said for every error, but, whatever may be said for it, the most important thing to be said about it is that it is erroneous. (78)

A man can no more possess a private religion than he can possess a private sun and moon. (79)

THE only argument against losing faith is that you also lose hope— and generally charity. (80)

A man may well be less convinced of a philosophy from four books, than from one book, one battle, one landscape, and one old friend. The very fact that the things are different kinds increases the importance of the fact that they all point to one conclusion. (81)

IT requires long years of plenitude and quiet, the slow growth of great parks, the seasoning of oaken beams, the dark enrichment of red wine in cellars and in inns, all the leisure and life of England through many centuries, to produce at last the generous and genial fruit of English snobbishness. (82)

REAL conviction and real charity are much nearer than people suppose. (83)

MY attitude toward progress has passed from antagonism to boredom. I have long ceased to argue with people who prefer Thursday to Wednesday because it is Thursday. (84)

PROGRESS is Providence without God. (85)

AN art school is a place where about three people work with feverish energy and everybody else idles to a degree that I should have conceived unattainable by human nature. (86)

THE honest poor can sometimes forget poverty. The honest rich can never forget it. (87)

IF there were no God, there would be no atheists. (88)

I believe in preaching to the converted; for I have generally found that the converted do not understand their own religion. (89)

THERE are only three things in the world that women do not understand; and they are liberty, equality, and fraternity. (90)

MANKIND has not passed through the Middle Ages. Rather mankind has retreated from the Middle Ages in reaction and rout. The Christian ideal has not been tried and found wanting. It has been found difficult; and left untried. (91)

THE madman is not the man who has lost his reason. The madman is the man who has lost everything except his reason. (92)

FEW except the poor preserve traditions. Aristocrats live not in traditions but in fashions. (93)

THE Bible tells us to love our neighbors, and also to love our enemies; probably because they are generally the same people. (94)

IT is much better to be tied to one wonderful thing than to allow a mere catalogue of wonderful things to deprive you of the capacity to wonder. (95)

WE do not really want a religion that is right where we are right. What we want is a religion that is right where we are wrong. (96)

WHEN the realist of the sex novel writes, "Red sparks danced in Dagmar Doubledick's brain; he felt the spirit of the cave man rising within him," the novelist's readers would be very much disappointed if Dagmar only went off and drew large pictures of cows on the drawing-room wall. (97)

FOR a man who does not believe in a miracle, a slow miracle would be just as incredible as a swift one. (98)

"MODERN conditions" are treated as fixed, though the very word "modern" implies that they are fugitive. "Old ideas" are treated as impossible, though their very antiquity often proves their permanence. (99)

THE Catholic Church is the only thing which saves a man from the degrading slavery of being a child of his age. (100)

SOURCES OF QUOTATIONS

⚜ 18 ⚜

SUNSETS, RAIN,
CAULIFLOWERS, ETC.

THIS particular evening, if it is remembered for nothing else, will be remembered in that place for its strange sunset. It looked like the end of the world. All the heaven seemed covered with a quite vivid and palpable plumage; you could only say that the sky was full of feathers, and of feathers that almost brushed the face. Across the great part of the dome they were grey, with the strangest tints of violet and mauve and an unnatural pink or pale green; but towards the west the whole grew past description, transparent and passionate, and the last red-hot plumes of it covered up the sun like something too good to be seen. The whole was so close about the earth, as to express nothing but a violent secrecy. The very empyrean seemed to be a secret. It expressed that splendid smallness which is the soul of local patriotism. The very sky seemed small.

[From *The Man Who Was Thursday*]

THE French windows, thus flung open, let in an evening even lovelier than that of the day before. The west was swimming with sanguine colours, and a sort of sleepy flame lay along the lawn. The twisted shadows of the one or two garden trees showed upon this sheen, not grey or black, as in common daylight, but like the arabesques written in vivid violet ink on some page of Eastern gold. The sunset was one of those festive and yet mysterious conflagrations in which common things by their colours remind us of costly or curious things. The slates upon the sloping roof burned like the plumes of a vast peacock, in every mysterious blend of blue and green. The red-brown bricks of the wall glowed with all the October tints of strong ruby and tawny wines. The sun seemed to set each object alight with a different coloured flame,

274

like a man lighting fireworks; and even Innocent's hair, which was of a rather colourless fairness, seemed to have a flame of pagan gold on it as he strode across the lawn towards the one tall ridge of rockery.

[From *Manalive*]

FOR indeed this is one of the real beauties of rainy weather, that while the amount of original and direct light is commonly lessened, the number of things that reflect light is unquestionably increased. There is less sunshine; but there are more shiny things; such beautifully shiny things as pools and puddles and mackintoshes. It is like moving in a world of mirrors.

And indeed this is the last and not the least gracious of the casual works of magic wrought by rain: that while it decreases light, yet it doubles it. If it dims the sky, it brightens the earth. It gives the roads (to the sympathetic eye) something of the beauty of Venice. Shallow lakes of water reiterate every detail of earth and sky; we dwell in a double universe. Sometimes walking upon bare and lustrous pavements, wet under numerous lamps, a man seems a black blot on all that golden looking-glass, and could fancy he was flying in a yellow sky. But wherever trees and towns hang head downwards in a pigmy puddle, the sense of Celestial topsy-turvydom is the same. This bright, wet, dazzling confusion of shape and shadow, of reality and reflection, will appeal strongly to anyone with the transcendental instinct about this dreamy and dual life of ours. It will always give a man the strange sense of looking down at the skies.

[From *A Miscellany of Man*]

A country girl I know in the county of Buckingham had never seen the sea in her life until the other day. When she was asked what she thought of it she said it was like cauliflowers. Now that is a piece of pure literature—vivid, entirely independent and original, and perfectly true. I had always been haunted with an analogous kinship which I could never locate; cabbages always remind me of the sea and the sea always reminds me of cabbages. It is partly, perhaps, the veined mingling of violet and green, as in the sea a purple that is almost dark red may mix with a green that is almost yellow, and still be the blue sea as a whole. But it is more the grand curves of the cabbage that curl over cavernously like waves, and it is partly again that dreamy repetition, as of a pattern, that made two great poets, Aeschylus and Shakespeare, use a word like "multitudinous" of the ocean. But just where my fancy halted the Buckinghamshire young woman rushed (so to speak) to my imaginative rescue. Cauliflowers are twenty times better than cabbages, for they show the wave breaking as well as curling, and the efflorescence of the branching foam, blind, bubbling, and opaque. Moreover, the strong lines of life are suggested; the arches of the rushing waves have all the rigid energy of green stalks, as if the whole sea were one great green plant with one immense white flower rooted in the abyss.

[From *Alarms and Discursions*]

B UT the splendour of furrowed fields is this: that like all brave things they are made straight, and therefore they bend. In everything that bows gracefully there must be an effort at stiffness. Bows are beautiful when they bend only because they try to remain rigid; and sword-blades can curl like silver ribbons only because they are certain to spring stright again. But the same is true of every tough curve of the tree trunk, of every strong-backed bend of the bough; there is hardly any such thing in Nature as a mere droop of weakness. Rigidity yielding a little, like justice swayed by mercy, is the whole beauty of the earth. The cosmos is a diagram just bent beautifully out of shape. Everything tries to be straight; and everything just fortunately fails.

The foil may curve in the lunge; but there is nothing beautiful about beginning the battle with a crooked foil. So the strict aim, the strong doctrine, may give a little in the actual fight with facts; but that is no reason for beginning with a weak doctrine or a twisted aim. Do not be an opportunist; try to be theoretic at all the opportunities; fate can be trusted to do all the opportunistic part of it. Do not try to bend, any more than the trees try to bend. Try to grow straight, and life will bend you.

[From *Alarms and Discursions*]

A blaze of lightning blanched the grey woods, tracing all the wrinkled foliage down to the last curled leaf, as if every detail were drawn in silver-point or graven in silver. The same strange trick of lightning by which it seems to record millions of minute things in an instant of time, picked out everything, from the elegant litter of the picnic spread under the spreading tree to the pale lengths of winding road, at the end of which a white car was waiting. In the distance a melancholy mansion with four towers like a castle, which in the grey evening had been but a dim and distant huddle of walls like a crumbling cloud, seemed to spring into the foreground, and stood up with all its embattled roofs and blank and staring windows. And in this, at least, the light had something in it of revelation. For to some of those grouped under the tree that castle was, indeed, a thing faded and almost forgotten, which was to prove its power to spring up again in the foreground of their lives.

[From *The Secret of Father Brown*]

IF I were to ask myself where and when I have been happiest, I could of course give the obvious answers, as true of me as of everybody else; at some dance or feast of the romantic time of life; at some juvenile triumph of debate; at some sight of beautiful things in strange lands. But it is much more important to remember that I have been intensely and imaginatively happy in the queerest because the quietest places. I have been filled with life from within in a cold waiting-room in a deserted railway-junction. I have been completely alive sitting on an iron seat under an ugly lamp-post at a third-rate watering place. In short, I have experienced the mere excitement of existence in places that could commonly be called as dull as ditch-water. And by the way, is ditch-water dull? Naturalists with microscopes have told me that it teems with quiet fun. Even that proverbial phrase will prove that we cannot always trust what is proverbial, when it professes to describe what is prosaic. I doubt whether the fifteen gushing fountains to be found in your ornamental garden contain creatures so amusing as those the microscope reveals; like the profiles of politicians in caricature. And that is only one example out of a thousand, of the things in daily life we call dull that are not really so dull after all. And I am confident that there is no future for the modern world, unless it can understand that it has not merely to seek what is more and more exciting, but rather the yet more exciting business of discovering the excitement in things that are called dull.

[From *The Spice of Life*]

IMMEDIATELY beneath and about them the lines of the Gothic building plunged outwards into the void with a sickening swiftness akin to suicide. There is that element of Titan energy in the architecture of the Middle Ages that, from whatever aspect it be seen, it always seems to be rushing away, like the strong back of some maddened horse. This church was hewn out of ancient and silent stone, bearded with old fungoids and stained with the nests of birds. And yet, when they saw it from below, it sprang like a fountain at the stars; and when they saw it, as now, from above, it poured like a cataract into a voiceless pit. For these two men on the tower were left alone with the most terrible aspect of Gothic; the monstrous foreshortening and disproportion, the dizzy perspectives, the glimpses of great things small and small things great; a topsy-turvydom of stone in the mid-air. Details of stone, enormous by their proximity, were relieved against a pattern of fields and farms, pygmy in their distance. A carved bird or beast at a corner seemed like some vast walking or flying dragon wasting the pastures and villages below. The whole atmosphere was dizzy and dangerous, as if men were upheld in the air amid the gyrating wings of colossal genii; and the whole of that old church, as tall and rich as a cathedral, seemed to sit upon the sunlit country like a cloudburst.

[From *The Innocence of Father Brown*]

SCRIPTURE says that one star differeth from another in glory, and the same conception applies to noses. To insist that one type of face is ugly because it differs from that of Venus of Milo is to look at it entirely in a misleading light. It is strange that we should resent people differing from ourselves; we should resent much more violently their resembling ourselves. This principle has made a sufficient hash of literary criticism, in which it is always the custom to complain of the lack of sound logic in a fairy tale, and the entire absence of true oratorical power in a three-act farce. But to call another man's face ugly because it powerfully expresses another man's soul is like complaining that a cabbage has not two legs. If we did so, the only course for the cabbage would be to point out with severity, but with some show of truth, that we were not a beautiful green all over.

But this frigid theory of the beautiful has not succeeded in conquering the art of the world, except in name. In some quarters, indeed, it has never held sway. A glance at Chinese dragons or Japanese gods will show how independent are Orientals of the conventional idea of facial and bodily regularity, and how keen and fiery is their enjoyment of real beauty, of goggle eyes, of sprawling claws, of gaping mouths and writhing coils. In the Middle Ages men broke away from the Greek standard of beauty, and lifted up in adoration to heaven great towers, which seemed alive with dancing apes and devils. In the full summer of technical artistic perfection the revolt was carried to its real consummation in the study of the faces of men. Rembrandt declared the sane and manly gospel that a man was dignified, not when he was like a Greek god, but when he had a strong, square nose like a cudgel, a boldly-blocked head like a helmet, and a jaw like a steel trap.

[From *The Defendant*]

THE world must not only be the tragic, romantic, and religious, it must be nonsensical also. And here we fancy that nonsense will, in a very unexpected way, come to the aid of the spiritual view of things. Religion has for centuries been trying to make men exult in the "wonders" of creation, but it has forgotten that a thing cannot be completely wonderful so long as it remains sensible. So long as we regard a tree as an obvious thing, naturally and reasonably created for a giraffe to eat, we cannot properly wonder at it. It is when we consider it as a prodigious wave of the living soil sprawling up to the skies for no reason in particular that we take off our hats, to the astonishment of the park-keeper. Everything has in fact another side to it, like the moon, the patroness of nonsense. Viewed from that other side, a bird is a blossom broken loose from its chain of stalk, a man a quadruped begging on its hind legs, a house a gigantesque hat to cover a man from the sun, a chair an apparatus of four wooden legs for a cripple with only two. This is the side of things which tends most truly to spiritual wonder.

[From *The Defendant*]

❧ 19 ❧

LITERATURE AND SOME OF ITS CREATORS

Essay Excerpts

O NE general description of madness, it seems to us, might be found in the statement that madness is a preference for the symbol over that which it represents. The most obvious example is the religious maniac, in whom the worship of Christianity involves the negation of all those ideas of integrity and mercy for which Christianity stands. But there are many other examples. Money, for example, is a symbol; it symbolises wine and horses and beautiful vesture and high houses, the great cities of the world and the quiet tent by the river. The miser is a madman, because he prefers money to all these things; because he prefers the symbol to the reality. But books are also a symbol; they symbolise man's impression of existence, and it may at least be maintained that the man who has come to prefer books to life is a maniac after the same fashion as the miser. A book is assuredly a sacred object. In a book certainly the largest jewels are shut in the smallest casket. But that does not alter the fact that superstition begins when the casket is valued more than the jewels. This is the great sin of idolatry, against which religion has so constantly warned us.

[From *Lunacy and Letters*]

Note: An example of what has been called Chesterton's "ephemeral journalism," the following paragraph pokes fun at *Britannia*, the journal published by Mrs. Pankhurst, the dynamic suffragette.

280

I should really like to ask . . . critics what they can make of the following sentence, for I confess I can make nothing of it. Like a great part of *Britannia*, it is printed in large capitals, which seems to exclude the idea of a misprint. For though all papers, including our own, have been known to have misprints, it is very unusual to see Pears' Soup instead of Pears' Soap in large letters on an advertisement. The headline runs "AVERT A PAN AND ISLAMIC REVOLT!" Why should Miss Pankhurst avert a pan? Who threw the pan? What is a pan revolt? Can it be a Suffragette rising of oppressed wives armed with kitchen utensils? These questions crowd upon my mind, and are somewhat bewildering at first; but on consideration I conclude that some political description must be intended. To all mortal appearance it would seem that these ladies attach to the word "Pan-Islamic" the idea that there are two great Eastern religions now in alliance, the religion of Islam and the worship of Pan. Perhaps they think the Greeks worship Pan. Or must that divine monosyllable always be separated by a conjunction from everything else? Ought we to describe Miss Pankhurst herself as the firm of Pan and Khurst? A singular business.

[From *The Living Age*, 8 January 1916]

I find that there really are human beings who think fairy tales bad for children. . . . A lady has written me an earnest letter saying that fairy tales ought not to be taught to children even if they are true. She says that it is cruel to tell children fairy tales, because it frightens them. You might just as well say that it is cruel to give girls sentimental novels because it makes them cry. All this kind of talk is based on that complete forgetting of what a child is like which has been the firm foundation of so many educational schemes. If you keep bogies and goblins away from children they would make them up for themselves. One small child in the dark can invent more hells than Swedenborg. One small child can imagine monsters too big and black to get into any picture, and give them names too unearthly and cacophonous to have occurred in the cries of any lunatic. The child, to begin with, commonly likes horrors, and he continues to indulge in them even when he does not like them.

There is just as much difficulty in saying exactly where pure pain begins in his case, as there is in ours when we walk of our own free will into the torture-chamber of a great tragedy. The fear does not come from fairy tales; the fear comes from the universe of the soul.

The timidity of the child or the savage is entirely reasonable; they are alarmed at this world, because this world is a very alarming place. They dislike being alone because it is verily and indeed an awful idea to be alone. Barbarians fear the unknown for the same reason that Agnostics worship it—because it is a fact. Fairy tales, then, are not responsible for producing fear in children, or any of the shapes of fear; fairy tales do not give the child the idea of the evil or the ugly; that is in the child already, because it is in the world already. Fairy tales do not give a child his first idea of bogey. What fairy tales give the child is his first clear idea of the possible defeat of bogey. The baby has known the dragon intimately ever since he had an imagination. What the fairy tales provide for him is a St. George to kill the dragon.

Exactly what the fairy tale does is this: it accustoms him for a series of clear pictures to the idea that these limitless terrors have a limit, that these shapeless enemies have enemies, that these strong enemies of man have enemies in the knights of God, that there is something in the universe more mystical than darkness, and stronger than strong fear.

[From *Tremendous Trifles*]

A distinguished doctor has written a book about the madmen of Shakespeare. By which he did not mean those few fantastic and manifest madmen, whom we might almost call professional madmen, who merely witnessed to the late Elizabethan craze for lurid and horrible grotesques. Ford or Webster, or some of their fellows, would hardly have hesitated to have a ballet or chorus of maniacs, like a chorus of fairies or fashionable beauties. But the medical gentleman seems to have said that any number of the serious characters were mad. Macbeth was mad; Hamlet was mad; Ophelia was congenitally mad; and so on. If Hamlet was really mad, there does not seem much point in his pretending to be mad. If Ophelia was always mad, there does not seem much point in her going mad. But anyhow, I think a saner criticism will always maintain that Hamlet was sane. He must be sane even in order to be sad; for when we get into a world of complete unreality, even tragedy is unreal. No lunatic ever had so good a sense of humour as Hamlet. A homicidal maniac does not say, "Your wisdom would show itself more richer to signify that to his doctor"; he is a little too sensitive on the subject of doctors. The whole point of Hamlet is that he is really saner than anybody else in the play; though I admit that being sane is not identical with what some call being sensible. Being outside the world, he sees all round it, where everybody else sees his own side of the world, his own worldly ambition, or hatred of love. But, after all, Hamlet pretended to be mad in order to deceive fools. We cannot complain if he has succeeded.

But, whatever we may say about Hamlet, we must not say this about Macbeth. Hamlet was only a mild sort of murderer; a more or less accidental and parenthetical murderer; an amateur. But Macbeth was a good, solid, serious, self-respecting murderer; and we must not have any nonsense about him. For the play of *Macbeth* is, in the supreme and special sense, the Christian Tragedy; to be set against the Pagan Tragedy of Oedipus. It is the whole point about Oedipus that he does not know what he is doing. And it is the whole point about Macbeth that he does know what he is doing. It is not a tragedy of Fate but a tragedy of Freewill. He is tempted of a devil, but he is not driven by a destiny. If the actor pronounces the words properly, the whole audience ought to feel that the story may yet have an entirely new ending, when Macbeth says suddenly, "We will proceed no further in this business." The incredible confusion of modern thought is always suggesting that any indication that men have been influenced is an indication that they have been forced. All men are always being influenced; for every incident is an influence. The question is, which incident shall we allow to be most influential. Macbeth was influenced; but he consented to be influenced. He was not, like a blind tragic pagan, obeying something he thought he ought to obey. He does not worship the Three Witches like the Three Fates. He is a good enlightened Christian, and sins against the light.

[From *Come to Think of It*]

From a review of one of Chesterton's American lectures:
Mr. Chesterton made an astounding revelation, which was received by the audience with great merriment. In reply to a question as to the psychological significance of the use of paradox in his books, he declared gravely, "I never use paradox. The statements I make are wearisome and obvious common sense. I have even been driven to the tedium of reading through my own books, and have been unable to

find any paradox. In fact, the thing is quite tragic, and some day I shall hope to write an epic called 'Paradox Lost.'"

[From *The New York Times*, 7 February 1921]

A poor man is a man who has not got much money. This may seem a simple and unnecessary description, but in the face of a great mass of modern fact and fiction, it seems very necessary indeed; most of our realists and sociologists talk about a poor man as if he were an octopus or an alligator. There is no more need to study the psychology of poverty than to study the psychology of bad temper, or the psychology of vanity, or the psychology of animal spirits. A man ought to know something of the emotions of an insulted man, not by being insulted, but simply by being a man. And he ought to know something of the emotions of a poor man, not by being poor, but simply by being a man. Therefore, in any writer who is describing poverty, my first objection to him will be that he has studied his subject. A democrat would have imagined it.

[From *Heretics*]

THERE exists by accident an early and beardless portrait of him [George Bernard Shaw] which really suggests in the severity and purity of its lines some of the early ascetic pictures of the beardless Christ. However he may shout profanities or seek to shatter the shrines, there is always something about him which suggests that in a sweeter and more solid civilisation he would have been a great saint. He would have been a saint of a sternly ascetic, perhaps of a sternly negative type. But he has this strange note of the saint in him; that he is literally unworldly. Worldliness has no human magic for him; he is not bewitched by rank nor drawn on by conviviality at all. He could not understand the intellectual surrender of the snob. He is perhaps a defective character; but he is not a mixed one. All the virtues he has are heroic virtues. Shaw is like the Venus of Milo; all that there is of him is admirable.

[From *George Bernard Shaw*]

NO man now alive in England deserves the name of genius more than Mr. H. G. Wells; and no man offers a more startling case of [the] contradiction between the public impression and the private fact. In most sketches, satires, and allusions to Mr. Wells he is referred to as a kind of mental skeleton; a man made of diagrams; a spirit of endless logic, at once trivial and ghostly; a vision of steel machinery by moonlight. He has written "The Time Machine"; therefore he himself is a machine; his heart must tick rather than beat. He has written "The First Men in the Moon"; therefore he is the first man out of the moon and has clinging to him the cold splendour of space. Above all (and this he will admit laughingly himself) he has a universally recognized copyright in the word "efficiency"; he started the political use of that term, with which Lord Rosebery, Lord Milner, and the Fabian Society have since wearied the world. His Socialism is supposed to be a dreary officialism, pointed with the metallic punctuality of little electric bells.

All this notion does not so much fall dead in the presence of Mr. Wells as actually turn upside down. I do not mean merely in his physical presence; though that is the reverse of metallic. A small, sturdy man with a warm, good-humored face, sunburned like an apple, in light gray country clothes, he looks the very reverse of a diagram; his mouth is full of strong humor, his eyes of an amiable doubt.

But the legend of the mechanical Wells is even more contradicted by his humane and responsive temperament than by his cheerful and almost rustic exterior. He has the largest hospitality of both head and heart; he will not only entertain a new idea, but domesticate it. No man's mind has grown less like clockwork construction and more like a living organism; feeding itself from every food and soil; perpetually modifying and modified by its environment. He goes far less by reason than by instinct; his farthest flights of thought are more like the homing of birds or the strange exodi of the silent fish. His theoretic morality is a maze of almost bewildering charity; he is always softening formulae, finding exceptions, thinking tenderly of hard cases. His philosophy is all anti-rationalist; and he sometimes comes near to saying that two and

285

two may not make four so exactly as is commonly supposed. If in his brilliant mass of gifts, wild imagination, warm sympathy, and swift and unhesitating analysis, there be one gift omitted, it is the great last gift of dogma—of announcing the final victory of thought.

[From *The American Magazine*, November 1910]

FOR the character of [Rudyard Kipling's] *Just-So Stories* is really unique. They are not fairy tales; they are legends. A fairy tale is a tale told in a morbid age to the only remaining sane person, a child. A legend is a fairy tale told to men when men were sane. We grant a child a fairy tale just as some savage king might grant a missionary permission to wear clothes, not understanding what we give, not knowing that it would be infinitely valuable if we kept it to ourselves, but simply because we are too kind to refuse. The true man will not buy fairy tales because he is kind; he will buy them because he is selfish. If Uncle John, who has just bought the *Just-So Stories* for his niece, were truly human (which, of course, Uncle John is not), it is doubtful whether the niece would ever see the book. . . .

But the peculiar splendour, as I say, of these new Kipling stories is the fact that they do not read like fairy tales told to children by the modern fireside, so much as like fairy tales told to men in the morning of the world. They see animals, for instance, as primeval men saw them; not as types and numbers in an elaborate biological scheme of knowledge, but as walking portents, things marked by extravagant and peculiar features. An elephant is a monstrosity with his tail between his eyes; a rhinoceros is a monstrosity with his horn balanced on his nose; a camel, a zebra, a tortoise are fragments of a fantastic dream, to see which is not seeing a scientific species, but like seeing a man with three legs or a bird with three wings, or men as trees walking. The whole opens a very deep question, the question of the relations between the old wonder and the new wonder, between knowledge and science. The hump of a camel is very likely not so much his characteristic from a scientific point of view as the third bone in the joint of his hind leg, but to the eyes of the child and the poet it remains his feature. And it is more important in this sense that it is more direct and certain: there is a relation between the human soul and the hump of a camel, which there is not between the human soul and the bone in his hind leg. The hump still remains and the bone vanishes, if all these physical phenomena are nothing but a grotesque shadow-show, constructed by a paternal deity to amuse a universe of children.

This is the admirable achievement of Kipling, that he has written new legends. We hear in these days of continual worship of old legends, but not of the making of new; which would be the real worship of legends. Just in the same way we hear of the worship of old ceremonies, but never of the making of new ones. If men decided that Mr. Gladstone's hat was to be carried three times around the House of Commons, they would have offered the best tribute to the Eleusinian mysteries. That is the tribute which "How the Whale Got His Throat" offers to the story of Sigurd and Hercules.

[From *The Bookman*, December 1902]

POETRY deals with primal and conventional things—the hunger for bread, the love of woman, the love of children, the desire for immortal life. If men really had new sentiments, poetry could not deal with them. If, let us say, a man did not feel a bitter craving to eat bread; but did, by way of substitute, feel a fresh, original craving to eat brass fenders or mahogany tables, poetry could not express him. If a man, instead of falling in love with a woman, fell in love with a fossil or a sea anemone, poetry could not express him. Poetry can only express what is original in one sense—the sense in which we speak of original sin. It is original, not in the paltry sense of being new, but in the deeper sense of being old; it is original in the sense that it deals with origins.

[From *Robert Browning*]

WE shall not get the tale of the modern and recent writers and thinkers told intelligently until it is told as a study in heresies. By which I do not mean that we should blame them for theological errors of which they were quite unconscious, and which they had no guidance to avoid. I mean that we shall assist and enlighten ourselves, in making sense of the story, because we alone can fall back on the old intelligent human custom of defining errors as errors, and tracing them to sources.

We shall not blame the Victorians for being vague, since they could be nothing else. But it will save us from being vague, if we can say, "It is the Calvinist fallacy that misleads Ruskin here," or "Dickens is very nearly right, and would be quite right but for his Pelagianism." . . .

For instance, I am deeply distrustful of Carlyle; not because he was a Victorian or praised or over-praised by Victorians; but because he was a heretic, and that of a deeper sort than Dickens or Tennyson. Even Mr. Noyes cannot persuade me that Carlyle did not really disregard Justice, when it was apparently overwhelmed by Success. . . .

What I mean, at any rate, is consistent with the most unfailing gratitude and the most unexhausted enthusiasm for those great Protestant men of genius who made the English culture of the nineteenth century; it is simply an attempt to study what they themselves would have called their wanderings in an unwandering and unwavering light, and to apply to some of the noblest men in history that lost and neglected thing, a moral science of mankind.

[From *America*, 22 February 1930]

Excerpts on pp. 288–290 from *Appreciations and Criticisms of the Work of Charles Dickens:*

NOW the really odd thing about England in the nineteenth century is this—that there was one Englishman who happened to keep his head. The men who lost their heads lost highly scientific and philosophical heads; they were great cosmic systematizers like Spencer, great social philosophers like Bentham, great practical politicians like Bright, great political economists like Mill. The man who kept his head kept a head full of fantastic nonsense; he was a writer of rowdy farces, . . . a man without education in any serious sense whatever, a man whose whole business was to turn ordinary cockneys into extraordinary caricatures. Yet when all these other children of the revolution went wrong he, by a mystical something in his bones, went right. He knew nothing of the Revolution; yet he struck the note of it. He returned to the original sentimental commonplace upon which it is for ever founded, as the Church is founded on a rock. In an England gone mad about a minor theory he reasserted the original idea—the idea that no one in the State must be too weak to influence the State. This man was Dickens.

HIS [Dickens'] revolt was simply and solely the eternal revolt; it was the revolt of the weak against the strong. He did not dislike this or that argument for oppression; he disliked oppression. He disliked a certain look on the face of a man when he looks down on another man. And that look on the face is, indeed, the only thing in the world that we have really to fight between here and the fires of Hell.

DICKENS attacks the modern workhouse with a sort of inspired simplicity as of a boy in a fairy-tale who has wandered about, sword in hand, looking for ogres and who has found an indisputable ogre. All the other people of his time are attacking things because they are bad economics or because they are bad politics, or because they are bad science; he alone is attacking things because they are bad. All the others are Radicals with a large R; he alone is a radical with a small one. He encounters evil with that beautiful surprise which, as it is the beginning of all real pleasure, is also the beginning of all righteous indignation. He enters the workhouse just as Oliver Twist enters it, as a little child.

PICKWICK is in Dickens's career the mere mass of light before the creation of sun or moon. It is the splendid, shapeless substance of which all his stars were ultimately made. You might split up *Pickwick* into innumerable novels as you could split up that primeval light into innumerable solar systems. The *Pickwick Papers* constitute first and foremost a kind of wild promise, a pre-natal vision of all the children of Dickens. He had not yet settled down into the plain, professional habit of picking out a plot and characters, of attending to one thing at a time, of writing a separate, sensible novel and sending it off to his publishers. He is still in the youthful whirl of the kind of world that he would like to create. He has not yet really settled what story he will write, but only what sort of story he will write. He tries to tell ten stories at once; he pours into the pot all the chaotic fancies and crude experiences of his boyhood; he sticks in irrelevant short stories shamelessly, as into a scrapbook; he adopts designs and abandons them, begins episodes and leaves them unfinished; but from the first page to the last there is a nameless and elemental ecstasy—that of the man who is doing the kind of thing that he can do. Dickens, like every other honest and effective writer, came at last to some degree of care and self-restraint. He learned how to make his dramatis personae assist his drama; he learned how to write stories which were full of rambling and perversity, but which were stories. But before he wrote a single real story, he had a kind of vision. It was a vision of the Dickens world—a maze of white roads, a map full of fantastic towns, thundering coaches, clamorous market-places, uproarious inns, strange and swaggering figures. That vision was *Pickwick*.

DICKENS stands first as a defiant monument of what happens when a great literary genius has a literary taste akin to that of the community. For this kinship was deep and spiritual. Dickens was not like our ordinary demagogues and journalists. Dickens did not write what the people wanted. Dickens wanted what the people wanted. And with this was connected that other fact which must never be forgotten, and which I have more than once insisted on, that Dickens and his school had a hilarious faith in democracy and thought of the service of it as a sacred priesthood. Hence there was this vital point in his popularism, that there was no condescension in it. The belief that the rabble will only read rubbish can be read between the lines of all our contemporary writers, even of those writers whose rubbish the rabble reads. Mr. Fergus Hume has no more respect for the populace than Mr. George Moore. The only difference lies between those writers who will consent to talk down to the people, and those writers who will not consent to talk down to the people. But Dickens never talked down to the people. He talked up to the people. He approached the people like a deity and poured out his riches and his blood. This is what makes the immortal bond between him and the masses of men. He had not merely produced something they could understand, but he took it seriously, and toiled and agonized to produce it. They were not only enjoying one of the best writers, they were enjoying the best he could do. His raging and sleepless nights, his wild walks in the darkness, his note-books crowded, his nerves in rags, all this extraordinary output was but a fit sacrifice to the ordinary man. He climbed towards the lower classes. He panted upwards on weary wings to reach the heaven of the poor.

[From *Charles Dickens*]

On a Censorship for Literature

THE recurring discussion about a Censorship for Literature or the Arts is a good example of the extreme difficulty in these days of discussing anything. Nobody seems to know where to begin. Nobody seems able to distinguish between one thing and another. For instance, to take a minor point, it is one thing to believe in A Censor and quite another thing to believe in The Censor. If I had to have my books censored, I would much rather they were censored by the Spanish Inquisition than by the British Home Office. The Spanish Inquisition was not an institution that I specially admire, but it did act on some intelligent principles; I know what the principles were and I agree with a great many of them. As to the principles of Sir William Johnson-Hicks, my difficulty is threefold. Not only do I not agree with them, but I do not know what they are. Not only do I not know what they are, but I am sure that he does not know what they are.

To begin with, supposing that the Censorship deals only with sexual decorum (which is generally far from being the case), there are at least three totally distinct things that are now generally discussed under that head. First, there is the preaching or propagating of some theory about sex considered anti-social or anarchical. Second, there is a certain sort of descriptive writing likely to excite appetites that may be anti-social or anarchical. Third, there is the use of certain terms, often merely old-fashioned, for things which later convention covers in some other way. I can understand a man wanting none of these things censored. I can understand him wanting all of these things censored. I can understand him wanting some censored and not others. But, anyhow, they have nothing to do with each other. No two of them need be found together in the same sentence or the same book. A man could preach sexual anarchy in language as cold as that of an astronomical treatise, and about as seductive as a page of Bradshaw. A man could describe sensual things with an unscrupulous appeal to the senses, without preaching any theory at all and without using any coarse words at all. Lastly, a man might use all the coarse words in Rabelais and make the theme rather repulsive than attractive. He might use all the coarse words in the Bible and be every bit as moral as the Bible, or even as Puritan as the grimmest expositor of the Bible.

One would think that the very first thing that anybody discussing the question would realize would be the distinction between these three tests. But, if we read a column in a newspaper, or a page in a popular book, professing to deal with the problem, we generally find them all mixed up together, whether the writer is denouncing the mixture or defending the mixture. The truth is that in this matter most people's moral ideas are now already mixed. To take the first section: in order to suppress false doctrine, we must have a definition of true doctrine. And very few people now know exactly what doctrine is true, even if they feel a great many current ones are false. For the second, it is, after all, a moral doctrine which declares that mere appeals to mere appetites are wrong. It is a moral doctrine most decent people vaguely feel, but now a little too vaguely to be applied vigilantly. But, of these first two divisions, I may be allowed to add that they do emphatically involve immortal and unalterable truth. The fact that a chaotic and ill-educated time cannot clearly grasp that truth does not alter the fact that it always will be the truth.

There is a right relation of the sexes; there is a right rule about it; and there is a wrong appeal calculated to encourage a wrong relation. But of the third thing it is not so. It is worth remarking that this third section, of the mere use of words, is the *only* one of which the modern talk is true. Of this it *is* true to say that it is only a question of convention, of custom, of different periods of history, of different stages of progress. It was not as gross of Shakespeare to use a certain word in a playhouse as it would have been gross of Dickens to use it in a drawing-room. But it would be just as wrong for Shakespeare to neglect his wife as for Dickens to neglect his wife. I am not here raising the delicate controversy about whether either of these authors did neglect his wife. The point is that if they did they were wrong; and I will wager that they knew they were wrong; for they were traditional Christian men. The notion that, because language can change, therefore life and love can change, is one of the many muddles of a thoroughly muddled mind. We might as well say that because Shakespeare had trunkhose and Dickens had trousers, it is but natural that the next great English author should have three legs.

So long as the modern world plays with the preposterous idea that everything changes with the fashion, it is useless for it to attempt to control the changes in anything so fanciful as fiction. People will pursue the moment that is just passing; but they will not be persecuted for the moment that has just passed. You may send a man to prison for five years for writing a silly book, if you can say to him, "If you were in prison for five hundred years, it would still be a silly book." But you cannot say to a man, "If you had waited fifteen years, this sort of book might have been fashionable; but, as it is, I send you to prison in the interval for being in advance of your age." That sort of persecution will never have any effect; for it combines injustice with indifference. It is at once an undeserved condemnation and an undeserved compliment. The fanatics of the past are sometimes blamed because they played the tyrant while appealing to eternal truth. But it is far more intolerable to play the tyrant while not appealing to eternal truth. It is most intolerable of all to play the tyrant while appealing only to temporary fiction. Nobody can be expected to stand the Inquisitor who says, "I am burning you alive for what you said to-day, and what I shall probably think to-morrow." And that is the tone of nearly all the tentative repressions and remonstrances of our time.

The plain truth is that modern society must have a morality before it can have a censor of morals. I should say that it must have a religion before it can have a morality. But that is another question which I should not discuss fully here. Anyhow, the trouble is that people are making a fuss about unreal romances when they ought to be making a fuss about real life. It is a case of taking care of the facts and the fictions will take care of themselves. If we cleanse the community, the community will cleanse its poetry and its prose. But it is absurd to expect that people who do not respect their own promises, made at their own weddings, will be horrified because every novel does not end in a Victorian manner with wedding-bells. It is ridiculous to expect that people will be stung to fury by the behaviour of Joan in *Green Pyjamas* or Peter in *Cocktail-Time*, when they have managed to get reconciled to it in their own daughters or sons-in-law. I do not mean, of course, that all our family life is like that. Nor is all our fiction like that. But many who demand a Censorship are really demanding that we should tolerate in life what we will not tolerate in literature.

[From *Come to Think of It*]

The Young Man in Fiction

THERE are some words which remain in current use like fossils of some primeval epoch embedded in a later deposit. One of these, of course, is the word "hero." The modern novelist steering a nondescript young man through trivial temptations and dreary embarrassments still insists on calling him the hero, the name which rings with the sound of the harp and sword. To a young gentleman of bewilderingly feeble character, to a young man who cannot decide which of three ladies he is in love with or which of six friends has really been his moral ruin, who covers trifling sins with transparent lies and a coarse vanity with a crude philosophy, who loses his faith in God when he reads half a page of German and loses his faith in his wife when he hears half a sentence in a club—to this watery Reuben of modernity, it is still correct to apply the most tremendous title of Sigurd or Achilles.

It would be interesting to trace, however roughly, this degeneration in the use of the word hero. Primarily, of course, in the great early epics, a hero means a hero, a being human indeed, but of so vast and towering a humanity that he is stronger than the circumstances which debase or limit human life. The victory of the divine part of man (for the hero was commonly partly of the blood of the gods) over the merely brutal part of the Cosmos is, of course, the central conception of all the fairy tales. In them, it is true, the victory is only a victory over dragons or ogres, but about the philosophical moral there can be no question; and the great gap in modern literature, a gap as wide as a howling desert, is the almost total absence of what may be called a story of heroic psychology. The typical intellectual romance of our day rings the changes perpetually upon one mournful bell: it is always concerned with the frustration or defeat of a human spirit by the savage irony of facts. This will appear to the lover of heroic literature a thing inverted and grotesque. It is as if he read a string of legends in which the dragon always ate St. George, or a story in which Cinderella's prince married one of the ugly sisters, or a Greek legend in which King Erystheus had to provide a new Hercules for each of the twelve labors. This kind of literature has for its great theme the manner in which man by faith and courage can beat down circumstance: of the victories of the body, the ancient literature spoke sublimely; of the similar victories of the soul, modern literature scarcely dares to speak at all. But when the work of genius shall come, which shall give us a psychological Hercules; which shall show that there is potentially a rejection of every temptation; a mastery for every mischance, much as there is a parry for every stroke of the sword, the event will certainly be something more important perhaps than the French Revolution. It will inaugurate a new literature and very possibly found a new religion.

To this primeval hero, youth was naturally attributed, and from the epics downwards we see this gradual transition from the hero to the young man who is still called by his title. But it is only very recently indeed that he has lost the last gleam from the sunset of the heroes. It might not strike the intellect at first that there was much resemblance between Hector and Nicholas Nickleby, or between Roland at Roncesvalles and Frank Fairleigh. But so it is when we consider the matter with a greater delicacy. Nicholas Nickleby, fallen and diminished, is still the hero, the Squeers slayer, and wears silver armor under his curious tight clothes; Frank Fairleigh, respectable as he appears, is undoubtedly the son of Jupiter. For these young men of early Victorian fiction move with a light step, the light step of the destined conqueror; they have a star of good luck above them and are marked by a kind of merry fatalism. Their ups and downs are indeed desolating; they are bandied about, as it were, from father to father; they think sometimes that they are orphans, sometimes that they are dukes, sometimes that they are hereditary criminals; they doubt their friends and their title-deeds, and almost their own faces in the glass. But one thing they never doubt—not one of them ever doubts that he is the third brother in the fairy tale.

Thus down to the time of Dickens we have the first walking gentleman, the young man, carrying with him a certain ancestral light and atmosphere of legend. And about the time of Dickens's later work that light fades into the light of common day. The first great creation in the new manner in England is the character of Arthur Pendennis. This is the young man lit from head to foot suddenly with the white light of realism, all the red lamps of legend being extinguished around him. Here we have the young man not engaged consistently in horsewhipping destiny, but fighting with it foolishly, irregularly, with tolerable courage, with frequent cowardice, and often getting horsewhipped himself. Here we have not merely St. George killing the dragon; we have St. George running away from the dragon, St. George forgetting the dragon, St. George bargaining with the dragon, St. George asking the dragon to dinner. It is a sobering picture but not a depressing one. Destructive realism is not by any means reality; it only tears up the flowers to find the garden, and so finds only a wilderness. But it has one great advantage when it is effected by a master of veracity like Thackeray: that, when all the illusions have been dispelled and the whole scene disenchanted, we do come upon the indestructible assurances, the things that remain. And the character of Arthur Pendennis is a translucent and amazing picture of the ordinary young man of the educated type: it reveals all his wanton and useless vices of intellect and temper, but it reveals also a fact about the coarse, selfish, vainglorious average young man of real life, an essential fact without a grasp of which no one can understand him for an instant—the fact that as surely as the sea or the heavens are unfathomably deep, he is quite unfathomably and quite idiotically well-meaning.

But more time has elapsed, and again a more curious thing has come about. We have travelled yet another stage along the downward track from the mountain of the heroes. Thackeray did not write of youth in the manner of Dickens or Dumas, who admired their heroes; far less did he write of it in the style of the great primitive poets, who may be said to have feared their heroes. But at least he sympathized with his hero. If he did not conceive him as the child of the gods, he realized to the full the pathos and the gallantry involved in the children of men; if he did not salute the hero's victory, as the poets did, he saluted his sublime defeat. But since Thackeray, there has come into fashion a fiction, of which some of the French and Russian novelists are able examplars, of which Mr. George Gissing is not innocent, a school which appears positively to despise the young man whom it calls hero. It has not for him even that dark and stormy kindliness which one sinner may have for another. At every point the hero is sacrificed to the author, as much as a dog to a vivisectionist; he goes through the ugliest antics of humiliation and meanness, that the author may parade his precious insight and candor: the one must be a cad that the other may be a prig. The story of the young man in fiction has travelled all this strange distance. It begins with the primitive bard, straining his voice and almost breaking his lyre in order to utter the greatness of youth and the greatness of masculinity; it ends with the novelist looking at both of them with a magnifying-glass; it begins with a delight in things above, and ends with a delight in things below us. I for one have little doubt about their relative value. For if a man can say, "I like to find something greater than myself," he may be a fool or a madman, but he has the essential. But if a man says, "I like to find something smaller than myself," there is only one adequate answer—"You couldn't."

[From *The Critic*, August 1903]

297

Dragooning the Dragon

WE all know the people who think it wicked to tell children fairy tales which they are not required to believe, though of course not wicked to teach them false doctrines or false news which they are required to believe. They hold that the child must be guarded from the danger of supposing that all frogs turn into princesses or that any pumpkin will at any minute turn into a coach and six, and that he must rather reserve his faith for the sober truth told in the newspapers, which will tell him that all Socialists are Satanists or that the next Act of Parliament will mean work and wealth for all. We ourselves have generally found that children were quite sufficiently intelligent to question the first and that grown-up people were quite sufficiently stupid to swallow the second. It almost looks as if there were something wrong about education; or perhaps something wrong about growing up. But the latest news in the educational world is that a more moderate reform is under consideration; and the reformers admit that there is a distinction to be made. One or two fairy tales about pretty things like flowers or butterflies, it is loftily admitted, may do no harm. But fairy tales about dragons and giants, because they are ugly things, may have a dreadful effect upon the delicate instinct for beauty. Schoolmasters discussed the question recently in the light of the most recent psychology of esthetics. For our part, we have seldom seen a schoolmaster who was half so decorative as a dragon. And though a giant may appear gross or grotesque, he is not necessarily less so when (as in the case of one or two professors) he is reduced to the dimensions of a dwarf. The human race must be a very horrible sight to the human child, if he is really so sensitive an esthete as all that. But it must be admitted that the objection was not exclusively esthetic, but also partly ethical. On moral grounds also it was urged that the child may read stories about beanstalks, but not stories about giants; the learned educationists having apparently forgotten that they both occur in the same story. Children, it appears, are not to read about giants and witches because it will encourage cruelty; as the child "will certainly sympathise with the torturers." This would seem to be an extreme dogma of Original Sin by the Calvinist rather than the Catholic definition of it. Why a little boy reading about another little boy pursued by a dragon should suppose himself to be a dragon, which he is not, instead of a boy, which he is, we have no idea;

we suppose it is the dragon complex. Anyhow, psychologists suffer from what may be called the contradiction complex; and we need not say that they contradict themselves flatly even on that one small point. For they also say that the tale of the dragon will produce morbid terror and panic; so that it would almost seem as if the little boy were a little boy after all. But he is a rather curious little boy, who exultantly enjoys eating himself at the same moment that he is mad and miserable with fear of being eaten by himself; his complex is evidently very complex indeed. Meanwhile, it might perhaps be pointed out that a child generally goes very eagerly to his father or his friend for the experience of fairy tales; whereas he can remain in complete isolation and ignorance, and still have the experience of fear. The child learns without being taught that life contains some element of enmity. His own dreams would provide him with dragons; what the legend provides is St. George.

[From *G. K.'s: A Miscellany of the First 500 Issues of G. K.'s Weekly*]

20

HUMANITY—AN INTERLUDE

EXCEPT for some fine works of art, which seem to be there by accident, the City of Brussels is like a bad Paris, a Paris with everything noble cut out, and everything nasty left in. No one can understand Paris and its history who does not understand that its fierceness is the balance and justification of its frivolity. It is called a city of pleasure; but it may also very specially be called a city of pain. The crown of roses is also a crown of thorns. Its people are too prone to hurt others, but quite ready also to hurt themselves. They are martyrs for religion, they are martyrs for irreligion; they are even martyrs for immorality. For the indecency of many of their books and papers is not of the sort which charms and seduces, but of the sort that horrifies and hurts; they are torturing themselves. They lash their own patriotism into life with the same whips which most men use to lash foreigners to silence. The enemies of France can never give an account of her infamy or decay which does not seem insipid and even polite compared with the things which the Nationalists of France say about their own nation. They taunt and torment themselves; sometimes they even deliberately oppress themselves. Thus, when the mob of Paris could make a government to please itself, it made a sort of sublime tyranny to order itself about. The spirit is the same from the Crusades or St. Bartholomew to the apotheosis of Zola. The old religionists tortured men physically for a moral truth. The new realists torture men morally for a physical truth.

Now Brussels is Paris without this constant purification of pain. Its indecencies are not regrettable incidents in an everlasting revolution. It has none of the things which make good Frenchmen love Paris; it has only the things which make unspeakable Englishmen love it. It has the part which is cosmopolitan—and narrow; not the part which is Parisian—and universal. You can find there (as commonly happens in modern centres) the worst things of all nations—the *Daily Mail* from England, the cheap philosophies from Germany, the loose novels of

France, and the drinks of America. But there is no English broad fun, no German kindly ceremony, no American exhilaration, and, above all, no French tradition of fighting for an idea. Though all the boulevards look like Parisian boulevards, though all the shops look like Parisian shops, you cannot look at them steadily for two minutes without feeling the full distance between, let us say, King Leopold and fighters like Clemenceau and Déroulède.

For all these reasons, and many more, when I had got into Brussels I began to make all necessary arrangements for getting out of it again; and I had impulsively got into a tram which seemed to be going out of the city. In this tram there were two men talking; one was a little man with a black French beard; the other was a baldish man with bushy whiskers, like the financial foreign count in a three-act farce. And about the time that we reached the suburb of the city, and the traffic grew thinner, and the noises more few, I began to hear what they were saying. Though they spoke French quickly, their words were fairly easy to follow, because they were all long words. Anybody can understand long words because they have in them all the lucidity of Latin.

The man with the black beard said: "It must that we have the Progress."

The man with the whiskers parried this smartly by saying: "It must also that we have the Consolidation International."

This is the sort of discussion which I like myself, so I listened with some care, and I think I picked up the thread of it. One of the Belgians was a Little Belgian, as we speak of a Little Englander. The other was a Belgian Imperialist, for though Belgium is not quite strong enough to be altogether a nation, she is quite strong enough to be an empire. Being a nation means standing up to your equals, whereas being an empire only means kicking your inferiors. The man with whiskers was the Imperialist, and he was saying:

"The science, behold there the new guide of humanity."

And the man with the beard answered him "It does not suffice to have progress in the science; one must have it also in the sentiment of the human justice."

This remark I applauded, as if at a public meeting, but they were much too keen on their argument to hear me. The views I have often heard in England, but never uttered so lucidly, and certainly never so fast. Though Belgian by nation they must both have been essentially French. Whiskers was great on education, which, it seems is on the march. All the world goes to make itself instructed. It must that the more instructed enlighten the less instructed. Eh, well then, the European must impose upon the savage the science and the light. Also (ap-

parently), he must impose himself on the savage while he is about it.
Today one travelled quickly. The science had changed all. For our
fathers, they were religious, and (what was worse) dead. Today humanity had electricity to the hand; the machines came from triumphing; all
the lines and limits of the globe effaced themselves. Soon there would
not be but the great empires and confederations, guided by the science,
always the science.

Here Whiskers stopped an instant for breath; and the man with the
sentiment of human justice had "la parole" off him in a flash. Without
doubt Humanity was on the march, but towards the sentiments, the
ideal, the methods moral and pacific. Humanity directed itself towards
Humanity. For your wars and empires on behalf of civilization, what
were they in effect? The war, was it not itself an affair of the barbarism?
The Empires, were they not things savage? The Humanity had passed
all that; she was now intellectual. Tolstoy had refined all human souls
with the sentiments the most delicate and just. Man was become a spirit:
the wings pushed. . . .

At this important point of evolution the tram came to a jerky stop-
page; and staring around I found, to my stunned consternation, that it
was almost dark, that I was far away from Brussels, that I could not
dream of getting back to dinner; in short, that through the clinging
fascination of this great controversy on Humanity and its recent complete alteration by science or Tolstoy, I had landed myself Heaven
knows where. I dropped hastily from the suburban tram and let it go on
without me.

I was alone in flat fields out of sight of the city. On one side of the
road was one of those small, thin woods which are common in all
countries, but of which, by a coincidence, the mystical painters of
Flanders were very fond. The night was closing in with cloudy purple
and grey; there was one ribbon of silver, the last rag of the sunset.
Through the wood went one little path, and somehow it suggested that
it might lead to some sign of life—there was no other sign of life on the
horizon. I went along it, and soon sank into a sort of dancing twilight of
all those tiny trees. There is something subtle and bewildering about
that sort of frail and fantastic wood. A forest of big trees seems like a
bodily barrier; but somehow that mist of thin lines seems like a spiritual
barrier. It is as if one were caught in a fairy cloud or could not pass a
phantom. When I had well lost the last gleam of the high-road a curious
and definite feeling came upon me. I had heard a lot about Humanity in
the tram. Now I suddenly felt something much more practical and
extraordinary—the absence of humanity: inhuman loneliness. Of
course, there was nothing really lost in my state; but the mood may hit

one anywhere. I wanted men—any men; and I felt our awful alliance over all the globe. And at last, when I had walked for what seemed a long time, I saw a light too near the earth to mean anything except the image of God.

I came out on a clear space and a low, long cottage, the door of which was open, but was blocked by a big grey horse, who seemed to prefer to eat with his head inside the sitting-room. I got past him, and found he was being fed idly by a young man who was sitting down and drinking beer inside, and who saluted me with heavy rustic courtesy, but in a strange tongue. The room was full of staring faces like owls, and these I traced at length as belonging to about six small children. Their father was still working in the fields, but their mother rose when I entered. She smiled, but she and all the rest spoke some rude language, Flamand, I suppose; so that we had to be kind to each other by signs. She fetched me beer, and pointed out my way with her finger; and I drew a picture to please the children; and as it was a picture of two men hitting each other with swords, it pleased them very much. Then I gave a Belgian penny to each child, for as I said on chance in French, "It must be that we have the economic equality." But they had never heard of economic equality, while all Battersea workmen have heard of economic equality, though it is true that they haven't got it.

I found my way back to the city, and some time afterwards I actually saw in the street my two men talking, no doubt still saying, one that Science had changed all in Humanity, and the other that Humanity was now pushing the wings of the purely intellectual. But for me Humanity was hooked on to an accidental picture. I thought of a low and lonely house in the flats, behind a veil or film of slight trees, a man breaking the ground as men have broken from the first morning, and a huge grey horse champing his food within a foot of a child's head, as in the stable where Christ was born.

[From *Tremendous Trifles*]

CHRISTMAS POEMS

The House of Christmas

There fared a mother driven forth
Out of an inn to roam;
In the place where she was homeless
All men are at home.
The crazy stable close at hand,
With shaking timber and shifting sand,
Grew a stronger thing to abide and stand
Than the square stones of Rome.

For men are homesick in their homes,
And strangers under the sun,
And they lay their heads in a foreign land
Whenever the day is done.
Here we have battle and blazing eyes,
And chance and honour and high surprise,
But our homes are under miraculous skies
Where the yule tale was begun.

A Child in a foul stable,
Where the beasts feed and foam;
Only where He was homeless
Are you and I at home;
We have hands that fashion and heads that know,
But our hearts we lost—how long ago!
In a place no chart nor ship can show
Under the sky's dome.

This world is wild as an old wives' tale,
And strange the plain things are,
The earth is enough and the air is enough
For our wonder and our war;

But our rest is as far as the fire-drake swings
And our peace is put in impossible things
Where clashed and thundered unthinkable wings
Round an incredible star.

To an open house in the evening
Home shall men come,
To an older place than Eden
And a taller town than Rome.
To the end of the way of the wandering star,
To the things that cannot be and that are,
To the place where God was homeless
And all men are at home.

[From *Poems*]

A Child of the Snows

There is heard a hymn when the panes are dim,
    And never before or again,
When the nights are strong with a darkness long,
    And the dark is alive with rain.

Never we know but in sleet and in snow,
    The place where the great fires are,
That the midst of the earth is a raging mirth
    And the heart of the earth a star.

And at night we win to the ancient inn
    Where the child in the frost is furled,
We follow the feet where all souls meet
    At the inn at the end of the world.

The gods lie dead where the leaves lie red,
    For the flame of the sun is flown,
The gods lie cold where the leaves lie gold,
    And a Child comes forth alone.

[From *Poems*]

The Wise Men

Step softly, under snow or rain,
　　To find the place where men can pray;
The way is all so very plain
　　That we may lose the way.

Oh, we have learnt to peer and pore
　　On tortured puzzles from our youth,
We know all labyrinthine lore,
We are the three wise men of yore,
　　And we know all things but the truth.

We have gone round and round the hill
　　And lost the wood among the trees,
And learnt long names for every ill,
And served the mad gods, naming still
　　The furies the Eumenides.

The gods of violence took the veil
　　Of vision and philosophy,
The Serpent that brought all men bale,
He bites his own accursed tail,
　　And calls himself Eternity.

Go humbly . . . it has hailed and snowed . . .
　　With voices low and lanterns lit;
So very simple is the road,
　　That we may stray from it.

The world grows terrible and white,
　　And blinding white the breaking day;
We walk bewildered in the light,
For something is too large for sight,
　　And something much too plain to say.

The Child that was ere worlds begun
　　(. . . We need but walk a little way,
We need but see a latch undone . . .)
The Child that played with moon and sun
　　Is playing with a little hay.

The house from which the heavens are fed,
　The old strange house that is our own,
Where tricks of words are never said,
And Mercy is as plain as bread,
　And Honour is as hard as stone.

Go humbly, humble are the skies,
　And low and large and fierce the Star;
So very near the Manger lies
　That we may travel far.

Hark! Laughter like a lion wakes
　To roar to the resounding plain,
And the whole heaven shouts and shakes,
For God Himself is born again,
And we are little children walking
　Through the snow and rain.

[From *Poems*]

The Nativity

The thatch on the roof was as golden,
　Though dusty the straw was and old,
The wind had a peal as of trumpets,
　Though blowing and barren and cold,
The mother's hair was a glory
　Though loosened and torn,
For under the eaves in the gloaming
　A child was born.

Have a myriad children been quickened,
　Have a myriad children grown old,
Grown gross and unloved and embittered,
　Grown cunning and savage and cold?
God abides in a terrible patience,
　Unangered, unworn,
And again for the child that was squandered
　A child is born.

What know we of aeons behind us,
  Dim dynasties lost long ago,
Huge empires, like dreams unremembered,
  Huge cities for ages laid low?
This at least—that with blight and with blessing,
  With flower and with thorn,
Love was there, and his cry was among them,
  "A child is born."

Though the darkness be noisy with systems,
  Dark fancies that fret and disprove,
Still the plumes stir around us, above us
  The wings of the shadow of love:
Oh! princes and priests, have ye seen it
  Grow pale through your scorn;
Huge dawns sleep before us, deep changes,
  A child is born.

And the rafters of toil still are gilded
  With the dawn of the stars of the heart,
And the wise men draw near in the twilight,
  Who are weary of learning and art,
And the face of the tyrant is darkened,
  His spirit is torn,
For a new king is enthroned; yea, the sternest,
  A child is born.

And the mother still joys for the whispered
  First stir of unspeakable things,
Still feels that high moment unfurling
  Red glory of Gabriel's wings.
Still the babe of an hour is a master
  Whom angels adorn,
Emmanuel, prophet, anointed,
  A child is born.

And thou, that art still in thy cradle,
  The sun being crown for thy brow,
Make answer, our flesh, make an answer,
  Say, whence art thou come—who art thou?
Art thou come back on earth for our teaching
  To train or to warn—?

Hush—how may we know?—knowing only
A child is born.

[From *Poems*]

Gloria in Profundis

There has fallen on earth for a token
A god too great for the sky.
He has burst out of all things and broken
The bounds of eternity:
Into time and the terminal land
He has strayed like a thief or a lover,
For the wine of the world brims over,
Its splendour is spilt on the sand.

Who is proud when the heavens are humble,
Who mourns if the mountains fall,
If the fixed suns topple and tumble
And a deluge of love drowns all—
Who rears up his head for a crown,
Who holds up his will for a warrant,
Who strives with the starry torrent
When all that is good goes down?

For in dread of such falling and failing
The Fallen Angels fell
Inverted in insolence, scaling
The hanging mountain of hell:
But unmeasured of plummet and rod
Too deep for their sight to scan,
Outrushing the fall of man
Is the height of the fall of God.

Glory to God in the Lowest
The spout of the stars in spate—
Where the thunderbolt thinks to be slowest
And the lightning fears to be late:
As men dive for a sunken gem
Pursuing, we hunt and hound it,

The fallen star that has found it
In the cavern of Bethlehem.

[From *Gloria in Profundis*]

A Christmas Carol

The Christ-child lay on Mary's lap,
His hair was like a light.
(O weary, weary were the world,
But here is all aright.)

The Christ-child lay on Mary's breast,
His hair was like a star.
(O stern and cunning are the kings,
But here the true hearts are.)

The Christ-child lay on Mary's heart,
His hair was like a fire.
(O weary, weary is the world,
But here the world's desire.)

The Christ-child stood at Mary's knee,
His hair was like a crown.
And all the flowers looked up at Him,
And all the stars looked down.

[From *The Wild Knight*]

CHESTERTON FOR TODAY

Since a significant aspect of Chesterton's expressiveness was his reasoned and religiously oriented battle against skepticism, subjectivism, and moral ambivalence—attitudes that are prevalent today—and since his argumentation was eminently logical and experiential, his insights and analyses can provide a basis of illuminating sanity for our generation. He upheld the primacy of selfless wonder and praise to God as the fundamental ground of life, in contrast to our secular humanism and frantic consumerism. And he upheld the absolute certainty of Faith, in contrast to our age of introspection, trendy and emasculated beliefs, and refined doubt.

One of the passionate concerns of his life was the assaults which modern culture had mounted upon the dignity and nature of man. Believing that man bears the imprint of his Creator, a source which gives him a sacred and inviolable nature, Chesterton resisted mightily the modern tendency to alter human nature to fit conditions, instead of altering conditions to fit human nature. Long before the advances in genetic engineering which have taken place in our time, Chesterton realized that, when once man began to be viewed as a shifting and provisional and alterable thing, it would always be easy for the strong and the clever to twist him into new shapes for all kinds of unnatural purposes. If man's nature is not fixed and elevated by God beyond human interference, then there is nothing to prevent the powerful from adapting it, fundamentally and endlessly. What is to prevent, Chesterton asked, the new marvels turning into the old abuses—the old abuses of debasement and slavery? "That is the nightmare with which the mere notion of adaptation threatens us," he wrote in 1910, in his great work of Christian sociology, *What's Wrong with the World.* "That is the nightmare that is not so very far from the reality."

[From Karl G. Schmude, *The Man Who Was Chesterton*]

One of the lectures that Chesterton delivered several times during his first trip to America is called "The Ignorance of the Educated." Chesterton was obviously not deceived by academic pomposity. His greatly diversified interests are reflected in his advocacy of a genuinely broad and integrated education that would be a basis for the multifarious aspects and duties of life.

For health and balance and perception and brilliance and common sense in the human mind, there is no medicine more indicated than the reading and re-reading of Chesterton. But I reject the word "medicine" in this connection; Chesterton is a feast of fun and jollity at the same time that he is a prescription labeled, "To learn how to think—take in liberal doses at least once a day."

[From Joe Breig, *Ave Maria*, 9 May 1959]

A further reason for Chesterton's importance is that he was not a doctrinaire adherent of an unexamined faith but was a *seeker* after truth. Many apologists for the Catholic Church have never been outside of it. But GKC deliberately chose orthodox Christianity after his youthful years of doubt, confusion, and reflection. He probed all beliefs and examined all of the alternatives, until he finally realized which one was true. And he argued for the truth with all the enthusiasm that comes from such a laborious and analytical personal discovery. Late in life, to encourage a friend who was bothered with certain difficulties about the Faith, he said, "I doubt if there is a doubt anywhere I have not entertained, examined, and dismissed."

As a young man, Chesterton suffered his way right through the lunatic nightmare of fundamental scepticism, and emerged with a firm commitment to basic sanity, to "the divine dogma that pigs is pigs." Beyond this, he emerged with a passionate and even hyperaesthetic awareness—expressed again and again throughout his *oeuvre*—of the astounding *goodness* of all being, the wrongness of the Manichees, and the necessity and rightness of gratitude, even for a little. Hence, while fully recognising the evils in this world and the consequent need for protest and even (occasionally) for revolution, he became that rare thing, a serious prophet and advocate of human happiness. "The voice of the special rebels and prophets recommending discontent should . . . sound now and then suddenly, like a trumpet. But the voices of the saints and sages, recommending contentment, should sound unceasingly, like the sea."

The peak of his mind lies here, the centre of his heart: this is what made him so sympathetic an interpreter of those very different saints, Thomas and Francis, and it is a theme which found its final and definitive statement in the last chapter of his *Autobiography*—a chapter which we can recommend everyone to read and study and make his own, even if he has no time to trace its message throughout the whole vast corpus of Chesterton's writings.

[From Christopher Derrick, *The Chesterton Review*, Spring-Summer 1980]

Though he spoke out against what he perceived as the ills of his times, Chesterton was by no means a grim denouncer of social and moral abnormalities. On the contrary, he was noted and revered for his kindness, humility, optimism, ebullient good humor, and sensitive respect for other people's opinions. Despite decades of controversy and debates, he made no enemies. He was a great man of ideas with a radiant Christian reasonableness. He gave off that aura of graciousness, courage, and faith that one perceives in the presence of a saintly person. And his outstanding achievement is that he not only expressed these virtues in his own life but was able to articulate them so well in his writing.

Very early in his career, C. F. G. Masterman wrote of him,

He crashes in upon the orderly scheme and the accepted wisdom and scatters them to the winds. The attitude of the child is restored: wonderland returns to the earth and the age of perpetual marvel. We are shown as still living in the atmosphere of miracle, in the visible presence of God.

[From *The Bookman*, February 1903]

When Chesterton was a well-known commentator on his times, J. C. Squire noted,

It is not as a critic of current politics, or of political history, that he is most essentially remarkable, great though his gifts may be in these regards. His greatest distinction lies in the hold he has upon the fundamentals of human life, considered both in its social and its metaphysical aspects. In an age of new questions he has reiterated old answers; in an age of skepticism he has laughed at the laughers with a hilarity less hollow than theirs; in an age which tends to excuse baseness, even when it does not explain it away, he has flown the banners of honor, fidelity, and generosity; in an age of mass-regimentation he has stood for the sanctities of the individual soul. And above all, . . . living in a period when the value of life itself has been widely questioned (and, by that very fact, impoverished), he has maintained that "it is something to have been," showing the world the spectacle of one man enjoying the thousand miracles of the day, though the sword of Damocles hang over his head as it hangs over the heads of us all.

[From *The Living Age,* August 1928]

And Father John Boyd effectively summed up Chesterton's great gift a decade after his death:

To Chesterton, our universe . . . is a vibrant reality, much too worth while ever to get used to. There is a shock of wonder about everything and this wonder is sacramental, for our universe is a sacrament, a tell-tale mystery, a great analogy of being where God and His creation join hands.

[From *Columbia,* December 1947]